What Can This Book Do for You?

Within a few years, your high school experience will lead you into a new world of college, military, work, travel, and more. This book is designed to give you guidance, ideas, and answers about the many options life offers and the steps you'll need to take for each.

What First?

Take a few minutes to claim ownership of this book. Write your name in it. In pencil, lay out your career and life goals as you see them today. Consider the obstacles you may have to overcome to achieve your goals. If you don't have a formal plan, that's OK. Answering these questions will spark your imagination and help you make one. The first steps might not be easy, but luckily there are no right or wrong answers. As you continue working through this book, refer to these goals and feel free to fill in any blanks you left or to change your ideas.

What Next?

Your needs, goals, ideas, and talents are unique to you. What is right for you may not be right for others. But the steps in the process of choosing a career direction (and understanding what education you might need to get there) are the same whether you aspire to repair car engines or design the next generation of space shuttles.

Think of This Book as a Road Map

Knowing where you want to go and what roads will lead you there are the first steps in the process. You can always change your destination and chart a new course. We're providing the map. The rest is up to you.

GETTING A JUMP ON THE ROAD TO SUCCESS

Name ________________________

Age ________________________

Grade ________________________

Date Started ________________________

My current goal after I graduate from high school is to:

____

____

At school, to reach my goal I'll need:

Curriculum planning:

____

____

Clubs, teams, associations:

____

____

Career research:

____

____

Outside school, to reach my goal I'll need:

Volunteer work:

____

____

Shadowing/mentor program:

____

____

Job experiences:

____

____

Extracurricular activities:

____

____

Challenges my goal presents:

____

____

Ideas to overcome these challenges:

____

____

____

About Peterson's Publishing

To succeed on your lifelong educational journey, you will need accurate, dependable, and practical tools and resources. That is why Peterson's is everywhere education happens. Because whenever and however you need education content delivered, you can rely on Peterson's to provide the information, know-how, and guidance to help you reach your goals. Tools to match the right students with the right school. It's here. Personalized resources and expert guidance. It's here. Comprehensive and dependable education content—delivered whenever and however you need it. It's all here.

For more information, contact Peterson's Publishing, 2000 Lenox Drive, Lawrenceville, NJ 08648; 800-338-3282 Ext. 54229; or find us online at www.petersonspublishing.com.

Bernadette Webster, Director of Publishing; Jill C. Schwartz, Editor; Ray Golaszewski, Publishing Operations Manager; Linda M. Williams, Composition Manager

ISBN-13: 978-0-7689-3382-6
ISBN-10: 0-7689-3382-X

Printed in the United States of America

10 9 8 7 6 5 4 3 2 1 13 12 11

Eleventh Edition

By printing this book on recycled paper (40% post-consumer waste) 112 trees were saved.

CONTENTS

PART 4: YOU AND THE WORKPLACE

SPECIAL ADVERTISING SECTION

A LETTER TO STUDENTS

Dear Student:

Whether graduation seems light-years away or alarmingly close, it's never too early—or too late—to think about what comes after high school. Do you know what your next step will be?

Teens' Guide to College & Career Planning can help you figure that out. This book is designed to help you launch your career, whether this means going on for more education or directly entering the work force. You have a multitude of options and some crucial choices to make. In the pages that follow, we have tried to give you a jump-start on planning the future that's right for you.

The book is arranged in four parts. Part 1 has all the guidance you'll need to make the transition to high school. Part 2 provides general introductory information about your options after high school and how to use your high school education to plan for the next phase of your life. Part 3 offers more detailed information about postsecondary education, whether you choose a two-year or four-year college or university, a vocational/career college, or the military. Finally, Part 4 provides useful information about the workplace and how to handle stress, peer pressure, conflict, cyberbullying, and other obstacles you may encounter.

We hope you will find this publication helpful as you begin thinking about the rest of your life. If you have questions or feedback on the Teens' Guide, please contact us at:

Peterson's Publishing
2000 Lenox Drive
Lawrenceville, NJ 08648

Sincerely,

Editorial Staff

A MESSAGE FOR PARENTS

Preparing for the future may seem daunting and overwhelming, but it doesn't have to be. Your teen can pursue a variety of options after high school: getting a job, entering the military, or seeking further education and training. Learning about the choices and creating a plan will help put your teen on the path to success. You can help your teen navigate these options and prepare for the future by using this book, *Teens' Guide to College & Career Planning*.

Preparing for the Future

With this comprehensive guide for high school students, *Teens' Guide to College & Career Planning*, you and your teen can learn how to explore career options, plan a career path, and find the colleges and career schools that will help your teen reach his or her goals. In addition, the *Teens' Guide* offers alternatives to traditional four-year colleges, facts about many of the standardized tests your teen may be expected to take during the next few years, and information about how you can finance your teen's education or training.

As you are getting ready to read through the *Teens' Guide*, discuss these options with your teen:

- **Going to college.** A college education allows students to exercise their minds and learn critical-thinking and analytical skills. Another bonus: studies show that college degrees lead to higher incomes. The United States alone has thousands of two- and four-year colleges, each of which offers dozens, sometimes hundreds, of majors that can lead to exciting careers. Today, everyone can pursue a college education, and you'll find out why in the *Teens' Guide*.
- **Enlisting in the military.** The U.S. military is the largest employer in the nation. It offers training and employment in more than 2,000 job specialties and provides service-people an opportunity to see the world. Plus, joining the military is a great way to finance a college education.
- **Getting a job.** College and the military aren't the only options out there. Your teen may want to experience the work world first and go to college as an adult student. In fact, students over the age of 25 compose more than 30 percent of today's campus population.
- **Alternatives.** Higher education isn't limited to traditional two- and four-year colleges. Apprenticeship programs, career schools, and technical institutes train young people for work as carpenters, auto mechanics, medical secretaries, computer technicians, and more.

Using the *Teens' Guide*

The *Teens' Guide* is designed to help you and your teen through the process of preparing for life after high school. The basic organization of the book is as follows:

Part 1: You're Going to Be a Freshman

While the main focus of the *Teens' Guide* is planning for life after high school, just making the transition to high school can be overwhelming. This section addresses all the questions and fears looming out there as your teen moves from middle or junior high school to high school.

Part 2: Jump-Start Your Future

This section contains exercises and information to encourage your teen to pursue higher education and explore career opportunities.

Part 3: The Road to More Education

Here you'll find the many educational opportunities available to your teen: traditional colleges, career schools, technical institutions, apprenticeship programs, and the military. Part 3 contains information about searching for and applying to schools, preparing for standardized tests, and locating financial aid.

Part 4: You and the Workplace

While many people go on to higher education right after high school, it isn't always the right option for every person. This section explores how your teen can succeed in his or her first job and offers essential survival skills.

Forming a Plan

When thinking about your teen's future, you have so many things to consider: career training, military service, college searches, standardized tests, and financial aid. Where do you begin? What should you and your teen be focusing on over the next few years? Forming a plan and staying organized will help you guide your son or daughter through the process of getting ready for a job, further education, or the military.

To get started, check out the "Planning Your Education While in High School" chapter of the *Teens' Guide*. It contains detailed planning time lines for students to follow in each grade. These time lines can show you what to do next and help you stay on track.

Communication Is Key

The most important thing you can do as a parent is to sit down and talk about your teen's future with him or her. Open communication allows each of you to discuss your expectations, hopes, and concerns. Approach your conversations with a positive attitude, ask questions, and listen. The last thing you want is for your teen to dread talking to you about his or her future!

PART 1
YOU'RE GOING TO BE A FRESHMAN

You know what it's supposed to be like—being in high school should be COOL. But what will it REALLY be like? Will you be able to figure it all out? Of course you will . . . especially since you are reading this! Your high school years will be like nothing else you have experienced, and, as a freshman, you're going to have questions about everything. Luckily, you'll be able to get answers right here. Whether you're wondering about how to keep your "stuff" organized, choosing your classes, or what a GPA is, we are here to help! So, come on, jump in—you're going to be a FRESHMAN!

CHAPTER 1

THE BIG JUMP TO HIGH SCHOOL

Even if you've never said anything to anyone else, chances are the thought of your first year of high school is totally scary, especially with all these questions whirling around in your head:

Who will I sit with at lunch?

What if my best friends don't have lunch when I do?

Where is the vending machine?

How will I find my way around the halls?

What will I do when I have only 4 minutes to get to my next class?

What happens if I get lost?

Will I remember my locker combination?

What happens if I can't open my locker?

What happens if there aren't any lockers?

Will all those books fit in my backpack?

What if my best friend isn't in any of my classes?

What if I don't know anyone in my classes?

What if I don't know where the bathroom is?

What if I forget where to go for my class?

What if the seniors are mean and treat me like dirt?

What if . . . What if . . . What if?

YOU'RE OFF TO HIGH SCHOOL

In middle school, you knew where everything was. You knew exactly who would be sitting next to you at lunch. You knew all the teachers. All the teachers knew you. You were at the top of the heap. Now you're starting all over again.

FIRST OF ALL, take a deep breath, sit back, and realize that it's okay to have the ups and downs, the doubts, and the feelings that zip back and forth between "I can't wait to get into high school" and "I'm hiding under my bed and never coming out." In the first few weeks of high school, you'll be surrounded by kids who are bigger, who seem to know an awful lot more than you do, and who know exactly where to go. You'll wonder what it will be like to try out for sports teams or shows and activities with the tenth, eleventh, and twelfth graders.

FROM THE GUIDANCE OFFICE

Freshmen are afraid the upper class students will pick on them, but honestly, that's not true. Upper class students are not the least bit interested in freshmen.

Guidance Counselor
Jackson Memorial High School
Jackson, New Jersey

SECOND, the friend of a friend's brother who told you he hated ninth grade isn't you. Everyone adjusts to high school in different ways and at different speeds. For some kids, the transition from junior high school/middle school to high school takes a short time, days or weeks. For others, the adjustment takes longer, especially if they're not admitting to themselves and others what their feelings are and letting others help them get over their insecurities.

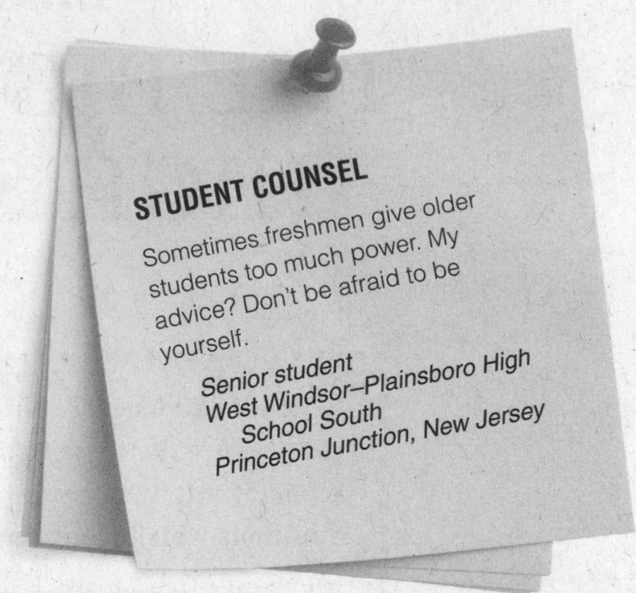

THIRD, you are not alone. All those older kids ahead of you have gone through the same fears and have had the same feelings, too. They made it through, and you will also. It's most likely that the sophomores, juniors, and seniors are too busy dealing with the problems of being sophomores, juniors, and seniors to be concerned if you forgot your locker combination and have to go slinking off to the school office to find out what it is.

THE DIFFERENCES: MIDDLE SCHOOL VS. HIGH SCHOOL

There's no getting around it. High school is a different ball game. It's like you're used to playing soccer and all of a sudden you're expected to throw the ball, rather than kick it, to score. The following are some of the major differences between middle school and high school:

You are more independent. In middle school, you were part of a group. You did the same things together—ate lunch, took the same classes, goofed off. Same teachers, same schedule. It's a big adjustment to realize that you'll have your own schedule of classes that could be very different from your best friend's. You'll be in classes with people you don't know because there are different levels of subjects. You could be in the middle level of a math class, and your friend could be in the upper-level section.

You have to take more responsibility. In middle school, you probably had fewer choices about which classes you could take. In high school, you have many more choices to make about your education, especially as you go into your sophomore year. You'll get to choose some classes, or electives as they're called. As a freshman, your choice of electives is limited. Most freshmen can choose only one elective. Sophomores only two. At the junior and senior levels, you'll have more and more choices to make, all depending on your goals and interests.

Explore your interests via elective classes.

The way you are graded is different in high school. Your teachers in junior high school were probably more lenient when it came to late homework. They were more likely to look at your past record and give you a little leeway. Teachers in high school aren't so likely to accept excuses. "I forgot" won't work. In high school, your grades are based on numbers. Some teachers will deduct points if you don't get your homework done and turned in on time.

You have to speak up for yourself. In middle school, your parents probably helped you if you got into a tough situation, say with a teacher. They were the ones making the phone call or visiting the teacher. In high school, you may have to deal with situations on your own, such as speaking with a teacher about homework or getting your voice heard in clubs and activities even though you're the youngest one there. In high school, you have to develop the ability to get advice from your parents and counselors, figure out how to solve the problem, and then take action.

THERE'S SO MUCH TO DO!

Your freshman year is a time for you to explore your interests—what's it like being a crime scene investigator, a computer graphics designer, a veterinarian, and so on.

Explore your interests via elective classes. One of the main purposes of high school electives is to allow you to investigate career interests. Though you'll be required to take a variety of basic classes such as math, English, history, and science, your choice of electives can point you in the direction of a future college major. Something you enjoy doing as a freshman could end up being the start of your career.

You can take electives in areas such as computers, art, accounting, or music. Say you think you'd like to be in business some day, sitting in an office overlooking the city. You can begin to realize that dream by taking accounting as an elective. You may find out you really like working with numbers. Or, you may find out you'd rather be building high-rises instead of sitting in a cubicle in one of them.

Explore your interests via clubs and activities. In addition to sports, high school offers many clubs and activities outside your classroom learning. You may think these activities are there just so you can have some fun. While that's true, they also give you the opportunity to find out what your interests are. Extracurricular activities can help you find what goals you want to set and then how to reach them.

Here's a sample list of clubs and activities in which you can participate. Every school is different, so you'll have to find out what your high school offers, but the following list will give you an idea of what you can expect.

- Auto club
- Band
- Bowling club
- Cheerleading
- Choir
- Forensics club
- Math club
- Mock trial
- Newspaper
- Science club

Explore your interests via volunteer work. High schools often offer opportunities for you to do volunteer work. Are you interested in working with younger kids? In being a lawyer? In helping those who are sick? You can volunteer to help out in a hospital or law office, for instance. By volunteering and working alongside people who are doing the things you may like to do, you can quickly judge if you really do like hospitals or law offices.

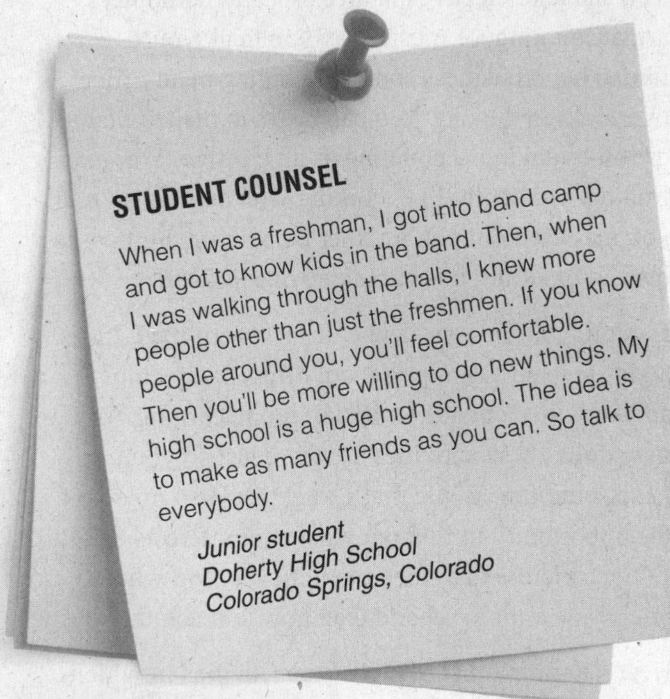

STUDENT COUNSEL

When I was a freshman, I got into band camp and got to know kids in the band. Then, when I was walking through the halls, I knew more people other than just the freshmen. If you know people around you, you'll feel comfortable. Then you'll be more willing to do new things. My high school is a huge high school. The idea is to make as many friends as you can. So talk to everybody.

Junior student
Doherty High School
Colorado Springs, Colorado

HONORS OR NONHONORS: CHOOSING CLASSES

One of the most critical decisions you're going to have to make in your first year of high school is whether to take classes on a regular level or on an honors level. You may have heard about Advanced Placement, or AP, classes. You can't take those until your junior or senior year, but the time to start planning for this high academic level is actually in your freshman year. If your goal is to take college-level courses in high school (that's what AP classes are), you should start in the ninth grade by taking honors classes. AP classes are very competitive, with little wiggle room for poor grades or performance as you move from freshman, to sophomore, to junior.

But first you need to know the difference between "regular," honors, and AP classes.

Classes at the "Regular" Level

Different high schools may have different labels for this level, but, basically, if you're in a "regular" class, you're getting what you need in that subject area to meet the requirements to graduate from high school in four years and go on to college. Do the work expected of you, turn in all your homework, do well on the tests, and you'll get that piece of paper in four years that says you've completed the necessary subjects to become a high school graduate.

Classes at the Honors Level

Honors-level classes require more from you. You'll do more reading and writing that demands more in-depth understanding of the subject matter. Classes at this level develop critical-thinking skills by asking you to interpret situations and events. Honors classes are designed to provide you with an in-depth investigation into a subject.

Teachers will expect you to participate in class discussions. You'll learn to feel comfortable with a subject so you'll be able to talk about it. For instance, when studying the Civil War in an honors class, you'll delve deeper into the conditions that brought about the war, in addition to dates, geographic locations, and famous names. Then you'll look at how the war affected history and learn something about the social and political issues that followed.

FROM THE GUIDANCE OFFICE

Some kids that I counsel know what they want to be. Others don't have a clue, and some have an inkling. Your high school courses can help you reach that goal and, if you don't have a goal, they can help you explore what you want to do.

Director of Guidance
Port Charlotte High School
Port Charlotte, Florida

Some Things to Consider Before Taking the Honors Plunge

Many students do well in honors classes. Others struggle, even though they may have done very well starting off in a regular-level class. Once they've become familiar with the different way classes are taught and what's expected academically of high school students, they may be able to handle an honors class with ease.

You must be honest with yourself and with your parents. Sometimes parents see their kids through rosy glasses and think their sons and daughters are geniuses. Meanwhile, the son or daughter struggles to cope with the whole change from junior high school to high school and falls behind. Your mind-set has a lot to do with how well you'll do in high school, so it's much better to begin high school at a level that fits you.

If you are terrible at writing but love science, that's your clue about which honors classes to take and in which sequence. You may take a science honors class in ninth grade and see how you do, and then add an English honors course in tenth grade.

If you're not confident about your study habits or organizational skills, the first semester of high school is a time to slowly dip your tootsies in the honors pool. Feel the temperature of the water by doing well in a regular class, flex your mind muscles, and then dive into honors. The goal is to excel in what you do well and then take the classes that challenge you.

The WORST mistake you can make is to select an honors class because your best friend decided to take it. How well you do in high school determines if many of the doors to your future plans will be open. If you do poorly, you begin to close some doors even in your freshman year.

PARENT PERSPECTIVE

"My son was nervous about starting ninth grade. After the first two or three days, he felt so much better. He learned the best route to all of his classes so he'd be on time, and he made a good number of new friends. So the things he most worried about were no longer a concern."

Mother of high school sophomore
Council Rock High School North
Newtown, Pennsylvania

Classes at the AP (Advanced Placement) Level

In AP classes, you're actually learning at the college level. You are expected to do the assignments and perform on the tests as you would if you were in college. No wonder you often can't take AP classes until your junior and senior years. Just to get into an AP class, you must be a high achiever.

While the hurdles to succeeding in an AP class are high, the advantages for those who do well are huge. The AP exams are given to students across the United States in May and are scored on a level from 1–5, with 5 being the top score. If you get a 3, 4, or 5 in the exam of a particular class, you may be able to waive the introductory level of that class in college. Some colleges may even award you college credit! You'll not only save time and money but also impress college admission offices with the fact that you're taking AP classes. Colleges look favorably on students who work hard in high school and do well in difficult subjects.

During the college admission process, some colleges "weight" the different levels of classes you take. For instance, they'll give you more points for an A in an honors or AP class than they would for an A in a regular class. An A in a class at a regular level may count as a 4, while an A in an honors or AP class would count as a 5, and a B in an honors or AP class would count as a 4.

What If You Want to Be a Chef and Your Parents Want You to Go to Harvard?

That's a tough situation and the above example is a little on the exaggerated side. But, as a freshman, now is the time to address a difference of opinion about your future plans with your parents. So, say you do want to be a chef. You know that honors classes demand a lot more studying and time and that to get into culinary schools or other vocational tracks, you don't need to get A's in honors classes. However, your parents know you could get A's without too much effort. High school counselors will probably encourage you to take the honors classes. Why not leave your options open? As a freshman, your plans can change a lot before you graduate. If you start out with the plan to be a chef set in concrete and leave no room for change, you could get to your junior year and decide that you hate the smell of burning food and would rather get a degree in business from a top college. If you'd taken honors classes, you'd be in a good position to go to the university of your choice.

Advice for Parents

Make sure your child can do well in honors or AP classes before you start pushing for all A's at that level. Each child has different skills. Let's imagine your child takes honors classes in everything that's offered that first year. Your child works extremely hard and comes home with a C in biology. You're devastated. Your child is devastated. You've never seen a C on a report card. To help your child make the right decisions about honors and AP classes, talk with your child and your child's guidance counselor.

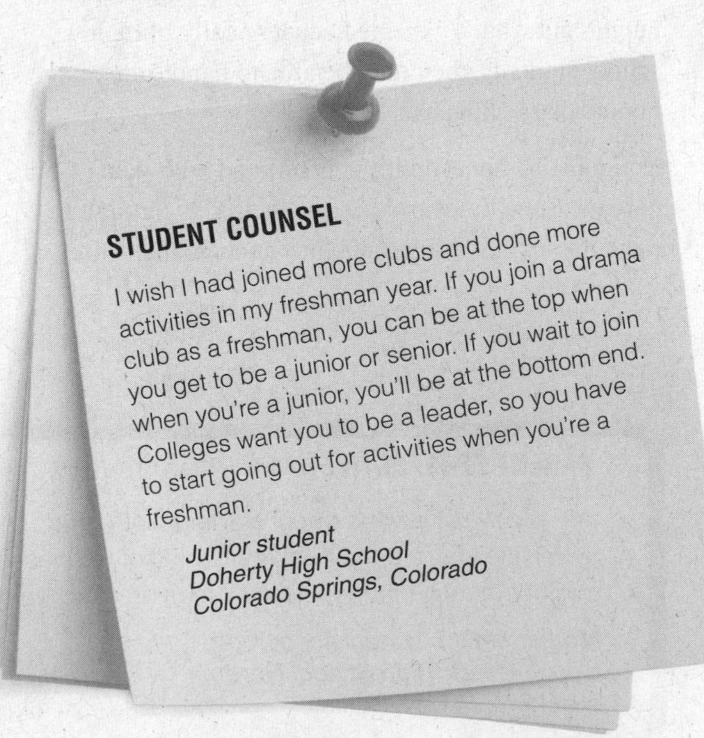

WHAT IN THE WORLD IS A GPA AND WHAT THE HECK IS A TRANSCRIPT?

Your GPA (Grade Point Average)

If you haven't already heard about the GPA, those three letters—G, P, and A—are going to mean a lot as you move from freshman to senior. There's no getting around the fact that the GPA is important to your future: what college you can attend, what kind of upper-level high school classes you can take (such as those AP classes), what academic and athletic scholarships you may get, or for what special programs you may qualify.

In short, the GPA is the average of all your grades starting from your freshman year. A little planning in your freshman year can go a long way toward a better GPA when you graduate. If you know the impact a GPA can have, you may do things a little differently in your freshman year.

It's good to know how your GPA is computed. Different schools have their own ways of totaling a GPA, but here is the basic idea.

In general, schools score letter grades as follows:

A = 4 points	D = 1 point
B = 3 points	F = 0 points
C = 2 points	

Some schools give higher points for grades earned in honors courses. That's something you'll need to check out in the guidance office. So, let's take a hypothetical student's grades for one semester:

English	A	4 points
History	B	3 points
Music	A	4 points
Math	C	2 points
Spanish	B	3 points
Physical Education	A	4 points

The points total 20 points. Divide that by the number of classes, which is 6, and you get a GPA of 3.33 for one semester.

Let's take the next semester and see how our student did.

English	A	4 points
History	A	4 points
Music	A	4 points
Math	B	3 points
Spanish	C	2 points
Physical Education	A	4 points

That totals 21 points divided by 6, which equals a 3.5 GPA. Now, add the total number of points over these last two semesters, which is 41 and divide by the number of classes (12) and you get a 3.42 GPA.

This is a simplified version of how schools score GPAs because some high schools give different points to different types of classes. For instance, an A in English may be worth more points than an A in physical education.

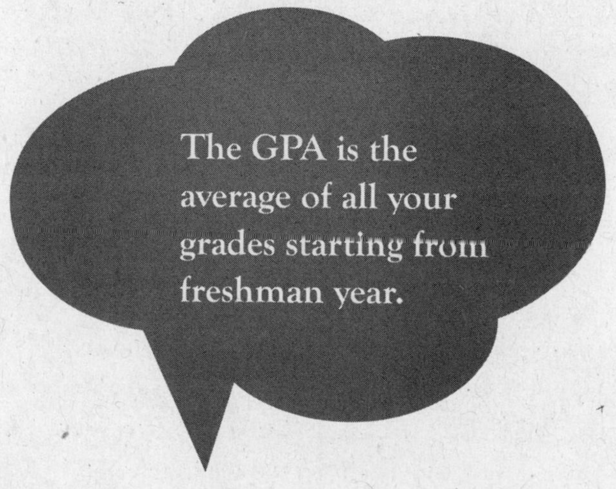

Your Transcript

Your transcript is a history of the classes you took and what grades you achieved in those classes. It's what colleges ask for to assess what kind of a student you are.

As a freshman, you need to lay a good foundation academically. Competitive colleges that attract thousands of applicants look carefully at transcripts. They're not only looking at your final GPA but also at how you challenged yourself during your high school years. Did you take courses that stretched you academically, such as honors and AP classes, or did you take only those classes you were required to take?

Some Important Things to Know About Transcripts

Transcripts differ from school to school. You need to find out what your school records on your transcript. For example, say you got good grades but missed a lot of classes because you just didn't feel like showing up. If your transcript shows the number of times you were not in class, and you're hoping to attend a top college or university, your good grades (and high GPA) won't look quite so good.

- Some schools show how many absences you had for each class.
- Some schools are on the trimester system, which means you'll have three sets of grades for each year.
- Some schools show plus and minus grades, such as a B+ or an A–, and some don't.
- Some schools don't count the freshman year when adding up your GPA.
- Some schools don't show your rank in your class, such as 168 out of 388, but instead use a quartile system, such as ranking you in the top 25% of your class.
- Some schools show your GPA as "weighted," which means that you get an extra credit point for an honors or AP class.
- Some schools show your "citizenship" record in classes. Did you contribute to the class or were you disruptive?
- Some schools will send a profile of your school with your transcript to colleges, showing the community in which the school is located, the student population, how many honors and AP classes are offered, the number of periods in a day that classes are offered, and so on.

Colorado Springs Dist 11 (H)

Unofficial Transcript

Doherty High School
4515 Barnes Rd
Colorado Springs, CO 80917

719-328-6400

	Entry Date	Counselor	Graduation Date
(I)	09/01/2007		05/20/2011
	Exit Date	**Exit Reason**	**Diploma Type**
(J)	06/06/2011	W19-Graduated	High School Diploma

GPA Type	GPA	Crdt Atmpt	Class Rank
Overall Weighted	3.0476	42.0000	168 of 388
(K)	(L)	(M)	(N)

Total Credits Earned 44.0000 (O)

Issued To	Print Date
(A)	02/01/11 1 of 1

Doherty High School Grd 09 Semester 1 01/08

Subject Cd	Course	Mrk1	Abs	Credits
(B) EN	English 1, Honors	B	3	1.0000
HU	Frhand Drwng1	A	5	1.0000
HU	Spanish 1	B	4	1.0000
MA	Algebra 1	B	5	1.0000
PE	PE 9	B	7	1.0000
SC	Intro to Science 1	C	6	1.0000
SS	Gov/Law 1	B	5	1.0000

TERM: GPA 3.1429 CREDITS 7.0000
(C) **CUMULATIVE: GPA 3.1429 CREDITS 7.0000**

Doherty High School Grd 09 Semester 2 06/08

Subject Cd	Course	Mrk1	Abs	Credits
CM	Computer Apps	B	1	1.0000
EN	English 2, Honors	C	1	1.0000
HU	Frhand Drwng2	A	2	1.0000
HU	Spanish 2	B (D)	4	1.0000
MA	Algebra 2	B	1	1.0000
SC	Intro to Science 2	A	1	1.0000
SS	Gov/Law 2	B	3	1.0000

TERM: GPA 3.2857 CREDITS 7.0000
CUMULATIVE: GPA 3.2143 CREDITS 14.0000

Doherty High School Grd 10 Semester 1 01/09

Subject Cd	Course	Mrk1	Abs	Credits
E3	English 3	B	3	1.0000
HL	Health	C	1	1.0000
HU	Spanish 3	B	1	1.0000
MA	Geometry 1	B	(E)	1.0000
PA	Todays Foods	B	2	1.0000
SC	Biology 1	B	3	1.0000
SS	World & US History 3	C	2	1.0000

TERM: GPA 2.7143 CREDITS 7.0000
CUMULATIVE: GPA 3.0476 CREDITS 21.0000

Doherty High School Grd 10 Semester 2 06/09

Subject Cd	Course	Mrk1	Abs	Credits
E4	English 4	B	1	1.0000
HU	Frhand Drwng3	A	6	1.0000
HU	Spanish 4	B	6	1.0000
MA	Geometry 2	C	3	1.0000 (F)
PE	PE 10	B	7	1.0000
SC	Biology 2	B	7	1.0000
SS	World & US History 4	C	6	1.0000

TERM: GPA 2.8571 CREDITS 7.0000
CUMULATIVE: GPA 3.0000 CREDITS 28.0000

Doherty High School Grd 11 Semester 1 01/10

Subject Cd	Course	Mrk1	Abs	Credits
A1	Hist: US & World 5	C	9	1.0000
E5	English 5	B	9	1.0000
HU	Psychology	B	3	1.0000
MA	Algebra 3	B	1	1.0000
PA	Automotive Tech 1	A	5	1.0000

TERM: GPA 3.0000 CREDITS 5.0000
CUMULATIVE: GPA 3.0000 CREDITS 33.0000

Doherty High School Grd 11 Semester 2 06/10

Subject Cd	Course	Mrk1	Abs	Credits
A2	Hist: US & World 6	B	7	1.0000
E6	English 6	B	1	1.0000
EL	Student Tutor (G)	G	4	1.0000
HU	Psychology, Advanced	A	9	1.0000
MA	Algebra 4	B	4	1.0000

TERM: GPA 3.2500 CREDITS 5.0000
CUMULATIVE: GPA 3.0270 CREDITS 38.0000

Doherty High School Grd 12 Semester 1 01/11

Subject Cd	Course	Mrk1	Abs	Credits
CE	Cons Econ	B	3	1.0000
EN	Creative Writing	A	5	1.0000
EN	Senior Speed Reading 1	B	7	1.0000
PE	PE	A	9	1.0000
PE	Physical Ed	G		1.0000
SC	College Prep Chem 1	C	9	1.0000

TERM: GPA 3.2000 CREDITS 6.0000
CUMULATIVE: GPA 3.0476 CREDITS 44.0000

Mrk 1: Course Grade

Student Notes	
(P)	

(Q)

School Official's Signature

See next page for details and explanation.

WHAT'S WHAT ON YOUR TRANSCRIPT

A. Your personal information:

Name

Address

Social Security Number (or Student ID number if you don't have this number)

Date of Birth

Ethnic Code

NOTE: Parents can request that your social security number, date of birth, and ethnic code be deleted from the transcript when it is sent to various colleges.

B. Abbreviations of the classes you've taken.

C. **Term GPA** is the number of grade points you earn each semester. In the transcript example on the following page, each letter grade is given a number of points, with honors classes getting an extra point:

English 1 Honors (with an extra point for honors)	B = 4 points
Freehand Drawing 1	A = 4 points
Spanish 1	B = 3 points
Algebra 1	B = 3 points
PE 9	B = 3 points
Intro to Science 1	C = 2 points
Government/Law 1	B = 3 points

Add the points up and you get 22 points. Then divide that total (22) by the number of classes this student took, which is 7. Carry that out to 4 decimal places and you get 3.1429 grade points.

Cumulative GPA is found by taking the number of grade points from all your previous semesters and adding them up and then dividing them by the number of semesters. Let's look again at this student's transcript for the second semester:

Computer Apps	B = 3 points
English 2 Honors (with an extra point for honors)	C = 3 points
Freehand Drawing 2	A = 4 points
Spanish 2	B = 3 points
Algebra 2	B = 3 points
Intro to Science 2	A = 4 points
Government/Law 2	B = 3 points

Add the points up and you get 23 points. Then divide that total (23) by 7 (the number of classes) and carry that figure out 4 decimals to get 3.2857 points. Add the two semesters' points (3.1429 and 3.2857) together and divide by the number of semesters, which is 2, and you get the cumulative GPA of 3.2143.

D. Letter grade you earned in each class.

E. Number of absences in each class.

F. Number of credits you earned in each class—you get one credit per class, and you need 44 to graduate at this high school. Every school district has a different number of classes you need to graduate or, in some states, every district might be the same.

G. In this transcript, the letter G instead of an A, B, C, D, or F indicates that this course is not taken into account when figuring out your GPA. An "H" would indicate that you dropped the class without a penalty, like an "F". This student didn't drop any classes.

H. **Unofficial Transcript** means that it hasn't been signed or stamped with an official stamp. Transcripts are mailed directly to the school or colleges of your choice. Sometimes they can be transported by the student in a sealed envelope.

I. The date you entered the high school.

J. The date you left the high school.

K. Overall weighted—if your school gives extra points for honors or AP classes when figuring out your GPA, it will be noted here.

L. Your final cumulative GPA.

M. The total amount of credits you attempted.

N. Your class standing and the number of students who were in your senior class when you graduated. This student was 168 out of 388 students in the senior class.

O. Total Credits Earned in high school.

P. Notes about the clubs, sports, and committees in which you participated can be added here with verification from the person responsible for that extracurricular activity.

Q. Signature—The transcript must be signed and have an official seal in order to be accepted as an official transcript.

TIPS FOR A SMOOTH START

Write down a list of things you want to accomplish. If you have a rough idea of where you're headed, you'll have an easier time getting there. You've already set goals for yourself. Maybe it was to score more points on a video game than the kid down the street. Maybe it was to ride a bike faster or do more maneuvers on a skateboard. When you get into high school, it's important to set goals for yourself from the start. Obviously, the goals will change over time, but having a list of goals—*I want to make the football team; I want to take some honors classes; I want to run for class president; I want to be the editor of the school yearbook*—will help you stay motivated and give you something to work toward.

Make your goals specific. For example:

A vague goal is:

I want to be a better student than I was in middle school.

A specific goal is:

The reason I wasn't a good student in middle school is because I didn't turn in my homework. Starting off in high school, I'm going to turn in all my homework on time.

Get involved in clubs and activities immediately. We've already talked about how clubs and activities help narrow your interests and focus you on what you want to do in the future. But extracurricular activities serve another very important purpose for high school freshmen. You'll find friends who like the same things you do. You'll be with older kids, so you'll get to know some juniors and seniors. You'll gain confidence in yourself as you work together with other kids. You'll become comfortable with being in high school a lot quicker than if you hang around on the fringes looking in instead of being in the middle of the action, whether it's on a soccer team, chess club, or—whatever!

Get organized. In high school, being organized does not mean showing up in class on time with your teeth brushed. Being organized is at a whole different level in high school. Some kids are naturally this way. In middle school, they knew what homework had to be done, when it was due, and what was required. In high school, the list of things to organize gets longer. You still have to show up on time and whether your teeth are brushed is up to you, but you do have to have all the supplies you need with you.

PARENT PERSPECTIVE

STUDENT COUNSEL

When I was a freshman, I was intimidated by the older kids' appearance of greatness and their accomplishments. I thought, 'Wow, I can't get to their level.' But don't give up because you think there's too much competition, especially if it's something you really want to do.

Senior student
West Windsor Plainsboro High School South
Princeton Junction, New Jersey

"Every Friday afternoon before leaving school, my daughter gets her locker organized. It's easy for it to get out of control because kids are stuffing things in there all week. Then they can't find something when they need it, and the time between classes is so short."

Mother of high school junior
Council Rock High School North
Newtown, Pennsylvania

That sparkly pink pen in your hand won't do to take the test the teacher just handed you. Your teacher specifically told you to bring a blue or black ballpoint. *Now where is it? I thought I put it in my backpack. Oh no, here's the sandwich I forgot to eat yesterday on top of my history homework.* Your room may be a disaster, but your notebooks, binders, and calendar need to be in tip-top shape.

You're organizing for more classes and carrying around a lot more books and papers than you ever did in middle school. You're going to be involved in sports and clubs. Unless you're organized, you're going to spend more time dealing with chaos and confusion and moldy sandwiches than getting your homework done and having all the fun there is to have in high school. Each week in high school goes by at blazing speed and things can get out of control very quickly.

TIPS FROM A TEACHER

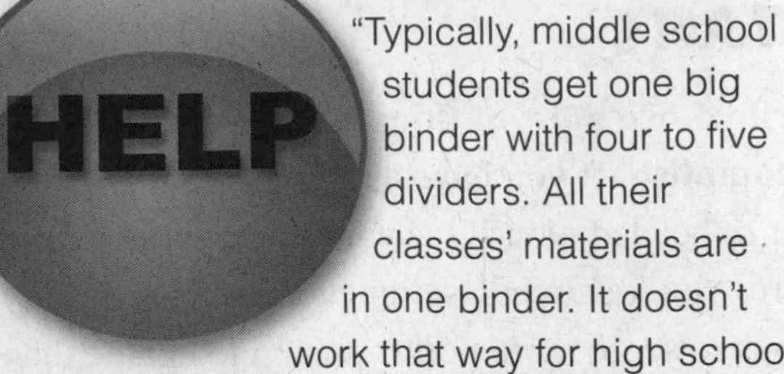

"Typically, middle school students get one big binder with four to five dividers. All their classes' materials are in one binder. It doesn't work that way for high school. They have too much. They can't put homework, notes, handouts, and other pieces of paper in one section of the binder. When the binder system fails by mid-October, then they take everything that was in the binder and stuff it in a backpack. Now it's a 15-minute ordeal to find something in the backpack."

Spanish teacher
Pioneer High School
San Jose, California

This is what organized students know:

- What was assigned in each class
- When the homework is due
- When the next test is scheduled
- What I need to bring to each class
- Where the supplies I need are located

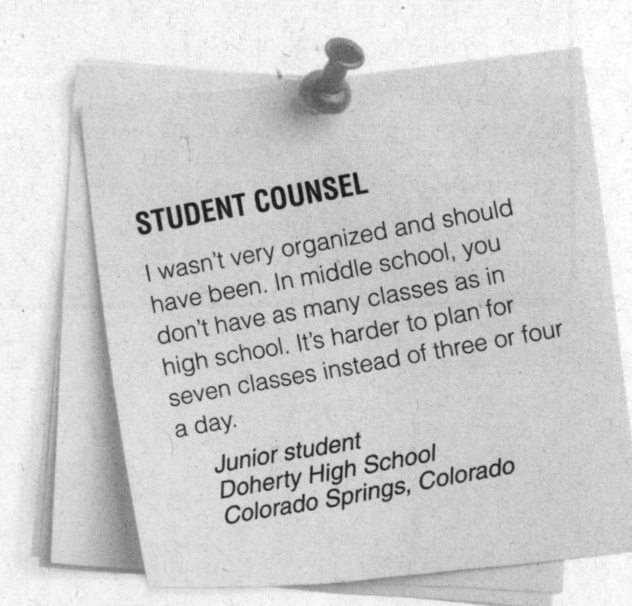

STUDENT COUNSEL

I wasn't very organized and should have been. In middle school, you don't have as many classes as in high school. It's harder to plan for seven classes instead of three or four a day.

Junior student
Doherty High School
Colorado Springs, Colorado

Organization skills will stay with you the rest of your life. Now's a great time to learn how much easier your life will be when you're organized.

The way to get organized is to set up a system. It can be someone else's system or your own. The important thing is to have some way to keep track of when assignments are due, when tests are coming, and what nights are taken up with practices or meetings. Each week, go through and set up a new schedule for the coming week. It sounds like a lot of work, but when Thursday hits and your head is spinning, you'll be glad you have a schedule to hang on to. You could have three tests on the same day. Wouldn't it be helpful to know that way ahead of time instead of remembering the day of the tests?

FROM THE GUIDANCE OFFICE

As students transition to high school, it's important to develop self-advocacy skills. If you need or want something, you will have to seek out the resources to get the help or support that you desire. If you are struggling academically in a particular subject, you need to seek out your teacher for extra help. Your school counselor is an excellent resource to help you develop your self-advocacy skills and to help problem-solve other situations. Once you are in college, your parents will not be there, so start early so you will feel comfortable approaching the resources available.

Guidance Counselor
West Windsor–Plainsboro High School South
Princeton Junction, New Jersey

Manage your time. Time management is a term that you've probably heard and put into the "I'll deal with that when I get older" category. Guess what, you're older! You have to take your time and manage it, which means figuring out what you have to do and how much time you have to do it.

It's going to be easy to say, "I'll do my homework after dinner," but you have to take into account that basketball practice doesn't end until 8 p.m., and when you get home you'll want something to eat. So, in reality, you're doing homework until 10 or 11 o'clock, and you have to get up at 6 o'clock.

In high school, your workload increases as you move into the upper classes. If you don't learn how to manage your time, you'll only have to struggle that much harder. Plus you have all those other activities eating away at the 24 hours in each day.

Ask questions. You've heard the saying, "No question is a stupid question." Well, kids going into ninth grade seem to forget the "NO" part of that sentence and instead rephrase it as "All my questions are stupid." No matter if you went down the wrong hall and can't find your classroom. No matter if you need help in signing up for a club you really want to join. No matter if you didn't understand what the teacher was saying. The guidance counselors and teachers are there to help you get adjusted and pointed in the right direction.

Take advantage of the help the guidance counselors can give you. You'd be amazed at the number of things you can find in the guidance office—advice on good study habits, advice on planning for college, advice about what to do with that class that seems over your head. Use it, because it's there for you.

Develop good study habits. If your study habits are lacking, you still have time to improve them. Studying should not happen only in the days or hours—or minutes!—before a test. As a high school student, it's your job to attend class, pay attention to your teachers, recognize what you don't understand, and get the help you need to be able to understand it. It's a good idea to review your notes daily—not right before a test.

Take good notes. Notes don't always have to be in written form, and they shouldn't be transcripts of everything your teacher says. If you determine the main idea of the lesson, you have to record only the details that support that idea. If you're a visual learner, try turning your notes into action-packed pictures. By turning the content into a visual representation, you'll probably understand it more and remember it better.

Stay motivated and committed. You've set your goals for high school, and now it's up to you to stay motivated and committed. View obstacles as a challenge to overcome and not a reason for throwing in the towel or giving up.

About 60 percent of jobs require training or education beyond high school. According to the Education Commission of the States, high school graduates earn higher salaries and are less likely to depend on public assistance, have health problems, or turn to criminal activity. Just as elementary school and middle school prepared you for high school, high school is the training ground for the rest of your life. When you look at it that way, it can be a little scary. The habits you develop in high school, however, will help you during the course of your life.

BEWARE THE BLACK HOLE OF THE BACKPACK

It looks like an ordinary backpack (or whatever it is you use to carry your books and school papers), but don't be fooled by its innocent appearance. Somewhere between when you get out of middle school and into high school, it turns into a black hole—casually destroying finished homework, cheerfully ripping through notes you saved for a test, cunningly hiding the special pen you like.

You may have been organized in junior high school, but once you get into high school, the backpack can turn into an endless pit into which you stuff everything, and whatever it is you need to find in its endless depths cannot be found without a major search and rescue.

The reason for this dilemma that will suddenly appear in your life is that in high school you've got a lot more papers to organize. Homework is given in most classes. You're getting handouts that have to be saved for a test that will come up in three weeks, along with that list of supplies you're supposed to bring to science class and the day planner you bought.

You must ramp up the way you keep things organized to keep up with high school. One suggestion is to get a three-subject spiral notebook for each class. Section one is for taking notes in class. Section two is for homework. Section three is for tearing out sheets of paper. You now have everything you need for one subject in one notebook. The pages can't come out unless you tear them out and it's chronological, so you can look back at past notes and tell what was discussed when.

With this system, or any other that suits you best, your backpack will turn into an ordinary useful bag, and when your history teacher asks you to pull out the notes from last week's class, you'll know exactly where to find them.

MAKE SURE YOUR PARENTS READ THIS!

Some of you have been through the process of transitioning a son or daughter from middle school to high school. For some of you, it's your first time. According to a guidance counselor who has worked in elementary, middle, and high school, the transitions from elementary to middle and middle to high school are the most traumatic for your kids. The range of emotions swings from fearful to happy and back again. The transition brings out all your child's insecurities. But the cumulative wisdom of other parents and guidance counselors can help you help your children. The following are some tried and tested tips.

- Find out what tryouts for high school clubs, activities, and sports take place in the summer and see if your child may be interested in joining.
- While your child is still in middle school, take her to the high school on casual trips, such as to the library, to the swimming pool, or to a play, so she will already be familiar with the building and things to do before ninth grade starts.
- Before high school starts, and if the school permits, take your child on a test run to walk the halls and meet teachers who are there early to set up their classrooms. Then let him come back by himself for another test run.
- Encourage involvement in school activities other than just sports. In general, the students who are involved in extracurricular activities enjoy school and have greater academic success. Advise your child to start gradually in the freshman year, with a few activities, and then add more as she moves toward her senior year.
- Help your child set up a system to organize homework assignments, test dates, and other activities.
- Give your children the space to try and do things by themselves. Get your children to advocate for their interests and needs on their own. School administrators and teachers love parent involvement, but it's important to let kids deal with some issues alone.
- Set realistic goals for your child. It's good for children to be challenged, but if the goals are too ambitious, children give up reaching for any goals.

TOP 10 MISTAKES

Everyone makes errors, but if you can avoid these Top 10 mistakes as you begin your freshman year, you'll be in much better shape. Drum roll, please. We'll start with the worst.

1 **My freshman year doesn't count. My senior year is far away. If I mess up, I can always get back on track in the tenth grade.** While it's true you can make up for bad choices and slip-ups, your freshman year is the foundation upon which the rest of your high school years, and then college, are built. Freshman year isn't practice or a trial period—it's the real thing!

2 **I'm picking this class because my friend is taking it.** Your friend picked the class in honors biology because she's always talked about becoming a doctor and can't wait to dissect a pig. You, on the other hand, would rather read poetry about the human body. You won't find out what a mistake you've made until you're way behind on your homework and have failed several tests, when you could have been getting A's in the honors English class that you should have taken.

3 **I'll just skip this class. One day won't make a difference.** Not so. In high school, attendance counts. Many schools have policies that cause you to lose credits if you miss class a certain number of times. Even the best of students will miss classes because of illness or other unforeseen events. But remember, much of the teaching in high school is cumulative, meaning that each day is built on what happened in the class the previous day. If you get out of the loop, it's really hard to get back in.

4 **I don't need to write down that assignment. I'll remember it.** Most likely, you'll only remember the assignment until you leave the classroom; then it's history. By the time you get home, you'll have a vague recollection of what the teacher said you had to do. Then you'll have to call someone in the class to ask about the assignment, and if that person isn't home, you'll be making a lot more calls. And you certainly don't want to skip doing the homework.

5 **I spilled soda on my homework. I know I'll be late turning it in if I do it over, so I'll just forget about it.** You should talk to your teacher about making up lost or forgotten homework. Even though the teacher will probably take off some points, you guarantee getting no points if you don't turn it in at all! So, while the assignment may be late, at least it will be counted. Don't be afraid to ask your teacher about turning in late assignments—better late than never!

6 **Sorry, I can't join that club, I have to study all the time.** In your freshman year, it's especially important to become part of the school community. You'll not only get to know other kids who like the same things you do, but you will also get to explore what you like to do.

7 **Everyone else in this class understood what the teacher just said except me, so I won't ask him to explain it.** You'll be surprised to know that if you didn't understand something or if you need further explanation, probably others feel the same way. Be brave. Ask the question, and you'll have everyone else in your class silently thanking you. Plus, more important, you'll understand what the teacher was saying.

8 **I don't want to talk to the teacher about the problems I'm having with her class.** Teachers aren't mind-readers. They have no clue that you're struggling until they see your work. If you're having problems, it's okay to say, "I just don't get fractions." Teachers love to teach, and part of teaching is helping students understand things.

9 **A situation at school is making me uncomfortable. I'll just tell my friend about it and not go to the counselor's office.** Big or small, serious or not, whatever problems you're having or whatever situations are bothering you, your high school counselors are there to help you, protect you, guide you, comfort you. Your best friend may be able to sympathize with your problem, but chances are your friend can't solve the issue so effectively as a counselor or teacher can.

10 **I really don't need all that much sleep.** That may have been true during the summer when you could sleep late. Now you're up and out with the sunrise. Trouble is, when you go to bed late, you find yourself nodding off in first period. All that brain power you are using to adjust to high school takes energy. Energy comes from a good night's sleep.

PART 2
JUMP-START YOUR FUTURE

Come on. Admit it. You know that big question—what will I do when I graduate from high school?—is right around the corner. Some of your classmates know what they want to do, but you're freaking out about all the decisions you still have to make.

You've got a lot of possibilities from which to choose. Maybe you'll attend a two-year or four-year college or a vocational or career college. Or maybe you'll join the armed services. Or perhaps you'll go right into the workplace with a full-time job. But before you march across that stage to get your diploma, the *Teens' Guide* will help you to begin thinking about your options and to open up doors you never knew existed.

CHAPTER 2

A LOOK AT YOURSELF

Deciding what to do with your life is a lot like flying. Just look at the many ways you can fly and the many directions your life can take.

A teacher once asked her students to bring something to class that flies. Students brought kites, balloons, and models of airplanes, blimps, hot-air balloons, helicopters, spaceships, gliders, and seaplanes. But when class began, the teacher explained that the lesson was about career planning, not flying.

She was making the point that your plans for life after high school can take many forms. How you'll make the journey is an individual matter. That's why it's important to know who you are and what you want—before taking off.

READY TO FLY?

Just having a high school diploma is not enough for many occupations. But, surprise, surprise, neither is a college degree. Different kinds of work require different kinds of training. Knowing how to operate a particular type of equipment, for instance, takes special skills and work experience that you might not learn in college. Employers always want to hire the best-qualified people available, but this does not mean that they always choose those applicants who have the most education. The *type* of education and training you have is just as important as *how much*. Right now, you're at the point in your life where you can choose how much and what kind of education and training you want to get.

If you have a definite career goal in mind, such as being a doctor, you probably already know what it will take in terms of education. You're looking at about four years of college, then four years of medical school, and, in most states, one year of residency. Cosmetologists, on the other hand, complete a state-approved training program that ranges from eight to eighteen months.

But for most of you, deciding what to do after high school is not so easy. Perhaps you haven't chosen a field of work yet. You might just know for certain that you want a job that will give you status and a big paycheck. Or maybe you know what you want to do, but you're not sure what kind of education you'll need. For instance, you may love fixing cars, and the idea of being an auto mechanic sounds great. But you need to decide whether to learn on the job, attend a vocational school, seek an apprenticeship, or pursue a combination of these options.

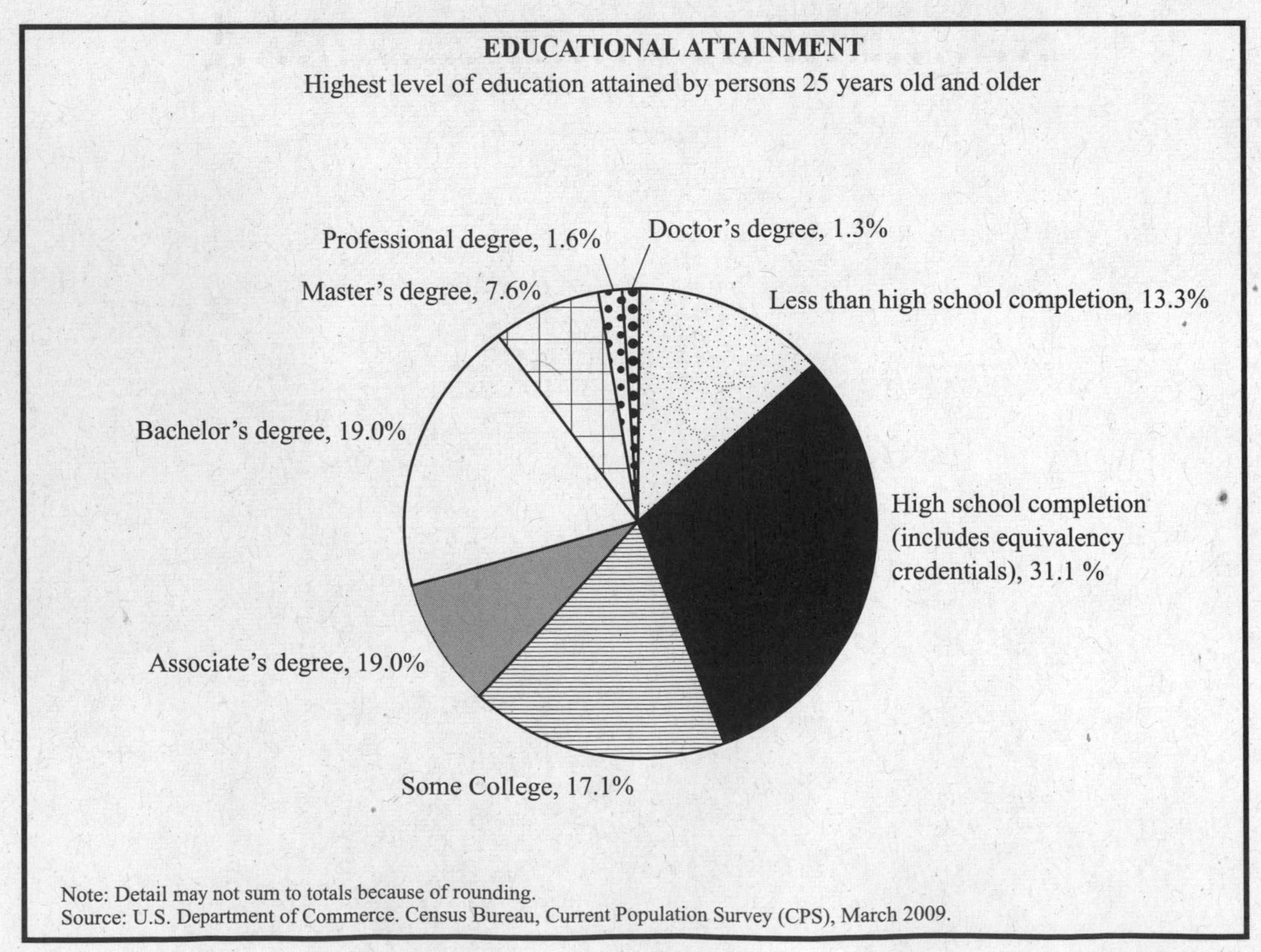

TOP 10 REASONS TO CONTINUE YOUR EDUCATION

Continuing your education after high school is one choice that can give you a good start no matter what your final career decision is. If you think college is not for you at all, take a look at this list, It just might change your mind.

10 **Fulfill a dream—or begin one.** Some people hope to become teachers or scientists. For many, continuing their education provides the opportunity to make that dream a reality for themselves or their families.

9 **Have fun.** Classes are an important part of continued education, but plenty of opportunities for some great times exist outside the classroom. You can join hundreds of sports, clubs, groups, activities, and associations. Many people say that their college years were the best years of their lives.

8 **Make connections.** The friends, professors, supervisors, and classmates you meet after high school will provide valuable leads for future jobs, committees, and associations within the community.

7 **Become part of a cultural stew.** As you have probably already figured out, not everyone is like you. Nor should they be. Being in college is a good way to meet many types of people from various backgrounds and geographic locations, with different viewpoints and opinions. You may discover that you like people and things you never knew existed.

6 **Meet new people.** By furthering your education, you'll widen your circle of friends and, chances are, form meaningful lifelong relationships.

5 **Do what you love doing and get paid for it.** Have you ever taken a test during which everything clicked or played a video game and caught on immediately? This is what happens when you combine education and training with the right job. Work becomes more like play, which is far more satisfying and rewarding than just going through the motions.

4 **Exercise your mind.** Just as physical exercise keeps your body in shape, mental exercise keeps your mind free of cobwebs. No matter what your area of interest, education holds the key to the most interesting and challenging information you can imagine. Explore your outer limits and become a lifelong learner.

3 **Earn a higher income.** Although money isn't everything, it is necessary for survival. A good education can lead to higher overall income.

2 **Learn critical-thinking, analytical, and writing skills.** Education teaches you to think critically, organize and analyze information, and write clearly.

1 **You won't get left behind.** In the twenty-first century, you need to be prepared to change jobs and continually learn new skills to keep up with changes in industry, communications, and technology. Education and training gives you that preparation.

INCREASE YOUR EARNING POWER

People with more education tend to earn more money. Look at the median income of workers over the age of 25 by educational level.

DEGREE	MEDIAN INCOME
Professional Degree	$100,000
Doctoral Degree	$86,171
Master's Degree	$71,097
Bachelor's Degree	$58,826
Associate Degree	$43,006
Some College	$37,447
High School Diploma	$31,337
Less Than High School Diploma	$20,643

Source: U.S. Census Bureau, March 2008

Breaking Down Barriers to Continuing Your Education

Some of you may say, "Forget the reasons why I *should* continue my education. I *can't* because (fill in the blank)." Let's see if your objections stand up.

I CAN'T.

Nobody in my family has ever gone to college.

You can!

You can be the first! It's a little scary and not always easy, but just think how great you'll feel being the first person in your family to receive a degree, diploma, or certificate.

I CAN'T.

My grades are not good enough.

You can!

Don't let less-than-perfect grades stand in your way. Different institutions have different requirements, including what grades they accept. Schools also evaluate you for admission as a whole person, including your participation in extracurricular activities; your talents, such as academics and athletics; and your employment and volunteer history. In addition, classes to help you improve your skills in various subject areas are available. Get a tutor now or form a study group to improve your grades as much as possible. Talk to your guidance counselor about what the appropriate curriculum for you is so you'll have more options when making decisions about continuing your education.

I CAN'T.

I can't afford it.

You can!

Many families cannot afford to pay education costs completely out of pocket. That's why there are so many opportunities for financial aid, scholarships, grants, and work-study programs. Federal, state, school-sponsored, private, and career-specific financial aid resources are available to students who take the time to look. Talk to a guidance counselor, go to the library, and look on the Internet. Read the "Financial Aid Dollars and Sense" chapter of this guide for more information about how to finance your continued education. Be creative and persistent. It can happen for you.

I CAN'T.

I don't know how to apply or where I want to go.

You can!

Fortunately, many resources are available to help you decide which institution to select. Talk to friends, family members, neighbors, your guidance counselor, pastor, coach, or librarian. Take a look online for listings of two-year and four-year colleges, as well as vocational and career colleges in your state.

I CAN'T.

I think it may be too difficult for me.

You can!

Think back to something you have done in your life that seemed too difficult in the beginning. Didn't you find that once you began, put your mind to it, and stuck with it that you succeeded? You can do almost anything if you set your mind to it and are willing to work for it.

I CAN'T.

I'm not sure I'll fit in.

You can!

One of the best things about furthering your education is the chance to meet new people and be part of new experiences in new surroundings. Colleges and other continuing education options attract a wide variety of students from many different backgrounds. Chances are you won't have any problem finding someone else with interests that are similar to yours. Because schools differ in size, location, student body, and lifestyle, you'll surely find one that meets your needs. Advance visits and interviews can help you determine which school is right for you.

I CAN'T.

I don't even know what I want to do with my life.

You can!

Many students don't know this about themselves until they get to experience some of the possibilities. Take the "Self-Assessment Inventory" to help you determine what your interests and talents are. Read "Choosing Your Major" in Chapter 9 for a listing of the most popular college majors and their related careers.

I CAN'T.

I need to work, so I'd need to be a part-time student.

You can!

Part-time students are becoming the norm. In fact, a recent study determined that 43 percent of undergraduate students attend school part-time. Most schools offer evening and weekend classes, and many offer work-study opportunities to help students pay for their education. Also, some employers will pay or reimburse you if you are working and want to further your education. If you are enrolled part-time, it does take longer to graduate. But if full-time enrollment is not an option for you, don't give up the opportunity to continue your education. You can achieve your goals in many nontraditional ways.

The greater the obstacle, the more glory in overcoming it.
~Moliere

FASTEST-GROWING OCCUPATIONS

Want to have a career that's going places? Check out this chart to see which occupations are expected to grow the fastest by the year 2018 and what type of training you'll need to get the job.

Occupation	Expected Openings	Required Education
Biomedical Engineers	12,000	Bachelor's degree
Network Systems and Data Communications Analysts	156,000	Bachelor's degree
Home Health Aides	461,000	On-the-job training
Personal and Home Care Aides	376,000	On-the-job training
Financial Examiners	11,000	Bachelor's degree
Medical Scientists, Except Epidemiologists	44,000	Doctoral degree
Physician Assistants	29,000	Master's degree
Skin Care Specialists	15,000	Postsecondary vocational award
Biochemists and Biophysicists	9,000	Doctoral degree
Athletic Trainers	6,000	Bachelor's degree
Physical Therapist Aides	17,000	On-the-job-training
Dental Hygienists	63,000	Associate degree
Veterinary Technologists and Technicians	29,000	Associate degree
Dental Assistants	106,000	On-the-job training
Computer Software Engineers, Applications	175,000	Bachelor's degree
Medical Assistants	164,000	On-the-job training
Physical Therapist Assistants	21,000	Associate degree
Veterinarians	20,000	First professional degree
Self-Enrichment Education Teachers	81,000	Work experience in a related occupation
Compliance Officers, Except Agriculture, Construction, Health and Safety, and Transportation	81,000	On-the-job training
Occupational Therapist Aides	2,000	On-the-job training
Environmental Engineers	17,000	Bachelor's degree
Pharmacy Technicians	100,000	On-the-job training
Computer Software Engineers, Systems Software	120,000	Bachelor's degree
Survey Researchers	7,000	Bachelor's degree
Physical Therapists	56,000	Master's degree
Personal Financial Advisors	63,000	Bachelor's degree
Environmental Engineering Technicians	6,000	Associate degree
Occupational Therapist Assistants	8,000	Associate degree
Fitness Trainers and Aerobics Instructors	7,000	Postsecondary vocational award

Source: Bureau of Labor Statistics, December 2009 Economic News Release

CHOOSING A CAREER THAT WILL MAKE YOU HAPPY

Take some time *now* to consider what it is you *really* want to do. Have you always dreamed of doing a particular job? What activities do you enjoy now that you might want to turn into a career someday? Perhaps you enjoy playing video games, putting together trendy outfits, listening to music on your iPod, texting your friends, or playing sports. Consider turning your current interests into a future career. By attending a school that specializes in preparing students for a specific career, you'll improve your chances of landing a career that you truly enjoy, and your job won't feel like work at all!

Earn a Living Doing What You Love

Video Gaming

Your parents have probably nagged you to stop playing video games and study more because "video games aren't going to get you anywhere in life." Not true! You can have a great career as a video game designer or developer by attending a traditional school, a game-specific school, or an art school.

Traditional schools are four-year colleges and universities or two-year community colleges that provide a well-rounded education, which helps you develop problem-solving skills and analytical and critical thinking, which are necessary to develop video games.

Game-specific schools cater to people who want to learn specific skills and exit school with a job offer to make games. Game-specific schools are in tune with the cutting-edge technologies and often have specific resources available to students to help them put together job applications specific to the video game industry. Most gaming schools take a team-oriented group project approach because the game development industry thrives on the team approach.

Art schools now offer more courses, certificates, and degrees in game-relevant subjects. Art schools offer courses in animation and 3-D art and design, which help in all careers in the gaming industry.

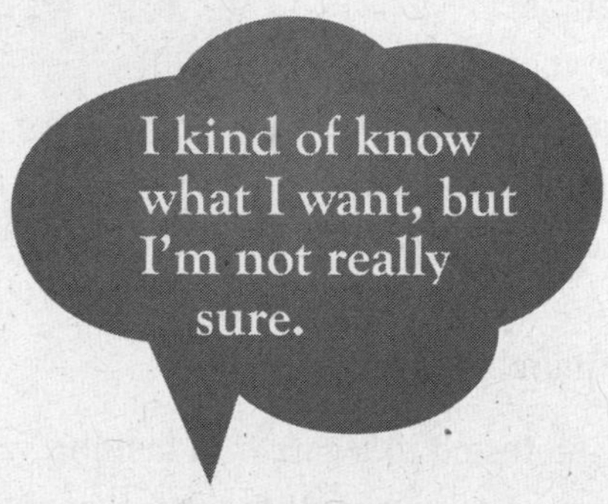

One of the best things you can do now to get into the video gaming industry later is make games. They don't have to be video games; they can be pen and paper, card games, or board games. Then, write down all the rules and instructions for playing them. You need to be able to make games if you want to someday make video games. For more information about game-specific schools and other schools for future game developers, visit www.gamecareerguide.com.

Fashion

A career in fashion can lead you in many different directions, such as design and production, media and promotions, or marketing and merchandising. The following is a list of possible careers in the fashion industry:

- Accessories designer
- Boutique owner
- Buyer
- Clothing patternmaker
- Costume designer
- Fashion coordinator
- Fashion designer
- Fashion editor
- Fashion marketing and merchandising
- Fashion public relations specialist
- Fashion stylist
- Fashion writer

Graphic designer
Illustrator
Merchandiser
Model
Personal stylist
Photographer
Product manager
Retail merchandiser
Retail store manager
Sales representative
Showroom sales representative
Visual merchandiser

If you're interested in a career in fashion, you should consider applying to one of the many accredited fashion schools across the country. In addition, research the types of careers that are available to you. Think about your strengths, weaknesses, and interests and match them to a category in the fashion industry. Once you have narrowed your choice to the area of fashion that most interests you, find an accredited school with a knowledgeable faculty in a location that suits you.

Music

Being in a band is not your only career choice if you are interested in music. Music is a broad field with many career alternatives such as facility, arena, and club management; instrument work and development; merchandising; music education; recording; or radio station disc jockey or program director. The area of the music field that interests you most will determine the type of school you may want to attend. If you are more interested in writing and composing music, you'll likely want to go to a school that specializes in musical composition. If you think you'd prefer managing a musical facility or working in the wings at a concert, you'll want to attend a school that prepares you for the technical aspects of those careers.

Media and Communications

All that time you spend texting and communicating with your friends might set you up for a career in media and communication. Media and communication is a multibillion-dollar industry, and a degree in communication provides a valuable foundation for careers in almost any field because it lays the foundation for good listening, speaking, creative thinking, decision making, and problem solving. Some specialized careers in media and communication include the following:

Broadcast and sound engineering technicians and radio operators
Language interpreters and translators
News analysts, reporters, and correspondents
Public relations specialists
Television, radio, and sports announcers
Television, video, and motion picture camera operators and editors
Writers and editors

Sports

Love sports but don't think you'll make it as a professional athlete? Why not pursue a career in the sports industry instead. The National Football League (NFL), Major League Baseball (MLB), the National Basketball Association (NBA), the National Hockey League (NHL), Major League Soccer (MLS), and the National Collegiate Athletic Association (NCAA) are just a few potential employers for those interested in sports jobs. The schooling you need for such jobs can be obtained at many four-year colleges and universities. Some sports industry jobs include the following:

Administration and finance support
Fitness, coaching, and scouting
Management and agent
Marketing and sales
Media, public relations, and broadcasting
Promotions, events, and facilities
Retail manufacturing

ON THE HUNT FOR INFORMATION

Perhaps you're one of the many high school students who say:

"I Kind of Know What I Want, But I'm Not Really Sure."

A good way to gather information about potential occupations is by talking with people who have achieved goals that are similar to yours. Talk to teachers, neighbors, and adult friends about their work experiences. The formal name for that activity is an "informational interview." You're interviewing them about the work they do—not to get a job from them but to gather information about their jobs.

If you don't have any contacts in a field that sparks your interest, do some poking around in the workplace. For instance, if you're interested in a career in nursing, you could visit a hospital, doctor's office, or nursing home. Most people love to talk about themselves, so don't be afraid to ask if they'll chat with you about their profession. Offering to volunteer your services can be the best way to know whether you'll be happy doing that type of work.

"I Don't Have a Clue About What I Want to Do."

If you're completely unsure about what kind of work you'd like to do, contact a career counselor who can help you explore your options and possibly administer some interest and aptitude tests. You also might think about contacting a college career planning and placement office, a vocational school placement office, the counseling services of community agencies, or a private counseling service, which may charge you a fee. Many high schools offer job-shadowing programs, where students actually shadow someone in a particular occupation for an entire day or more. Don't forget that as a high school student, your best resource is your high school guidance counselor. Take a look at the list of the "Fastest-Growing Occupations" in this chapter to get a sampling of the careers with the largest projected job growth in the coming years.

Regardless of how unsure you may be about what you want to do after high school, the following is a list of actions you can take to get the information you need to head in the right direction. Many people start off thinking they want one career and end up doing something completely different. But this is a good place to begin:

- Investigate careers both in and out of school. Participate in mentoring, job shadowing, and career day opportunities whenever possible.
- Get some on-the-job experience in a field that interests you.
- Research two-year and four-year colleges, vocational/career colleges, and apprenticeship programs.
- Participate in school and state career-development activities.
- Prepare for and take aptitude and college entrance tests.

The following are a few Web sites where you can receive valuable direction by completing a career interest questionnaire or by reading about various occupations:

Occupational Outlook Handbook

www.bls.gov/oco

The Bureau of Labor Statistics, an agency within the U.S. Department of Labor, produces this Web site, which offers more information than you'll ever need about specific careers.

Mapping Your Future

www.mappingyourfuture.org

On this site, you can find out how to choose a career and how to reach your career goals. You can also pick up useful tips on job hunting, resume writing, and job interviewing techniques. This site also provides a ten-step plan for determining and achieving your career goals.

University of Waterloo Career Development eManual

www.cdm.uwaterloo.ca/

This site provides a thorough online career interest survey and strategies you can use to get the job that's right for you.

LiveCareer

www.livecareer.com

LiveCareer is a San Francisco–based company founded by Sigma Assessment Systems, Inc., and a group of leading career professionals and investors. Since 2004, LiveCareer has developed innovative practical assessment solutions that have helped more than 5 million people make important career decisions.

Monster

www.monster.com

This site includes information about thousands of job and career fairs, advice on resumes, and much more.

Today is your day! Your mountain is waiting. So get on your way.

~Dr. Seuss

SELF-ASSESSMENT INVENTORY

In addition to looking to outside sources for information, there's another rich source of data: yourself. Knowing what you want to do begins with knowing yourself—the real you. The better you understand your own wants and needs, the better you will be able to make decisions about your career goals and dreams. This self-assessment inventory can help.

Whom do you admire most, and why?

What is your greatest strength?

What is your greatest talent?

What skills do you already have?

DESCRIBE HOW YOU CURRENTLY USE THESE SKILLS IN YOUR LIFE:

Athletic ability

Mechanical ability

Ability to work with numbers

Leadership skills

Teaching skills

Artistic skills

Analytical skills

CHECK THE AREAS THAT MOST INTEREST YOU:

❑ Providing a practical service for people

❑ Self-expression in music, art, literature, or nature

❑ Organizing and record keeping

❑ Meeting people and supervising others

❑ Helping others in need, either mentally, spiritually, or physically

❑ Solving practical problems

❑ Working in forestry, farming, or fishing

❑ Working with machines and tools

❑ Taking care of animals

❑ Physical work outdoors

❑ Protecting the public via law enforcement or fire fighting

❑ Medical, scientific, or mathematical work

❑ Selling, advertising, or promoting

WHAT GIVES YOU SATISFACTION?

Answer the following questions True (T) or False (F).

T F I get satisfaction not from personal accomplishment but from helping others.

T F I'd like to have a job in which I can use my imagination and be inventive.

T F In my life, money will be placed ahead of job security and personal interests.

T F It is my ambition to have a direct impact on other people's lives.

T F I am not a risk-taker and would prefer a career that offers little risk.

T F I enjoy working with people rather than by myself.

T F I would not be happy doing the same thing all the time.

WHAT MATTERS THE MOST TO YOU?

Rate the items on the list below from 1 to 10, with 10 being extremely important and 1 being not at all important.

___ Good health

___ Justice

___ Marriage/family

___ Faith

___ Fame

___ Beauty

___ Safety

___ Friendship

___ Respect

___ Accomplishment

___ Seeing the world

___ Love

___ Fun

___ Power

___ Individualism

___ Charity

___ Honor

___ Intelligence

___ Wealth

WHAT WOULD YOU DO IF YOU WERE IN A BLIZZARD SURVIVAL SITUATION?

Check the one that would be your most likely role.

❑ The leader

❑ The one who explains the situation to the others

❑ The one who keeps morale up

❑ The one who invents a way to keep warm and melt snow for water

❑ The one who listens to instructions and keeps the supplies organized

❑ The one who positions sticks and rocks to signal SOS

LOOKING AHEAD AND LOOKING BACK

What are your goals for the next five years?

Where would you like to be in ten years?

What was your favorite course, and why?

What was your least favorite course, and why?

Who was your favorite teacher, and why?

What are your hobbies?

What are your extracurricular activities?

What jobs have you held?

What volunteer work, if any, have you performed?

Have you ever shadowed a professional for a day? If so, what did you learn?

Do you have a mentor? If so, who? What have you learned from this person?

Do you want to stay close to home, or would you prefer to travel to another city after high school?

What are your career goals?

The interests, skills, and knowledge supporting my career goals are:

To fulfill my career goals, I will need additional skills and knowledge in:

I will obtain the additional skills and knowledge by taking part in the following educational activities:

I will need a degree, certification, and/or specialized training in:

When I look in the classified ads of the newspaper, the following job descriptions sound attractive to me:

WHAT ARE YOUR IMMEDIATE PLANS AFTER HIGH SCHOOL?

After high school, I plan to:

- ❑ Work full-time
- ❑ Work part-time and attend school
- ❑ Attend college full-time
- ❑ Attend technical college
- ❑ Enter the military

WHAT WILL YOU NEED TO GET WHERE YOU'RE GOING?

The information I have given indicates that I will be selecting courses that are primarily:

- ❑ College path (Four-year or two-year education that offers liberal arts courses combined with courses in your area of interest.)
- ❑ Vocational path (One or more years of education that include hands-on training for a specific job.)
- ❑ Combination of the two

MY PERFECT JOB WOULD BE ...

Let your imagination run wild. You can have any job you want. What's it like? Start by describing to yourself the following:

Work conditions What hours are you willing to work? Do you feel most satisfied in an environment that is indoors/outdoors, varied/regular, noisy/quiet, or casual/traditional?

Duties What duties do you feel comfortable carrying out? Do you want to be a leader, or do you perform best as a team player?

People Do you want to work with other people or more independently? How much people contact do you want/need?

Education How much special training or education is required? How much education are you willing to seek? Can you build upon the education or experience you have to date? Will you need to gain new education or experience?

Benefits What salary and benefits do you expect? Are you willing to travel?

Disadvantages There are disadvantages with almost any job. Can you imagine what the disadvantages may be? Can you confirm or disprove these beliefs by talking to someone or researching the industry or job further? If these disadvantages really exist, can you live with them?

Personal qualities What qualities do you want in the employer you ultimately choose? What are the most important qualities that you want in a supervisor? In your coworkers?

Look over your responses to this assessment. Do you see recurring themes in your answers that start to show you what kind of career you might like? If not, there are many more places to get information to decide where your interests lie. You can go to your guidance counselor for advice. You can take the Campbell™ Interest and Skills Inventory, the Strong Interest Inventory, the Self-Directed Search, or other assessment tests that your guidance counselor recommends.

CHAPTER 3

THE FIRST STEPS TO A CAREER

Don't be too surprised when your summer job turns into your career.

The word "career" has a scary sound to it when you're still in high school. Careers are for college graduates or those who have been in the workplace for years. But unless you grew up knowing for sure that you wanted to fly airplanes or be a botanist, what will you do? You'll be happy to know that interests you have now can very possibly lead to a college major or career. A job at a clothing store, for instance, could lead to a career designing clothes. Perhaps those hours you spend on your Xbox will lead to a career creating video games! Maybe you babysit and love being around kids, so teaching becomes an obvious choice. Perhaps cars fascinate you, and you find out you want to fix them for a living.

This chapter will show you how you can begin exploring your interests—sort of like getting into a swimming pool starting with your big toe, rather than plunging in. Vocational/career and tech-prep programs, summer jobs, and volunteering are all ways you can test various career paths to decide if you like them.

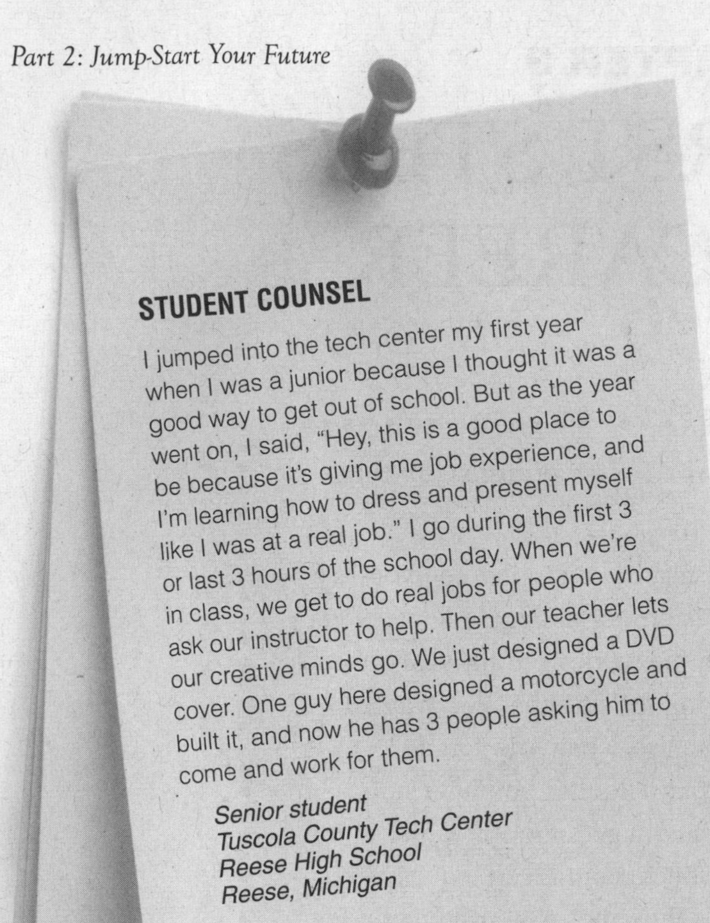

FROM THE GUIDANCE OFFICE

When adults ask kids what they want to do as a career, kids feel pressured. They think adults want them to identify with one single career. But there are more than 40,000 job titles a person can hold. We tell kids to pick a path first. When you exit high school, there are three paths you can take. One is to the workplace. One leads to the military as a career or as a stepping stone. The third leads to more education—a professional degree, a four-year degree, or a two-year degree. They have to determine which path they'll take.

One of the main selling points about getting career education in high school is that nearly every employer wants you to have some experience before you are hired. In career tech, students are in a workplace environment and can list their time as work experience, and they'll have previous employers who can vouch for them.

Counselor, Technology Center
Tuscola ISD
Caro, Michigan

THE VOCATIONAL/ CAREER EDUCATION PATH

If you're looking for a more real-world education, add yourself to the nearly 11 million youths and adults who are getting a taste of the workplace through vocational and career education programs offered in high schools across the nation. These programs are designed to help you develop competency in the skills you'll need in the workplace as well as in school.

What makes this kind of program different is that you learn in the classroom and in the "real world" of the workplace. You not only learn the academics in school, but you also get hands-on training by job shadowing, working under a mentor, and actually performing a job outside school. Your interests and talents are usually taken into consideration, and you can choose from a variety of traditional, high-tech, and service industry training programs. Take a look at the following categories and see what piques your interest.

Agricultural education. These programs prepare students for careers in agricultural production, animal production and care, agribusiness, agricultural and industrial mechanics, environmental management, farming, horticulture and landscaping, food processing, and natural resource management.

Business education. Students prepare for careers in accounting and finance and computer and data processing as well as administrative/secretarial and management/supervisory positions in professional environments (banking, insurance, law, public service).

Family and consumer sciences. These programs prepare students for careers in child care, food management and production, clothing and interiors, and hospitality and facility care. Core elements include personal development, family life and planning, resource management, and nutrition and wellness.

Trade and industrial and health occupations. Students prepare for careers in auto mechanics, the construction trades, cosmetology, electronics, graphics, public safety, and welding. Health occupation programs offer vocational training for careers in dental and medical assisting, practical nursing, home health care, and medical office assisting.

Marketing education. These programs prepare students for careers in sales, retail, advertising, food and restaurant marketing, and hotel management.

Many vocational/career education programs are available; the kinds just listed represent only a few of the possibilities. To get more information about vocational education programs, call 202-245-7700, e-mail ovae@ed.gov, or visit the U.S. Department of Education, Office of Vocational and Adult Education Web site, www.ed.gov/about/offices/list/ovae/index.html.

THE TECH-PREP PATH

An even more advanced preparation for the workplace and/or an associate degree from a college is called tech-prep. It's an educational path that combines college-prep and vocational/technical courses of study.

During the sequence of courses, the focus is on blending academic and vocational/technical competencies. When you graduate from high school, you'll be able to jump right into the work force or get an associate degree. But if you want to follow this path, you've got to plan for it starting in the ninth grade. Ask your guidance counselor for more information.

People ask me what career do I want. I don't know. Where do I get help?

USING THE SUMMER TO YOUR ADVANTAGE

When you're sitting in class, a summer with nothing to do might seem appealing. But after you've downloaded and listened to all of your favorite new songs, aced all of your video games, hung out at the same old mall, and talked to your friends on the phone about being bored, what's left? How about windsurfing on a cool, clear New England lake? Horseback riding along breathtaking mountain trails? Parlez français in Paris? Trekking through spectacular canyon lands or living with a family in Costa Rica, Spain, Switzerland, or Japan? Exploring college majors or possible careers? Helping out on an archaeological dig or a community-service project? Along the way, you'll meet some wonderful people and maybe even make a couple of lifelong friends.

Interested? Get ready to pack your bags and join the 1 million kids and teens who will be having the summer of a lifetime at thousands of terrific camps, academic programs, sports clinics, arts workshops, internships, volunteer opportunities, and travel adventures throughout North America and abroad.

Oh, you don't have the money, you say? Not to worry. There are programs to meet every budget, from $50 workshops to $5000 world treks and sessions that vary in length from just a couple of hours to a couple of months.

FLIP BURGERS AND LEARN ABOUT LIFE

Many teenagers who are anxious to earn extra cash spend their summers in retail or food service since those jobs are plentiful. If you're flipping burgers or helping customers find a special outfit, you might think the only thing you're getting from the job is a paycheck. Think again. You'll be amazed to discover that you have gained far more.

Being employed in these fields will teach you how to get along with demanding (and sometimes downright unpleasant) customers, how to work on a team, and how to handle money and order supplies. Summer jobs not only teach you life skills but also offer ways to explore potential careers. What's more, when you apply to college or for a full-time job after high school graduation, the experience will look good on your application.

Sometimes summer jobs become the very thing you want to do later in life. Before committing to a college major, summer jobs give you the opportunity to try out many directions. Students who think they want to be engineers, lawyers, or doctors might spend the summer shadowing an engineer, being a gofer in a legal firm, or volunteering in a hospital.

FROM THE GUIDANCE OFFICE

Students have the opportunity to develop many skills through classes, student organizations, and career/technology classes during high school. These skills form an essential core that they can use when they continue on to college, enter the job market, or participate in additional training after graduation. When students can identify those skills and make the connection by applying and expanding their skills as lifelong learners, then the possibilities are endless.

Career and Technology Counselor
South San Antonio ISD
Career Education Center
San Antonio, Texas

Rather than grab the first job that comes along, however, find out where your interests are and build on what is natural for you. Activities you take for granted provide clues about your abilities. What about that bookcase you built? Or those kids you love to babysit? Same thing with that big party you arranged. The environments you prefer provide other hints, too. Perhaps you feel best in the middle of a cluttered garage instead of surrounded by people. That suggests certain types of jobs.

Getting a summer job while in high school is the first step in a long line of work experiences to come. And the more experience you have, the better you'll be at getting jobs all your life.

TRY YOUR HAND AT AN INTERNSHIP

Each year, thousands of interns work in a wide variety of places, including corporations, law firms, government agencies, media organizations, interest groups, clinics, labs, museums, and historical sites. How popular are internships? Consider the recent trends. In the early 1980s, only 1 in 36 students completed an internship or other experiential learning program. Compare this with 2006, when one study found that 62 percent of college students had planned for a summer internship. And an increasing number of high school students are signing up for internships now, too.

Use the summer and internships to your advantage.

The Employer's Perspective

Employers consider internships a good option in both healthy and ailing economies. In healthy economies, managers often struggle to fill their positions with eager workers who can adapt to changing technologies. Internships offer a low-cost way to get good workers "into the pipeline" without offering them a full-time position up front. In struggling economies, on the other hand, downsizing often requires employers to lay off workers without thinking about who will cover their responsibilities. Internships offer an inexpensive way to offset position losses resulting from disruptive layoffs.

The Intern's Perspective

If you are looking to begin a career or supplement your education with practical training, internships are a good bet for several reasons.

1 **Internships offer a relatively quick way to gain work experience and develop job skills.** Try this exercise. Scan the Sunday want ads of your newspaper. Choose a range of interesting advertisements for professional positions that you would consider taking. Look at the desired or required job skills and work experiences specified in the ads. How many of these skills and experiences do you have? Chances are, if you are still in school, you don't have most of the skills and experience that employers require of their new hires. What do you do?

The growing reality is that many entry-level positions require skills and experiences that schools and part-time jobs don't provide. Sure, you know your way around a computer. You have some customer service experience. You may even have edited your school's newspaper or organized your junior prom. But you still lack the relevant skills and on-the-job experiences that many hiring managers require. A well-chosen internship can offer a way out of this common dilemma by providing you job training in an actual career field. Internships help you take your existing knowledge and skills and apply them in ways that will help you compete for good jobs.

2 **Internships offer a relatively risk-free way to explore a possible career path.** Believe it or not, the best internship may tell you what you *don't* want to do for the

next ten or twenty years. Think about it. If you put all your eggs in one basket, what happens if your dream job turns out to be the exact opposite of what you want or who you are? Internships offer a relatively low-cost opportunity to "try out" a career field to see if it's right for *you.*

3 **Internships offer real opportunities to do career networking and can significantly increase your chances of landing a good full-time position.** Have you heard the saying "It's not what you know, but who you know"? The reality is that who you know (or who knows you) can make a big difference in your job search. Studies show that fewer than 20 percent of job placements occur through traditional application methods, including newspaper and trade journal advertisements, employment agencies, and career fairs. Instead, 60 to 90 percent of jobs are found through personal contacts and direct application.

4 **Career networking is the exchange of information with others for mutual benefit.** Your career network can tell you where the jobs are and help you compete for them. Isn't it better to develop your networking skills now, when the stakes aren't so high, than later when you are competing with everyone else for full-time jobs? The internship hiring process and the weeks you actually spend on the job provide excellent opportunities to talk with various people about careers, your skills, and ways to succeed.

VOLUNTEERING IN YOUR COMMUNITY

You've probably heard the saying that money isn't everything. Well, it's true, especially when it comes to volunteering and community service. You'll get a number of benefits from volunteering that don't add up in dollars and cents but do add up to open doors in your future.

Community service looks good on a college application. Admission staff members look for applicants who have volunteered and done community service in addition to earning good grades. You could have gotten top grades, but if that's all that's on your application, you won't come across as a well-rounded person.

Community service lets you try out careers. How will you know you'll like a certain type of work if you haven't experienced it? For instance, you might think you want to work in the health-care field. Volunteering in a hospital will let you know if this is really what you want to do.

Community service is an American tradition. You'll be able to meet some of your own community's needs and join with all of the people who have contributed their talents to our country. No matter what your talents are, the ways for you to serve your community are unlimited. Take a look at your interests, and then see how they can be applied to help others.

The following are some ideas to get you started:

- **Do you like kids?** Volunteer at your local parks and recreation department, for a Little League team, or as a Big Brother or Sister.
- **Planning a career in health care?** Volunteer at a blood bank, clinic, hospital, retirement home, or hospice. You can also help organizations that raise money for disease research.

- **Interested in the environment?** Volunteer to assist in a recycling program. Create a beautification program for your school or community. Plant trees and flowers or design a community garden.
- **Just say no.** Help others stay off drugs and alcohol by volunteering at a crisis center, hotline, or prevention program. Help educate younger kids about the dangers of drug abuse.
- **Lend a hand.** Collect money, food, or clothing for the homeless. Food banks, homeless shelters, and charitable organizations need your help.
- **Is art your talent?** Share your knowledge and skills with youngsters, the elderly, or local arts organizations that depend on volunteers to help present their plays, recitals, and exhibitions.
- **Help fight crime.** Form a neighborhood watch or organize a group to clean up graffiti.
- **Your church or synagogue may have projects that need youth volunteers.** The United Way, your local politician's office, civic groups, and special interest organizations also provide exceptional opportunities to serve your community. Ask your principal, teachers, or counselors for additional ideas.

For more information on joining in the spirit of youth volunteerism, write to the Federal Citizen Information Center (FCIC), Pueblo, Colorado 81009 or call 888-878-3256 (toll-free) and request the *Catch the Spirit* booklet. Also check out the FCIC's Web site at www.pueblo.gsa.gov.

PART 3

THE ROAD TO MORE EDUCATION

Some people wake up at age 3 and announce that they want to be doctors, teachers, or marine biologists—and they do it.

They're the exceptions. Many high school students don't have a clue about what they want to be. They dread the question, "So, what are you going to do after graduation?" Unfortunately, some of those same people are also the ones who end up in careers that don't satisfy them.

You don't have to plan the rest of your life down to the last detail, but you can start to take some general steps toward your future and lay the groundwork. Then, when you do decide what you want to do, you'll be able to seize hold of your dream and go with it.

CHAPTER 4

PLANNING YOUR EDUCATION WHILE IN HIGH SCHOOL

Some people are planners. Others are nonplanners. Either way, we've got a plan for you!

Nonplanners see the words "plan" and "future" and say, "Yeah, yeah, I know." Meanwhile, they're running out the door for an appointment they were supposed to be at 5 minutes ago.

Unfortunately, when it comes time to really do something about those goals and future hopes, the nonplanners often discover that much of what should have been done wasn't done—which is not good when they're planning their future after high school. What about those classes they should have taken? What about those jobs they should have volunteered for? What about that scholarship they could have had if only they'd found out about it sooner?

But there is hope for poor planners. Now that you've thought about the direction you might want to go after graduating, you can use this chapter to help you plan what you should be doing and when you should be doing it, while still in high school.

Regardless of what type of education you're pursuing after high school, here's a plan to help you get there.

YOUR EDUCATION TIME LINE

Use this time line to help you make sure you're accomplishing everything you need to accomplish on time.

Ninth Grade

- As soon as you can, meet with your guidance counselor to begin talking about colleges and careers.
- Make sure you are enrolled in the appropriate college-preparatory or tech-prep courses.
- Get off to a good start with your grades. The grades you earn in ninth grade may be included in your final high school GPA and class rank.
- College might seem a long way off now, but grades really do count toward college admission and scholarships.
- Explore your interests and possible careers. Take advantage of Career Day opportunities.
- Get involved in extracurricular activities (both school- and nonschool-sponsored).
- Talk to your parents about planning for college expenses. Continue or begin a savings plan for college.
- Look at the college information available in your counselor's office and school and public libraries. Use the Internet to check out college Web sites.
- Tour a nearby college, if possible. Visit relatives or friends who live on or near a college campus. Check out the dorms, go to the library or student center, and get a feel for college life.
- Investigate summer enrichment programs.

Tenth Grade

Fall

- In October, take the Preliminary SAT/ National Merit Scholarship Qualifying Test (PSAT/NMSQT) for practice. When you fill out your test sheet, check the box that releases your name to colleges so you can start receiving brochures from them.
- Ask your guidance counselor about the American College Testing program's PLAN® (Pre-ACT) assessment program, which helps determine your study habits and academic progress and interests. This test will prepare you for the ACT next year.
- Take geometry if you have not already done so. Take biology and a second year of a foreign language.
- Become familiar with general college entrance requirements.
- Participate in your school's or state's career development activities.

Winter

- Discuss your PSAT score with your counselor.
- The people who read college applications aren't just looking for grades. Get involved in activities outside the classroom. Work toward leadership positions in the activities that you like best. Become involved in community service and other volunteer activities.
- Read, read, read! Read as many books as possible from a comprehensive reading list, such as the one at the end of this chapter.
- Read the newspaper every day to learn about current affairs.
- Work on your writing skills—you'll need them no matter what you do.
- Find a teacher or another adult who will advise and encourage you to write well.

Spring

- Keep your grades up so you can have the highest GPA and class rank possible.
- Ask your counselor about postsecondary enrollment options and Advanced Placement (AP) courses.
- Continue to explore your interests and careers that you think you might like.

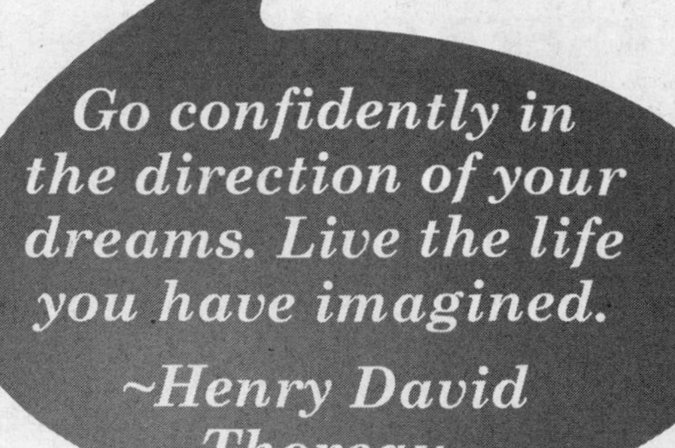

- Begin zeroing in on the type of college you would prefer (two-year or four-year, small or large, rural or urban).
- If you are interested in attending a military academy, such as West Point or Annapolis, now is the time to start planning and getting information.
- Write to colleges and ask for their academic requirements for admission.
- Visit college campuses. Read all of the mail you receive from colleges. You may see something you like.
- Attend college fairs.
- Keep putting money away for college. Get a summer job.
- Consider taking SAT Subject Tests in the courses you took this year while the material is still fresh in your mind. These tests are offered in May and June.

PARENT PERSPECTIVE

"The discussion about preparing for college needs to start in middle school. If parents don't expose their children to these concepts at that time, then it can be too late in the game. Children need to take the right courses in high school. Many kids here end up going to junior colleges because they don't meet the minimum requirements when they graduate. Many universities and private colleges don't count some of the classes kids take in high school. You can't wait until the child is 18 and then say, 'Maybe we should do something about getting into college.'"

Parent
Oak Park, California

CAREER CLUSTERS—TELL ME MORE!

Career Clusters in a Nutshell

The Career Clusters Initiative began in 1996 in the United States with the goal of creating curricular frameworks in broad career clusters that are designed to prepare students to transition successfully from high school to postsecondary education and employment in a career area.

HUH?

Let's try it this way. The U.S. Department of Education's 16 Career Clusters provide students with a focus for career-related learning and academic study and provide schools with a way of structuring curriculum, teaching resources, and grouping students. Students take classes around a particular career field, such as business, health, the arts, or technology. In selecting a career cluster, students learn about that particular field, along with their general academics (i.e., English, mathematics, social studies, and science) in the context of that career field.

Each Career Cluster has several associated Career Pathways. And then, each Career Pathway breaks down into numerous Career Specialties. Each layer requires more specific and advanced skills, but skills learned at the Cluster level are usually transferable to most of the Pathways and Specialties within the Cluster.

Presenting Your 16 Career Clusters

Just so we are all talking about the same thing, let's take a look at these 16 Career Clusters:

1 AGRICULTURE, FOOD, AND NATURAL RESOURCES

Creating and distributing food and other natural resources, including various plant and animal products. Employment opportunities range from farm workers to bioscientists.

2 ARCHITECTURE AND CONSTRUCTION

Designing, constructing, and maintaining buildings and structures. Employment opportunities range from construction workers to architects to engineers.

3 ARTS, AUDIO/VIDEO TECHNOLOGY, AND COMMUNICATIONS

Performing arts, journalism, and entertainment as well as developing and producing multimedia content. Employment opportunities range from actors to newscasters to Web site developers.

4 BUSINESS, MANAGEMENT, AND ADMINISTRATION

Planning, launching, and/or running a successful business. Employment opportunities range from receptionists to CEOs.

5 EDUCATION AND TRAINING

Educating and training people of all ages. Employment opportunities range from preschool teachers to university professors—and everything in between.

6 FINANCE

Handling money for individuals and businesses. Employment opportunities range from bank tellers to personal financial planners to economists.

7 GOVERNMENT AND PUBLIC ADMINISTRATION

Running a nation, state, county, city, or town by planning, protecting, and managing people and resources. Employment opportunities range from court clerk to city manager to the president.

8 HEALTH SCIENCE

Developing and providing medical diagnoses and treatment. Employment opportunities range from home-health aides to doctors to bioscientists.

9 HOSPITALITY AND TOURISM

Providing for the needs and comforts of restaurant or hotel guests. Employment opportunities range from cooks to tour guides to hotel owners.

10 HUMAN SERVICES

Caring for people's personal needs and/or problems. Employment opportunities range from hairdressers to funeral directors to counselors.

11 INFORMATION TECHNOLOGY

Developing and maintaining computers, software, and network systems. Employment opportunities range from help-desk technicians to database security experts to systems architects.

12 LAW, PUBLIC SAFETY, CORRECTIONS, AND SECURITY

Protecting people and enforcing laws. Employment opportunities range from EMTs to police officers to lawyers.

13 MANUFACTURING

Creating products from raw materials. Employment opportunities range from welders to industrial engineers.

14 MARKETING, SALES, AND SERVICES

Selling products or services. Employment opportunities range from cashiers to sales agents.

15 SCIENCE, TECHNOLOGY, ENGINEERING, AND MATHEMATICS

Using science and math to understand and/or change the world. Employment opportunities range from nutritionists to geoscientists to nuclear physicists.

16 TRANSPORTATION, DISTRIBUTION, AND LOGISTICS

Moving people or things from one place to another. Employment opportunities range from bus drivers to auto mechanics to air traffic controllers.

Why are Career Clusters Important?

Technological advances and global competition have transformed the nature of work. Tomorrow's jobs will require more knowledge, better skills, and more flexible workers than ever before. That means you'll need to be prepared to change jobs and careers several times and continually update your knowledge and skills.

Career clusters link what you learn in school with the knowledge and skills you need for success in college and careers. Career clusters identify pathways from secondary school to two- and four-year colleges, graduate school, and the workplace, so you can learn in school what you may do in the future.

Everyone Wins

Think of Career Clusters as your own personal advising team made up of the following:

High schools, which can be organized around career clusters to prepare students to meet the demands of postsecondary education and the expectations of employers.

Educators, who can use assessments for each cluster to gauge how well they are meeting the academic and career needs of all students, regardless of their interests or employment goals.

Guidance counselors, who can use career clusters to help students explore options for the future by using current information on the academic, technical, and college requirements students need for a wide range of careers.

Employers and industry groups, which can partner with schools to contribute to the development of high academic standards that help students prepare for work.

Parents, who can learn what academic and technical courses their children need for college and a variety of career fields. Clusters and the high standards that go with them reassure parents that their children will be fully prepared for college and the workplace.

And you! Students can use career clusters to check out a wide range of career choices. The career cluster approach makes it easier for you to both understand the relevance of your required courses and wisely select your elective courses.

Learn More Online

Want to know more? Check out these Web sites:

www.careerclusters.org

www.achievetexas.org

www.theworksuite.com

Eleventh Grade

Fall

- Meet with your counselor to review the courses you've taken, and see what you still need to take.
- Check your class rank. Even if your grades haven't been that good so far, it's never too late to improve. Colleges like to see an upward trend.
- If you didn't do so in tenth grade, sign up for and take the PSAT/NMSQT. In addition to National Merit Scholarships, this is the qualifying test for the National Hispanic Recognition Program.
- Make sure that you have a social security number.
- Take a long, hard look at why you want to continue your education after high school so you'll be able to choose the best college or university for your needs.
- Make a list of colleges that meet your most important criteria (size, location, distance from home, majors, academic rigor, housing, and cost). Weigh each of the factors according to their importance to you.
- Continue visiting college fairs. You may be able to narrow your choices or add a college to your list.
- Speak to college representatives who visit your high school.
- If you want to participate in Division I or Division II sports in college, start the certification process. Check with your counselor to make sure you are taking a core curriculum that meets National Collegiate Athletic Association (NCAA) requirements.
- If you are interested in one of the military academies, talk to your guidance counselor about starting the application process now.

ADVICE FROM COLLEGE PARENTS OF AMERICA

"Parents are getting more involved than ever before in supporting their children in the college process. This phenomenon is due to two factors:

"(1) This generation of parents has been much more involved with their children in dealing with the outside world than were their parents.

"(2) The investment made by today's parents is much more than that made by parents 20 or 30 years ago. As parents focus on the cost of this big-ticket item, there's interest to be more involved, to get the proper return.

"Parents can certainly be involved in the college selection and application process. Studies clearly indicate that parental support in this process and throughout the college years can make a big difference in the success of a student. But this process also should be a learning opportunity in decision making for students. In that regard, parents shouldn't direct the student but provide input and the framework to assist their students.

"Parents should not feel uncomfortable making suggestions to help their children through the thought and selection process—especially when it comes to identifying schools that their pocketbooks can accommodate. However, the child must be comfortable with the final decision and must have ultimate responsibility for the selection of the school. When students have made the final decision, it can help in their level of commitment because they're invested in it. They have a responsibility to do well and complete their academics at that location."

Richard Flaherty, Former President, College Parents of America

SIX STUDY SKILLS THAT LEAD TO SUCCESS

1 **SET A REGULAR STUDY SCHEDULE.** No one at college is going to hound you to do your homework. Develop the study patterns in high school that will lead to success in college. Anyone who has ever pulled an all-nighter knows how much you remember when you are on the downside of your fifth cup of coffee and no sleep—not much! Nothing beats steady and consistent study habits.

2 **SAVE EVERYTHING.** To make sure your history notes don't end up in your math notebook and your English papers don't get thrown at the bottom of your friend's locker, develop an organized system for storing your papers. Stay on top of your materials, and be sure to save quizzes and tests. It is amazing how questions from a test you took in March can miraculously reappear on your final exam.

3 **LISTEN.** Teachers give away what will be on the test by repeating themselves. If you pay attention to what the teacher is saying, you will probably notice what is being emphasized. If what the teacher says in class repeats itself in your notes and in review sessions, chances are that material will be on the test. So really listen.

4 **TAKE NOTES.** If the teacher has taken the time to prepare a lecture, then what he or she says is important enough for you to write down. Develop a system for reviewing your notes. After each class, rewrite them, review them, or reread them. Try highlighting the important points or making notes in the margins to jog your memory.

5 **USE TEXTBOOKS WISELY.** What can you do with a textbook besides lose it? Use it to back up or clarify information that you don't understand from your class notes. Reading every word may be more effort than it is worth, so look at the book intelligently. What is in boxes or highlighted areas? What content is emphasized? What do the questions ask about in the review sections?

6 **FORM A STUDY GROUP.** Establish a group that will stay on task and ask one another the questions you think the teacher will ask. Compare notes to see if you have all the important facts. And discuss your thoughts. Talking ideas out can help when you have to respond to an essay question.

Winter (Eleventh Grade)

- Collect information about college application procedures, entrance requirements, tuition and fees, room and board costs, student activities, course offerings, faculty composition, accreditation, and financial aid. The Internet is a good way to visit colleges and obtain this information. Begin comparing the schools by the factors that you consider to be most important.
- Discuss your PSAT score with your counselor.
- Begin narrowing down your college choices. Find out if the colleges you are interested in require the SAT, ACT, or SAT Subject Tests for admission.
- Register for the SAT and additional SAT Subject Tests, which are offered several times during the winter and spring of your junior year (see the "Tackling the Tests" chapter for a schedule). You can take them again in the fall of your senior year if you are unhappy with your scores.
- Register for the ACT, which is usually taken in April or June. You can take it again in the fall of your senior year, if necessary.
- Begin preparing for the tests you've decided to take.
- Have a discussion with your parents about the colleges in which you are interested. Examine financial resources, and gather information about financial aid. Check out the "Financial Aid Dollars and Sense" chapter for a step-by-step explanation of the financial aid process.
- Set up a filing system with individual folders for each college's correspondence and printed materials.

Spring

- Meet with your counselor to review senior-year course selection and graduation requirements.
- Discuss ACT/SAT scores with your counselor. Register to take the ACT and/ or SAT again if you'd like to try to improve your score.
- Discuss the college essay with your guidance counselor or English teacher.
- Stay involved with your extracurricular activities. Colleges look for consistency and depth in activities.
- Consider whom you'll ask to write your recommendations. Think about asking teachers who know you well and who will write positive letters about you. Letters from a coach, an activity leader, or an adult who knows you well outside school (e.g., volunteer work contact) are also valuable.
- Inquire about personal interviews at your favorite colleges. Call or write for early summer appointments. Make necessary travel arrangements.
- See your counselor to apply for on-campus summer programs for high school students. Apply for a summer job or internship. Be prepared to pay for college applications and testing fees in the fall.
- Request applications from schools you're interested in by mail or via the Internet.

Summer

- Visit the campuses of your top five college choices.
- After each college interview, send a thank-you letter to the interviewer.
- If you know anyone who has attended the colleges in which you are interested, try to talk to them.
- Continue to read books, magazines, and newspapers.

- Practice filling out college applications, and then complete the final application forms or apply online through the Web sites of the colleges in which you're interested.
- Volunteer in your community.
- Compose rough drafts of your college essays. Have a teacher read and discuss them with you. Polish them and prepare final drafts. Proofread your final essays at least three times.
- Develop a financial aid application plan, including a list of the aid sources, requirements for each application, and a timetable for meeting the filing deadlines.

ADMISSIONS ADVICE

At the University of Houston, we consider the types of classes students have taken. A grade of a B in an honors class is competitive to an A in a regular course. We seek not only academically talented students but those who are well-rounded. They need to submit their interests and activities, letters of recommendation, and writing samples in addition to their test scores. We look for someone who's involved in his or her community and high school, someone who holds leadership positions and has a balance of activities outside of academics. This gives us a look at that person as a whole.

Admission Counselor
University of Houston
Houston, Texas

Twelfth Grade

Fall

- Continue to take a full course load of college-prep courses.
- Keep working on your grades. Make sure you have taken the courses necessary to graduate in the spring.
- Continue to participate in extracurricular and volunteer activities. Demonstrate initiative, creativity, commitment, and leadership in each.
- To male students: You must register for selective service on your eighteenth birthday to be eligible for federal and state financial aid.
- Talk to counselors, teachers, and parents about your final college choices.
- Make a calendar showing application deadlines for admission, financial aid, and scholarships.
- Check resource books, Web sites, and your guidance office for information on scholarships and grants. Ask colleges about scholarships for which you may qualify.
- Give recommendation forms to the teachers you have chosen, along with stamped, addressed envelopes so your teachers can send them directly to the colleges. Be sure to fill out your name, address, and school name on the top of the form. Talk to your recommendation writers about your goals and ambitions.
- Give School Report forms to your high school's guidance office. Fill in your name, address, and any other required information. Verify with your guidance counselor the schools to which transcripts, test scores, and letters are to be sent. Give your counselor any necessary forms at least two weeks before they are due or whenever your counselor's deadline is, whichever is earlier.

- Register for and take the ACT, SAT, or SAT Subject Tests, as necessary.
- Be sure you have requested (either by mail or online) that your test scores be sent to the colleges of your choice.
- Mail or send electronically any college applications for early decision admission by November 1.
- If possible, visit colleges while classes are in session.
- If you plan to apply for an ROTC scholarship, remember that your application is due by December 1.
- Print extra copies or make photocopies of every application you send.

Winter

- Attend whatever college-preparatory nights are held at your school or by local organizations.
- Send midyear grade reports to colleges. Continue to focus on your school work!
- Fill out the Free Application for Federal Student Aid (FAFSA) and, if necessary, the PROFILE®. These forms can be obtained from your guidance counselor or go to www.fafsa.ed.gov/ to download the forms or to file electronically. These forms may not be processed before January 1, so don't send them before then.
- Mail or send electronically any remaining applications and financial aid forms before winter break. Make sure you apply to at least one college that you know you can afford and where you know you'll be accepted.
- Meet with your counselor to verify that all forms are in order and have been sent out to colleges.
- Follow up to make sure that the colleges have received all application information, including recommendations and test scores.

Spring

- Watch your mail between March 1 and April 1 for acceptance notifications from colleges.
- Watch your mail between April 1 and May 1 for notification of financial aid awards.
- Compare the financial aid packages from the colleges and universities that have accepted you.
- Make your final choice, and notify all schools of your intent by May 1. If possible, do not decide without making at least one campus visit. Send your nonrefundable deposit to your chosen school by May 1 as well. Request that your guidance counselor send a final transcript to your college in June.
- Be sure that you have received a FAFSA acknowledgment.
- If you applied for a Pell Grant (on the FAFSA), you'll receive a Student Aid Report (SAR) statement. Review this notice, and forward it to the college you plan to attend. Make a copy for your records.
- Complete follow-up paperwork for the college of your choice (scheduling, orientation session, housing arrangements, and other necessary forms).

Summer

- If applicable, apply for a Stafford Loan through a lender. Allow eight weeks for processing.
- Receive the orientation schedule from your college.
- Get housing assignment from your college.
- Obtain course scheduling and cost information from your college.
- Congratulations! You are about to begin the greatest adventure of your life. Good luck.

Suggested Reading List for Grades 9 Through 12

Instead of flipping on the TV or downloading tunes to your iPod, how about picking up a book instead? Reading not only will take you to wonderful, unexplored worlds through your imagination, but it also will provide practical gains. Reading gives you a more well-rounded background. College admission officers and future employers pick up on that. And you'll be able to answer questions like these: Did you read that book? What did you think of it? How many of the books on this list have you read?

Achebe, Chinua *Things Fall Apart*
Agee, James *A Death in the Family*
Angelou, Maya *I Know Why the Caged Bird Sings*
Anonymous *Beowulf*
Austen, Jane *Pride and Prejudice*
Baldwin, James *Go Tell It on the Mountain*
The Bible *Old Testament and New Testament*
Bolt, Robert *A Man for All Seasons*
Brontë, Charlotte *Jane Eyre*
Brontë, Emily *Wuthering Heights*
Buck, Pearl *The Good Earth*
Camus, Albert *The Stranger*
Cather, Willa *My Ántonia*
Cervantes, Miguel de *Don Quixote*
Chaucer, Geoffrey *The Canterbury Tales*
Chekhov, Anton *The Cherry Orchard*
Collins, Wilkie *The Moonstone*
Conrad, Joseph *Lord Jim*
Crane, Stephen *The Red Badge of Courage*
Dante *The Divine Comedy*
Defoe, Daniel *Moll Flanders*
Dickens, Charles *Great Expectations*
Dickinson, Emily *Poems*
Dostoevsky, Fyodor *Crime and Punishment*
Dreiser, Theodore *An American Tragedy*
Eliot, George *Silas Marner*
Eliot, T.S. *Murder in the Cathedral*
Ellison, Ralph *Invisible Man*
Emerson, Ralph *Waldo Essays*
Faulkner, William *The Sound and the Fury*
Fielding, Henry *Tom Jones*
Fitzgerald, F. Scott *The Great Gatsby*
Flaubert, Gustave *Madame Bovary*
Forster, E.M. *A Passage to India*
Franklin, Benjamin *The Autobiography of Benjamin Franklin*
Galsworthy, John *The Forsythe Saga*
Golding, William *Lord of the Flies*
Goldsmith, Oliver *She Stoops to Conquer*
Graves, Robert *I, Claudius*
Greene, Graham *The Power and the Glory*
Hardy, Thomas *Tess of the D'Urbervilles*
Hawthorne, Nathaniel *The Scarlet Letter*
Hemingway, Ernest *For Whom the Bell Tolls*
Henry, O. *Stories ("The Gift of the Magi," "The Ransom of Red Chief,"* etc.)
Hesse, Hermann *Steppenwolf*
Homer *The Iliad, The Odyssey*
Hughes, Langston *Poems*
Hugo, Victor *Les Misérables*
Hurston, Zora Neale *Their Eyes Were Watching God*
Huxley, Aldous *Brave New World*
Ibsen, Henrik *A Doll's House*
James, Henry *The Turn of the Screw*
Joyce, James *A Portrait of the Artist as a Young Man*
Kafka, Franz *The Trial*
Keats, John *Poems*
Kennedy, John F. *Profiles in Courage*
Koestler, Arthur *Darkness at Noon*
Lawrence, D.H. *Sons and Lovers*
Lawrence, Jerome and Robert E. Lee *Inherit the Wind*
Lee, Harper *To Kill a Mockingbird*
Lewis, Sinclair *Babbitt*
Llewellyn, Richard *How Green Was My Valley*
Mann, Thomas *The Magic Mountain*
Marlowe, Christopher *Dr. Faustus*
Maugham, W. Somerset *Of Human Bondage*
McCullers, Carson *The Heart Is a Lonely Hunter*
Melville, Herman *Moby-Dick*
Miller, Arthur *The Crucible*
Monsarrat, Nicholas *The Cruel Sea*
O'Connor, Flannery *Wise Blood*
O'Neill, Eugene *Long Day's Journey into Night*
Orwell, George *1984*
A Collection of Essays
Pasternak, Boris *Doctor Zhivago*
Poe, Edgar Allan *Short stories*
Remarque, Erich Maria *All Quiet on the Western Front*
Rostand, Edmond *Cyrano de Bergerac*
Salinger, J.D. *The Catcher in the Rye*
Sandburg, Carl *Abraham Lincoln*
Sayers, Dorothy *L. The Nine Tailors*
Shakespeare, William *Hamlet, King Lear, Much Ado About Nothing, Sonnets*
Shaw, George Bernard *Pygmalion*
Sheridan, Richard Brinsley *The School for Scandal*
Shute, Nevil *A Town Like Alice*
Sinclair, Upton *The Jungle*
Sophocles *Oedipus Rex*
Steinbeck, John *Of Mice and Men*
Stowe, Harriet Beecher *Uncle Tom's Cabin*
Swift, Jonathan *Gulliver's Travels*
Thackeray, William *Makepeace Vanity Fair*
Thoreau, Henry David *Walden*
Tolstoy, Leo *Anna Karenina*
Trollope, Anthony *Barchester Towers*
Turgenev, Ivan *Fathers and Sons*
Twain, Mark *Adventures of Huckleberry Finn*
Updike, John *Rabbit Run*
Virgil *The Aeneid*
Voltaire *Candide*
Warren, Robert Penn *All the King's Men*
Waugh, Evelyn *A Handful of Dust*
Wharton, Edith *The Age of Innocence*
White, T.H. *The Once and Future King*
Wiesel, Elie *Night*
Wilde, Oscar *The Picture of Dorian Gray*
Wilder, Thornton *Our Town*
Williams, Tennessee *A Streetcar Named Desire*
Wolfe, Thomas *Look Homeward, Angel*
Woolf, Virginia *To the Lighthouse*
Wouk, Herman *The Caine Mutiny*
Wright, Richard *Native Son*

CLASSES TO TAKE IF YOU'RE GOING TO COLLEGE

Did you know that classes you take as early as the ninth grade will help you get into college? Make sure you take at least the minimum high school curriculum requirements necessary for college admission. Even if you don't plan to enter college immediately, take the most demanding courses you can handle.

Review the list of Suggested Courses. Some courses, categories, and names vary from state to state, but this list may be used as a guideline. Talk with your guidance counselor to select the curriculum that best meets your needs and skills.

Of course, learning also occurs outside school. While outside activities will not make up for poor academic performance, skills learned from jobs, extracurricular activities, and volunteer opportunities help you become a well-rounded student and can strengthen your college or job application.

Getting a Head Start on College Courses

You can take college courses while still in high school so that when you're in college, you'll be ahead of everyone else. The formal name is "postsecondary enrollment." (In Texas, the formal names are "dual credit"—academic credit and articulated credit—and "Tech-Prep.") What it means is that some students can take college courses and receive both high school and college credit for the courses taken. It's like a two-for-one deal!

Postsecondary enrollment is designed to provide an opportunity for qualified high school students to experience more advanced academic work. Participation in a postsecondary enrollment program is not intended to replace courses available in high school but rather to enhance the educational opportunities available to students while in high school. Two options for postsecondary enrollment exist:

Option A: Qualified high school juniors and seniors take courses for college credit. Students enrolled under Option A must pay for all books, supplies, tuition, and associated fees.

Option B: Qualified high school juniors and seniors take courses for high school and college credit. For students enrolled under this option, the local school district covers the related costs, provided the student completes the selected courses. Otherwise, the student and parent are assessed the costs.

Certain pre-established conditions must be met for enrollment, so check with your high school counselor for more information.

Suggested Courses

College-Preparatory Curriculum

- **English.** Four units, with emphasis on composition (English 9, 10, 11, 12)
- **Mathematics.** Three units (algebra I, algebra II, geometry) are essential; trigonometry, precalculus, calculus, and computer science are recommended for some fields of study
- **Social Science.** Three units (American history, world history, government/economics)
- **Science.** Four units (earth science, biology, chemistry, physics)
- **Foreign Language.** Three units (at least 2 years in the same language)
- **Fine Arts.** One to two units
- **Other.** Keyboarding, computer applications, computer science I, computer science II, physical education, health

College-Preparatory Curriculum Combined with a Career Education or Vocational Program

- **English.** Four units
- **Mathematics.** Three units (algebra I, algebra II, geometry)
- **Social Science.** Three units (American history, world history, government/economics)
- **Science.** Two units (earth science, biology)
- **Foreign Language.** Three units (at least 2 years in the same language)
- **Fine Arts.** One to two units
- **Other.** Keyboarding, computer applications, physical education, and health and half-days at the Career Center during junior and senior years

Earning Credit Elsewhere

Earning college credits in high school doesn't have to be boring. It might seem hard to believe, but trekking through the jungles of Costa Rica or traveling to a foreign country can help you earn college credits and valuable life experiences that will add some extra oomph to your college applications.

Outward Bound Costa Rica

Outward Bound is a nonprofit educational organization that offers active learning expeditions to people of all ages and backgrounds. Outward Bound Costa Rica is an option for students who are at least 14 years old. Outward Bound offers two ways to earn academic credit through their Outward Bound Costa Rica courses.

1. Outward Bound has teamed with Western State College of Colorado to offer courses in Recreation Outdoor Education, which include challenging, group-focused, introspective courses. It is important to check with your school or university to determine whether the credits you earn will transfer. For more information, contact Erica Boucher at eboucher@western.edu or call 970-943-2885.

2. Outward Bound also offers an independent study program through which students can receive credits in several courses of study, such as Spanish and Coastal Ecology. If this option appeals to you, keep in mind that you may have to do a certain amount of selling because not all schools and universities are familiar with the program. Visit www.costaricaoutwardbound.org for more information or contact Outward Bound's Student Enrollment Coordinator at enrollment@crrobs.org or call 800-676-2018 (toll-free).

Study Abroad

Study abroad can be done when you're in high school or while in college. An advantage of studying abroad while in high school is that you'll earn a competitive edge over other students when applying to colleges. It also gives you an advantage later in life when you are looking for a job because you will have gained valuable knowledge about other cultures and languages.

Studying abroad in high school is also sometimes referred to as foreign exchange. In a foreign exchange program, students normally live with a host family in a foreign country, where they attend high school and have the opportunity to participate in school and community activities. Various foreign exchange programs are available, depending on the length of time you wish to live abroad. You can choose to study abroad for a full academic year, one semester, or during the summer. In most cases, credits earned while away will go toward credits you need to graduate from your American high school. However, it is recommended that you begin planning early and speak with your school guidance counselor to get written documentation about what you'll need to do to receive credit.

Fees for the program vary by duration of study and country and range from about $4,000 to $23,000. In some cases, scholarships and discounts are available. For more information, visit AYUSA Global Youth Exchange at www.ayusa.org.

SEVEN STEPS TO LANDING YOUR DREAM JOB

By Rachel Gutter, Director of the Center for Green Schools, U.S. Green Building Council

1 **Be willing to start at the bottom of the totem pole and work your way up.** Figure out where there are gaps in your knowledge base and/or resume and find a position that will allow you to fill them. If you can afford to take an unpaid internship at a place that will give you good access or relevant experience, do it—even if you have to live with your parents.

2 **Zero in on a few organizations or companies that most interest you and haunt their job pages.** Even in this economy, Washington, D.C., is always hiring ... eventually.

3 **Find a mentor who has your dream job and wow him or her.** If your mentor is your supervisor or someone else you work with, make yourself indispensable to him/her. If you don't work with him/her, try to do extra research or a side project to show how interested you are in the work he or she does. Shadow him/her for a week.

4 **Be persistent.** Always follow up. Always check back in. Always remind them you are still interested.

5 **Do your homework.** It's not so much about the job itself, it is about the culture of the organization. If you don't like the latter, you probably won't like the former.

6 **There's a lot more to life than work; it's always important to keep that in mind.** There is something to be said for having an employer that values personal sustainability.

7 **In the first few years of your career (not necessarily your first years of work experience, but your first years of work on a career track), you should work harder than you ever have and possibly harder than you ever will.**

CHAPTER 5

TACKLING THE TESTS

Unless you've been on another planet for the last two or three years, you've probably heard older high school students buzzing about the alphabet soup list of college entrance exams—PSAT/NMSQT, SAT, and ACT.

Some students who are getting ready to take one of these tests look like they're in various states of hysteria. Others have been studying for months on end, so when they open their mouths, out pops the definition for "meretricious" or the answer to "What is the ratio of 3 pounds to 6 ounces?" Well, the talk that you've heard about the tests is partly true. They are a big deal and can be crucial to your academic plans. On the other hand, you don't have to walk in cold. Remember that word "planning"? It's a whole lot nicer than the word "panic." Preparing for the tests takes a lot of planning and time, but if you're reading this chapter, you're already ahead of the game.

WHAT THE TESTS ARE . . . AND AREN'T

The major standardized tests students take in high school are the PSAT, SAT, and ACT. Colleges across the country use them to get a sense of a student's readiness to enter their ivy-covered walls. These tests, or "boards" as they are sometimes called, have become notorious because of how important they can be. A certain mystique surrounds them. People talk about the "magic number" that will get you into the school of your dreams.

Beware! A lot of misinformation is out there. First and foremost, these are not intelligence tests; they are reasoning tests designed to evaluate the way you think. These tests assess the basic knowledge and skills you have gained through your classes in school, and they also gauge the knowledge you have gained through outside experience. The tests emphasize academic and nonacademic experiences that educational institutions feel are good indicators of your probable success in college.

THE ACT

The ACT is a standardized college entrance examination that measures knowledge and skills in English, mathematics, reading, and science reasoning and the application of these skills to future academic tasks. The ACT consists of four multiple-choice tests.

Test 1: English

- 75 questions, 45 minutes
- Usage and mechanics
- Rhetorical skills

Test 2: Mathematics

- 60 questions, 60 minutes
- Pre-algebra
- Elementary algebra
- Intermediate algebra
- Coordinate geometry
- Plane geometry
- Trigonometry

Test 3: Reading

- 40 questions, 35 minutes
- Prose fiction
- Humanities
- Social studies
- Natural sciences

Test 4: Science

- 40 questions, 35 minutes
- Data representation
- Research summary
- Conflicting viewpoints

STUDENT COUNSEL

QUESTION: What kept you from stressing out about the tests?

ANSWER: The best way I found to prepare was to take the practice tests to get to know the questions. At first, I'd set the kitchen timer and practice while ignoring the time, just to see what I could do. Then I made sure that I could answer all of the questions in the right amount of time. Practice is the best because they don't really change the types of questions. You read that in every review book, and it's true.

My advice for dealing with the stress on test day? The night before, I watched movies and had popcorn. When you take the test, definitely bring candy. A candy bar in between each section helps.

Senior student
Edgemont High School
Scarsdale, New York

Each section is scored from 1 to 36 and is scaled for slight variations in difficulty. Students are not penalized for incorrect responses. The composite score is the average of the four scaled scores. The ACT also has a 30-minute optional Writing Test.

To prepare for the ACT, ask your guidance counselor for a free guidebook called *Preparing for the ACT*. In addition to providing general test-preparation information and test-taking strategies, this guidebook describes the content and format of the four ACT subject area tests, summarizes test administration procedures followed at ACT test centers, and includes a practice test. Peterson's publishes *The Real ACT Prep Guide* that includes five official ACT tests.

THE SAT

The SAT measures developed verbal and mathematical reasoning abilities as they relate to successful performance in college. It is intended to supplement the secondary school record and other information about the student in assessing readiness for college. There is one unscored, experimental section on the exam, which is used for equating and/or pretesting purposes and can cover either the mathematics or verbal subject area.

Critical Reading

- 67 questions, 70 minutes
- Sentence completion
- Passage-based reading

Mathematics

- 54 questions, 70 minutes
- Multiple-choice
- Student-produced response (grid-ins)

Writing

- 49 questions plus essay, 60 minutes
- Identifying sentence errors
- Improving paragraphs
- Improving sentences
- Essay

Students receive one point for each correct response and lose a fraction of a point for each incorrect response (except for student-produced responses). These points are totaled to produce the raw scores, which are then scaled to equalize the scores for slight variations in difficulty for various editions of the test.

The critical reading, writing, and mathematics scaled scores range from 200–800 per section. The total scaled score range is from 600–2400. To prepare for the SAT, check out libraries' and bookstores' large selection of material about the SAT and other standardized tests, including Peterson's *Master the SAT,* which offers 6 full-length practice tests, plus access to 3 online via CD, all with detailed answer explanations.

SHOULD I TAKE THE ACT OR THE SAT?

It's not a bad idea to take both. This ensures that you'll have the test scores required for admission to all schools because some colleges accept the results of one test and not the other, although nearly all colleges do accept both ACT and SAT scores at this time. Some institutions use test results for proper placement of students in English and math courses.

You should take the ACT and SAT during the spring of your junior year, if not earlier. This enables you to retake the test in the fall of your senior year if you're not satisfied with your scores. Also, this makes it possible for institutions to receive all test scores before the end of January. Institutions generally consider the better score when determining admission and placement. Because most scholarship applications are processed between December and April of the senior year, your best score results can then be included in the application.

THE PSAT/NMSQT

The Preliminary SAT/National Merit Scholarship Qualifying Test (NMSQT), better known as the PSAT, is a practice test for the SAT. Many students take the PSAT more than once because scores tend to increase with repetition and because it allows students to become more comfortable with taking standardized tests. During the junior year, the PSAT/NMSQT is also used as a qualifying test for the National Merit Scholarship Program and in designating students for the National Hispanic Scholar Recognition Program. The PSAT includes a writing-skills section, which consists entirely of multiple-choice questions. The PSAT/NMSQT does not include an essay section.

Critical Reading

- 48 questions, two 25-minute sections
- Sentence completion
- Passage-based reading

Math

- 38 questions, two 25-minute sections
- Multiple-choice
- Student-produced response (grid-ins)

Writing Skills

- 39 questions, one 30-minute section
- Identifying sentence errors
- Improving sentences
- Improving paragraphs

Students receive a score in each content area (critical reading, math, and writing skills). Each score ranges from 20 to 80 and is totaled with the others for the combined score. The total score ranges from 60 to 240.

RECOMMENDED TEST-TAKING DATES

	Sophomore Year
October	PSAT/NMSQT and PLAN (for practice, planning, and preparation)
May/June	SAT Subject Tests (if necessary)
	Junior Year
October	PSAT/NMSQT (for the National Merit Scholarship Program and practice)
January–June	
	ACT and/or SAT
	SAT Subject Tests (if necessary)
	Senior Year
October–December	
	ACT and/or SAT
	SAT Subject Tests (if necessary)

SAT SUBJECT TESTS

Subject Tests are required by some institutions for admission and/or placement in freshman-level courses. Each Subject Test measures one's knowledge of a specific subject and the ability to apply that knowledge. Students should check with each institution for its specific requirements. In general, students are required to take three Subject Tests (one English, one mathematics, and one of their choice).

Subject Tests are given in the following areas: biology, chemistry, Chinese, French, German, Italian, Japanese, Korean, Latin, literature, mathematics, modern Hebrew, physics, Spanish, U.S. history, and world history. These tests are 1 hour long and are primarily multiple-choice tests. Three Subject Tests may be taken on one test date.

Scored like the SAT, students gain a point for each correct answer and lose a fraction of a point for each incorrect answer. The raw scores are then converted to scaled scores that range from 200 to 800.

ADVICE FROM AN ADMISSION COUNSELOR

We encourage students to take the SAT or ACT more than once and see how they do. There are options for students who may not meet the academic requirements because they've had to work or are gifted in other areas, such as art or athletics, or who perhaps have been through something tragic. We ask them to submit letters of recommendation, a personal statement, and any other documentation that might help support their cases. What were the factors that affected their grades? What else can they offer the university?

We often encourage students who still may not meet the requirements to start at a community college and then transfer. We'll look at their college credit vs. their high school credit. They can prove to us that they can handle a college curriculum.

Admission Counselor
University of Houston
Houston, Texas

THE TOEFL INTERNET-BASED TEST (iBT)

The Test of English as a Foreign Language Internet-Based Test (TOEFL iBT) is designed to help assess a student's grasp of English if it is not the student's first language. Performance on the TOEFL may help interpret scores on the verbal sections of the SAT. The test consists of four integrated sections: speaking, listening, reading, and writing. The TOEFL iBT emphasizes integrated skills. The paper-based versions of the TOEFL will continue to be administered in certain countries until the Internet-based version is fully administered by Educational Testing Service (ETS). For further information, visit www.toefl.org.

WHAT OTHER TESTS SHOULD I KNOW ABOUT?

The Advanced Placement (AP) Program

The AP program allows high school students to try college-level work and build valuable skills and study habits in the process. Subject matter is explored in more depth in AP courses than in other high school classes. A qualifying score on an AP test—which varies from school to school—can earn you college credit or advanced placement. Getting qualifying grades on enough exams can even earn you a full year's credit and sophomore standing at more than 1,500 higher-education institutions.

At present, thirty-three AP courses are offered in a variety of subject areas: Art History, Biology, Calculus AB, Calculus BC, Chemistry, Chinese Language and Culture, Computer Science A, English Language and Composition, English Literature and Composition, Environmental Science, European History, French Language, German Language, Government and Politics: Comparative, Government and Politics: United States, Human Geography, Italian Language and Culture, Japanese Language and Culture, Latin Vergil, Macroeconomics, Microeconomics, Music Theory, Physics B, Physics C: Electricity and Magnetism, Physics C: Mechanics, Psychology, Spanish Language, Spanish Literature, Statistics, Studio Art: 2-D Design, Studio Art: 3-D Design, Studio Art: Drawing, United States History, and World History.

Speak to your guidance counselor for information about the AP courses offered your high school.

College-Level Examination Program (CLEP)

The CLEP enables students to earn college credit for what they already know, whether it was learned in school, through independent study, or through experiences outside the classroom. Approximately 2,900 colleges and universities now award credit for qualifying scores on one or more of the 33 CLEP exams. The exams, which are approximately 90 minutes in length, include primarily multiple-choice questions and are administered at participating colleges and universities. For more information, go online to http://clep.collegeboard.org.

Armed Services Vocational Aptitude Battery (ASVAB)

ASVAB is a career exploration program consisting of a multi-aptitude test battery that helps students explore their interests, abilities, and personal preferences. A career exploration workbook gives students information about the workplace, and a career information resource book helps students match their personal characteristics to the working world. Finally, an occupational outlook handbook describes in detail more than 250 civilian and military occupations. Students can use ASVAB scores for military enlistment up to two years after they take the test. A student can take the ASVAB as a sophomore, junior, or senior, but students cannot use their sophomore scores to enter the armed forces. Ask your guidance counselor or your local recruiting office for more information. Also, see Chapter 11, "The Military Option."

GED® Tests

The **Tests of General Education Development,** or **GED® Tests,** are standardized tests that measure skills required of high school graduates in the United States and Canada. The ultimate goal in passing these exams is a certificate that is equivalent to a high school diploma. The battery of five GED Tests are designed and administered by the GED Testing Service of the American Council of Education.

Knowing that you can take the GED test, however, is not a legitimate reason for dropping out of school. In fact, it is more difficult to get into the armed services with only a GED, and some employees have difficulty getting promoted without a high school diploma.

The GED test has five sections, which cover writing skills, social studies, science, reading comprehension, and mathematics. Part II of the Language Arts, Writing Test requires writing an essay. Call 800-62-MYGED (toll-free) or go online to www.my-ged.com to find your local GED office and more information.

For practice tests and subject review for preparing for the GED, check out *Peterson's Master the GED* or *Peterson's GED Basics*.

WHAT CAN I DO TO PREPARE FOR THESE TESTS?

Know what to expect. Get familiar with how the tests are structured, how much time is allowed, and the directions for each type of question. Get plenty of rest the night before the test and eat breakfast that morning.

A variety of products, from books to software to videos, are available to help you prepare for most standardized tests. Find the learning style that suits you best. As for which products to buy, you have two major categories from which to choose—those created by the test makers and those created by private companies. The best approach is to talk to someone who has been through the process and find out which product or products he or she recommends.

Some students report significant increases in scores after participating in coaching programs. Longer-term programs (40 hours) seem to raise scores more than short-term programs (20 hours), but beyond 40 hours, score gains are minor. Math scores appear to benefit more from coaching than do verbal scores.

Resources

You can prepare for standardized tests in a variety of ways—find a method that fits your schedule and your budget. But you should definitely prepare. Far too many students walk into these tests cold, either because they find standardized tests frightening or annoying or they just haven't found the time to study.

The key is that these exams are standardized. That means these tests are largely the same from administration to administration; they always test the same concepts. They have to, or else you couldn't compare the scores of people who took the tests on different dates. The numbers or words may change, but the underlying content doesn't.

So how do you prepare? At the very least, you should review relevant material, such as math formulas and commonly used vocabulary words, and know the directions for each question type or test section. You should take at least one practice test and review your mistakes so you don't make them again on test day. Beyond that, you know best how much preparation you need. You'll also find lots of material in libraries or bookstores to help you: books and software from the test makers and from other publishers (including Peterson's) or live courses that range from national test-preparation companies to teachers at your high school who offer classes.

TOP 10 WAYS NOT TO TAKE THE TEST

10 **Cramming the night before the test.**

9 **Not becoming familiar with the directions before you take the test.**

8 **Not becoming familiar with the format of the test before you take it.**

7 **Not knowing how the test is graded.**

6 **Spending too much time on any one question.**

5 **Not checking spelling, grammar, and sentence structure in essays.**

4 **Second-guessing yourself.**

3 **Writing a one-paragraph essay.**

2 **Forgetting to take a deep breath to keep from—**

1 **Losing It!**

CHAPTER 6
THE COLLEGE SEARCH

Now that you have examined your interests, talents, wants, and needs in great detail, it's time to start investigating colleges.

Finding the college that's right for you may feel like a daunting task. But if you plan carefully and use the available resources, you'll make the choice that's best for you—and for the chosen college!

THE BEST RESOURCES

Across the United States, you'll find thousands of colleges and universities, so before you start filling out applications, you need to narrow down your search. A number of sources are available to help you do this.

Your Guidance Counselor

Your guidance counselor is your greatest asset in the college-search process. He or she has access to a vast repository of information, from college bulletins and catalogs to financial aid applications. She knows how well graduates from your high school have performed at colleges across the country and has probably even visited many of the colleges to get some firsthand knowledge about the schools she has recommended. The more your guidance counselor sees you and learns about you, the easier it is for her to help you. So make sure you stop by her office often, whether it's to talk about your progress or just to say "hi."

Your Teachers

Use your teachers as resources, too. Many of them have had years of experience in their field. They have taught thousands of students and watched them go off to college and careers. Teachers often stay in contact with graduates and know about their experiences in college and may be familiar with the schools you are interested in attending. Ask your teachers how they feel about the match between you and your choice of schools and if they think you'll be able to succeed in that environment.

Your Family

Your family needs to be an integral part of the college-selection process, regardless of whether they are financing your education. They have opinions and valuable advice. Listen to them carefully. Try to absorb all their information and see if it applies to you. Does it fit with who you are and what you want? What works and what doesn't work for you? Is some of what they say dated? How long ago were their experiences, and how relevant are they today? Take in the information, thank them for their concern, compare what they have said with the information you are gathering, and discard what doesn't fit.

Colleges and Universities

Don't forget to go to college fairs. Usually held in large cities in the evening, they are free and sponsored by your local guidance counselors' association and the National Association for College Admission Counseling (NACAC). The admission counselors of hundreds of colleges, vocational/career colleges, and universities attend college fairs each year. Whether your questions are as general as what the overall cost of education is at a particular institution or as specific as how many biology majors had works published last year, the admission office works to assist you in locating the people who can answer your questions. Bring a shopping bag for all the information you'll get.

Admission officers also visit high schools. Don't forget to attend these meetings during your junior and senior years. In general, college admission counselors come to a school to get a general sense of the high school and the caliber and personality of the student body. Although it is difficult to make an individual impression at these group sessions, the college counselors do take names on cards for later contact, and you'll occasionally see them making notes on the cards when they are struck by an astute questioner. It is helpful to attend these sessions because consistent contact between a student and a college is tracked by colleges and universities. An admission decision may come down to examining the size of your admission folder and the number of interactions you have had with the school over time.

College and university brochures and catalogs are a good place to look, too. After reading a few, you'll discover that some offer more objective information than others. You'll also start to learn what information college admission officials consider essential to present. That's important. If one college's brochure does not present the same information as most of the other college brochures, you have to ask yourself why. What might this say about the college's academic offerings, athletic or extracurricular programs, or campus life? What does the campus look like? How is the campus environment presented in the brochure? The brochures should present clues about what schools believe are their important majors, what their mission is, and on which departments they are spending their budgets. Take the time to do these informational resources justice. They have a great deal to say to the careful reader.

A college's Web site can give you a glimpse of campus life that does not appear in the college's brochure and catalog. It is true that the virtual tour will show you the shots that the college marketing department wants you to see, highlighting the campus in the best light, but you can use the home page to see other things, too. Read the student newspaper. Visit college-sponsored chat rooms. Go to the department in the major you are investigating. Look at the Course Bulletin to see what courses are required.

ONLINE HELP

To help you find two-year and four-year colleges or universities, check out the following online resources for additional information on college selection, scholarships, student information, and much more.

Peterson's College Search. Petersons.com provides information and tools that will help you prepare, search, and pay for college. You can search for a school by name or location. In addition to college search and selection tools, Petersons.com also offers tips on financial aid, test preparation, and online applications.

The National Association for College Admission Counseling. This site offers information for professionals, students, and parents: www.nacacnet.org.

U.S. Department of Education. This federal agency's National Center for Education Statistics produces reports on every level of education, from elementary to postgraduate. Dozens are available for downloading. You can find these and other links at http://nces.ed.gov.

PARENT PERSPECTIVE

"Now that I've been through the college-admissions process with 3 of my children, here's my best advice. Apply early and meet deadlines. Both of my older sons were sitting there after high school graduation wondering why they were on college waiting lists. Each complained that they had good grades and just couldn't figure out why this happened to them. At age 18, they don't see tomorrow, much less way down the line. But do you want to deal with their heartbreak at not getting into the college where they want to be? It's their future. It's hard because they're in their senior year, and you want it to be fun for them. However, you see the reality out there that they'll be facing for the rest of their lives. They don't want to look at it, but you have to keep bringing them back to it—just not in a preachy way. If they start preparing earlier than their senior year, it won't be as much of a shock when they become seniors."

Mother of 3 former high school students
San Antonio, Texas

CAMPUS VISITS

How will I know if the college is right for me?

You've heard the old saying, "A picture is worth a thousand words." Well, a campus visit is worth a thousand brochures. Nothing beats walking around a campus to get a feel for it. Some students report that all they needed was to drive through a campus to know whether they loved or hated it. Then there is the true story of the guy who applied to a school because it had a prestigious name. He got accepted, but never visited the school. Then when he arrived to move into the dorms, discovered to his horror it was an all-male school. A visit would have taken care of that problem.

The best time to experience the college environment is during the spring of your junior year or the fall of your senior year. Although you may have more time to visit colleges during the summer, your observations will be more accurate when you can see the campus in full swing. Open houses are a good idea and provide you with opportunities to talk to students, faculty members, and administrators. Write or call in advance to take student-conducted campus tours. If possible, stay overnight in a dorm to see what living at the college is really like.

Bring your transcript so that you are prepared to interview with admission officers. Take this opportunity to ask questions about financial aid and other services that are available to students. You can get a good snapshot of campus life by reading a copy of the student newspaper. The final goal of the campus visit is to study the school's personality and decide if it matches yours. Your parents should be involved with the campus visits so that you can share your impressions. The following are some additional campus visit tips:

- ❑ Read campus literature prior to the visit.
- ❑ Ask for directions, and allow ample travel time.
- ❑ Make a list of questions before the visit.
- ❑ Dress in neat, clean, and casual clothes and shoes.
- ❑ Ask to meet one-on-one with a current student.
- ❑ Ask to meet personally with a professor in your area of interest.
- ❑ Ask to meet a coach or athlete in your area of interest.
- ❑ Offer a firm handshake.
- ❑ Use good posture.
- ❑ Listen, and take notes.
- ❑ Speak clearly, and maintain eye contact with people you meet.
- ❑ Don't interrupt.
- ❑ Be honest, direct, and polite.
- ❑ Be aware of factual information so that you can ask questions of comparison and evaluation.
- ❑ Be prepared to answer questions about yourself. Practice a mock interview with someone.
- ❑ Don't be shy about explaining your background and why you are interested in the school.
- ❑ Ask questions about the background and experiences of the people you meet.
- ❑ Convey your interest in getting involved in campus life.
- ❑ Be positive and energetic.
- ❑ Don't feel as though you have to talk the whole time or carry the conversation yourself.
- ❑ Relax, and enjoy yourself.
- ❑ Thank those you meet, and send thank-you notes when appropriate.

After you have made your college visits, use the "College Comparison Worksheet" (later in this chapter) to rank the schools in which you're interested. This will help you decide not only which ones to apply to but also which one to attend once you receive your acceptance letters.

CRITERIA TO CONSIDER

Depending on your personal interests, the following characteristics should play a role in helping you narrow down the field of colleges you are considering.

AFFILIATION

Public
Private, independent
Private, church affiliated
Proprietary

SIZE

Very small (fewer than 1,000 students)
Small (1,000–3,999 students)
Medium (4,000–8,999 students)
Large (9,000–19,999 students)
Very large (more than 20,000 students)

COMMUNITY

Rural
Small town
Suburban
Urban

LOCATION

In your hometown
Less than 3 hours from home
More than 3 hours from home

HOUSING

Dorm
Off-campus apartment
Home
Facilities and services for students with disabilities

STUDENT BODY

All male
All female
Coed
Minority representation
Primarily one religious denomination
Primarily full-time students
Primarily part-time students
Primarily commuter students
Primarily residential students

ACADEMIC ENVIRONMENT

Majors offered
Student-faculty ratio
Faculty teaching reputation
Instruction by professors versus teaching assistants
Facilities (such as classrooms and labs)
Libraries
Independent study available
International study available
Internships available

FINANCIAL AID

Scholarships
Grants
Loans
Work-study program
Part-time or full-time jobs

SUPPORT SERVICES

Academic counseling
Career/placement counseling
Personal counseling
Student health facilities

ACTIVITIES/SOCIAL CLUBS

Clubs, organizations
Greek life
Athletics, intramurals

ATHLETICS

Division I, II, or III
Sports offered
Scholarships available

SPECIALIZED PROGRAMS

Honors programs
Services for students with disabilities or special needs

THE COLLEGE INTERVIEW

Not all schools require or offer an interview. If you are offered an interview, however, use this one-on-one time to evaluate the college in detail and to sell yourself to the admission officer. The following list of questions can help you collect vital information you'll want to know.

- How many students apply each year? How many are accepted?
- What are the average GPAs and average ACT or SAT score(s) for those accepted?
- How many students in last year's freshman class returned for their sophomore year?
- What is the school's procedure for credit for Advanced Placement (AP) high school courses?
- As a freshman, will I be taught by professors or teaching assistants?
- How many students are there per instructor?
- When is it necessary to declare a major?
- Is it possible to have a double major or to declare a major and a minor?
- What are the requirements for the major in which I am interested?
- How does the advising system work?
- Does this college offer study abroad, cooperative programs, or academic honors programs?
- What is the likelihood, due to overcrowding, of getting closed out of the courses I need?
- What technology is available, and what are any associated fees?
- How well equipped are the libraries and laboratories?
- Are internships available?
- How effective is the job placement service of the school?
- What is the average class size in my area of interest?
- Have any professors in my area of interest recently won any honors or awards?
- What teaching methods (lecture, group discussion, fieldwork) are used in my area of interest?
- How many students graduate in four years in my area of interest?
- What are the special requirements for graduation in my area of interest?

WRITING TO A COLLEGE FOR INFORMATION

If neither you nor your guidance counselor has enough information for a college that you are interested in, write a brief letter to the college admissions office to request an application.

Date

Your Name
Street Address
City, State Zip

Office of Admission
Name of College
Street Address
City, State Zip

To Whom It May Concern:

I am a (freshman, sophomore, junior, senior) at (name of your school) and will graduate in (month) (year).

Please send me the following information about your college: a general information brochure, program descriptions, an admission application, financial aid information, and any other information that might be helpful. I am considering ________________ as my major field of study (optional, if you know your preferred field of study).

I am interested in visiting your campus, taking a campus tour, and meeting with an admission counselor and a financial aid officer. I would also like to meet with an adviser or professor in the (your preferred field of study) department, if possible. I will contact you in a week to set up a time that is convenient.

If you would like to contact me directly, I can be reached at (your phone number with area code and e-mail address). Thank you.

Sincerely,

(Signature)

Your Name

- What is the student body like? Age? Sex? Race? Geographic origin?
- What percentage of students lives in dormitories? In off-campus housing?
- What percentage of students goes home for the weekend?
- What are some of the regulations that apply to living in a dormitory?
- What are the security precautions taken on campus and in the dorms?
- Is the surrounding community safe?
- Are there problems with drug and alcohol abuse on campus?
- Do faculty members and students mix on an informal basis?
- How important are the arts to student life?
- What facilities are available for cultural events?
- How important are sports to student life?
- What facilities are available for sporting events?
- What percentage of the student body belongs to a sorority/fraternity?
- What is the relationship between those who belong to the Greek system and those who don't?
- Are students involved in the decision-making process at the college? Do they sit on major committees?
- In what other activities can students get involved?
- What percentage of students receives financial aid based on need?
- What percentage of students receives scholarships based on academic ability?
- What percentage of a typical financial aid offer is in the form of a loan?
- If a family demonstrates financial need on the FAFSA (and PROFILE®, if applicable), what percentage of the established need is generally awarded?
- How much did the college increase the cost of room, board, tuition, and fees from last year?
- Do opportunities for financial aid, scholarships, or work-study increase each year?
- When is the admission application deadline?
- When is the financial aid application deadline?
- When will I be notified of the admission decision?
- Is a deposit required and is it refundable?

Keep in mind that you don't need to ask all these questions—in fact, some of them may have already been answered for you in the catalog, on the Web site, or in the interview. Ask only the questions for which you still need answers.

THE MATCHING GAME

Read each question and respond by circling Y (Yes), N (No), or C (Combination). Complete all the questions and return to the top. Highlight each action that coordinates with your answer, and then read it. Where you chose C, highlight both actions. Is there a pattern? Do the questions seem to lead to a certain type of college or university? Certain size? Certain location? Read the suggestions at the end of "The Matching Game" for more ideas.

	Question	Yes/No/ Combination	Action
1.	Do I have a goal in life?	Y N C	Y: State it.________________________. N: Don't worry, many students start college without knowing what they want to do. Look into colleges that specialize in the arts and sciences.
2.	Do I know what I want to achieve with a college degree?	Y N C	Y: List specifically what your goals are. ________________________ N: Think about what college can offer you.
3.	Do I want to broaden my knowledge?	Y N C	Y: Consider a liberal arts college. N: You might need to consider other options or educational opportunities.
4.	Do I want specific training?	Y N C	Y: Investigate technical colleges or professional training programs in universities. N: You don't know what you want to study? Don't worry, only 20 pecent of seniors who apply to college are sure.
5.	Am I looking for a balanced workload?	Y N C	Y: When you are visiting colleges, ask students about how they handle the workload. N: Check the workload carefully. If no one is on campus on a sunny day, it may not be the school for you
6.	Am I self-directed enough to finish a four-year college program?	Y N C	Y: Consider only four-year colleges and universities. N: Maybe a two-year junior or community college is a better way to begin your college experience. Also consider a vocational/career college.
7.	Do I know what I do well?	Y N C	Y: Identify majors related to your abilities. ________________________ N: Spend a little more time asking yourself questions about your interests. Speak to your counselor and do an interest inventory.
8.	Do I like to spend time learning any one subject more than others?	Y N C	Y: List majors related to that area. ________________ ________________________ N: Look at your high school courses. Which ones do you like better than others? ________________
9.	Do I know what matters to me and what my values are?	Y N C	Y: Look for the schools that talk about the values on their campus. Do the values mesh or conflict with your values? N: Values are less important to you, so places that really expound their values may seem confining to you.
10.	Do I need to be in affluent surroundings?	Y N C	Y: Look at the schools that deliver that package. Check the small, private liberal arts colleges. N: How strong is your reaction against this setting? If it is strong, check larger, more diverse settings, like an urban school.
11.	Am I going to college for the financial gains?	Y N C	Y: What majors are going to give you the payback you want? Look at business colleges and professional programs, like premed. N: If a big financial payback does not interest you, look at social service majors, like counseling, teaching, and social work.
12.	Am I focused?	Y N C	Y: Search out the programs that will offer you the best options. N: Avoid those schools whose programs are not strong in your focused area.
13.	Am I conservative in my views and behavior?	Y N C	Y: The political policies of schools are important. Look into them carefully. You might look at the schools in the Midwest or the South. N: If you're a liberal, look closely at the political climate. Check the schools in the Northeast and on the West Coast.

14.	Do I need to be around people who are similar to me?	Y N C	Y: If you are African American, check the historically black colleges. If socioeconomic level or a certain look is important to you, study the student populations carefully during campus visits. If it is religious orientation you are interested in, look into religiously sponsored colleges and universities. N: Look at large, midsize, and small universities in urban settings.
15.	Are the name and prestige of the school important to me?	Y N C	Y: Look into the Ivies and the competitive schools to see if you are eligible and what they offer you. Broaden your search to include other colleges and compare their offerings to your specific needs and interests. N: Don't exclude the well-known institutions if they fit in every other way.
16.	Do I like sports?	Y N C	Y: Large universities with Division I teams will give you all the sports you need—as a competitor or a fan. If you do not want to compete at that level, check schools in other divisions. Look at the liberal arts colleges for athletes. N: Look into smaller universities and liberal arts colleges with good teams.
17.	Am I a techie?	Y N C	Y: Check for computer engineering courses at technical universities and large universities near research centers and major computer business areas. Ask about hardwiring, e-mail, and computer packages before you enroll. N: It still helps to know what computer services are available where you enroll.
18.	Do I need to live in or be near a city?	Y N C	Y. How close to a city do you need to be? In the city or an hour away? Do you still want a campus feel? Consider these questions as you visit campuses. N: Do you need space, natural beauty, and peaceful surroundings to think? Look into small liberal arts schools in rural and suburban settings. Explore universities in the Midwest and South.
19.	Will I need counseling for support?	Y N C	Y: Investigate the quality of student services and the mechanism for accessing them. Smaller schools often pride themselves on their services. Look at liberal arts colleges. Universities connected to medical centers often provide extensive services. N: It is still good to know what is offered.
20.	Do I need an environment in which questioning is important?	Y N C	Y: Liberal arts colleges, honors colleges, and smaller universities place an emphasis on academic inquiry. N: You like to hear others discuss issues, gather as much information and opinions as you can, and think it over by yourself. Try the university setting.

Suggestions

Here are some ideas for you to consider based on the way you answered the questions.

1. If you answered *no* to numbers 2 and 3, why not investigate apprenticeships, vocational/career colleges, armed services options, and certification or two-year college programs?
2. If you answered *yes* to numbers 4, 11, and 17, technical or professional colleges and universities with hands-on training may give you the education you want.
3. If you answered *yes* to numbers 9, 10, and 20, you are leaning toward a liberal arts setting.
4. If you answered *yes* to numbers 5 and 6, examine the competitive and Ivy League colleges.
5. If you answered *no* to numbers 9, 10, 14, and 20 and *yes* to 16, 17, and 18, larger universities may offer you the best options.

Once you have completed your self-evaluation, made a decision whether college is for you, have some ideas about your personality and likes and dislikes, and can relate them to the different personalities of colleges, it is time to gather information. It needs to be quality information from the right sources. The quality of information you put into your search now will determine whether your list of colleges will represent a good or a bad match.

SHOULD YOU HEAD FOR THE IVY LEAGUE?

Determining whether to apply to one of the eight Ivy League schools is something about which you should think long and hard. Sure, it can't hurt to toss your application into the ring if you can afford the application fee and the time you'll spend writing the essays. But if you want to figure out if you'd be a legitimate candidate for acceptance at one of these top-tier schools, you should understand the type of student that they look for and how you compare. Take a look at these statistics:

- On average only 15 percent or fewer applicants are accepted at Ivy League colleges each year.
- Most Ivy League students have placed in the top 10 percent of their class.
- Because Ivy League schools are so selective, they want a diverse student population. That means they want students who represent not only the fifty states but also a wide selection of other countries.

Being accepted at an Ivy League school is a process that starts in the ninth grade. You should select demanding courses and maintain good grades in those courses throughout all four years of high school. Get involved in extracurricular activities as well, and, of course, do well on your standardized tests. When it comes time to apply for college, select at least three schools: one ideal, one possible, and one shoe-in. Your ideal can be an Ivy League if you wish.

While the ultimate goal is to get the best education possible, students are sometimes more concerned about getting accepted than with taking a hard look at what a school has to offer them. Often, a university or college that is less competitive than an Ivy League school may have exactly what you need to succeed in the future. Keep that in mind as you select the colleges that will offer you what *you* need.

COLLEGE COMPARISON WORKSHEET

Fill in your top five selection criteria and any others that may be of importance to you. Once you narrow your search of colleges to five, fill in the colleges across the top row. Using a scale of 1 to 5, where 1 is poor and 5 is excellent, rate each college by your criteria. Total each column to see which college rates the highest based upon your criteria.

SELECTION CRITERIA	COLLEGE 1	COLLEGE 2	COLLEGE 3	COLLEGE 4	COLLEGE 5
1.					
2.					
3.					
4.					
5.					
OTHER CRITERIA					
6.					
7.					
8.					
9.					
10.					
TOTAL					

Sample criteria (Use this list as a starting point—there may be other criteria important to you not listed here.): Arts facilities, athletic facilities, audiovisual center, campus setting, class size, classrooms/lecture halls, computer labs, dining hall, dorms, financial aid, fraternity/sorority houses, majors offered, religious facilities, professor profiles, student-faculty ratio, student profile, student union, surrounding community.

MINORITY STUDENTS

African American, Hispanic, Asian American, and Native American high school students have a lot of doors into higher education opening for them. In fact, most colleges want to respond to the social and economic disadvantages of certain groups of Americans. They want to reflect the globalization of our economy. They want their student populations to look like the rest of America, which means people from many different backgrounds and ethnic groups. You'll find that most colleges have at least one member of the admission staff who specializes in recruiting minorities.

One of the reasons a college admission staff is recruiting minorities and want to accommodate their needs is because more minorities are thinking of attending college—and graduating. Let's put some numbers to these statements. In its October 2010 *Minorities in Higher Education 2010—Twenty-Fourth Status Report,* the American Council on Education (ACE) found that between 1997 and 2007 minority enrollment at U.S. colleges and universities increased by 52 percent—from 3.6 million to 5.4 million. Colleges and universities became more diverse during the past decade, with the minority share of the student body rising from 25 to 30 percent.

STUDENT COUNSEL

QUESTION: How did you choose the college you're attending?

ANSWER: I followed my instincts in not going for a big name school. I went where I thought I would get the most out of school, not necessarily because of its reputation. I considered seven schools, and once I was accepted, I looked at the location and courses they offered and the financial aid I could get.

College student
Pacific University

Academic Resources for Minority Students

In addition to churches, sororities and fraternities, and college minority affairs offices, minority students can receive information and assistance from the following organizations:

ASPIRA

ASPIRA's mission is to empower the Puerto Rican and Latino community through advocacy and the education and leadership development of its youth.

1444 I Street NW, Suite 800
Washington, D.C. 20005
202-835-3600
www.aspira.org

INROADS

INROADS is a national career-development organization that places and develops talented minority youth (African American, Hispanic American, and Native American) in business and industry and prepares them for corporate and community leadership.

10 South Broadway, Suite 300
St. Louis, Missouri 63102
314-241-7488
www.inroads.org

National Action Council for Minorities in Engineering (NACME)

NACME is an organization that aims to provide leadership and support for the national effort to increase the representation of successful African American, American Indian, and Latino women and men in engineering and technology and math- and science-based careers.

440 Hamilton Avenue, Suite 302
White Plains, New York 10601-1813
914-539-4010
www.nacme.org

National Association for the Advancement of Colored People (NAACP)

The purpose of the NAACP is to ensure the political, educational, social, and economic equality of all citizens; to achieve equality of rights and eliminate race prejudice among the citizens of the United States; to remove all barriers of racial discrimination through democratic processes; to seek enactment and enforcement of federal, state, and local laws securing civil rights; to inform the public of the adverse effects of racial discrimination and to seek its elimination; and to educate persons as to their constitutional rights and to take all lawful action to secure the exercise thereof, and to take any other lawful action in furtherance of these objectives, consistent with the efforts of the national organization.

4805 Mt. Hope Drive
Baltimore, Maryland 21215
877-NAACP-98 (toll-free)
www.naacp.org

The National Urban League

The National Urban League's Education & Youth Development division strives to improve educational opportunities for African American and underserved students. The division has developed a number of programs to prepare students for success after graduation. Among these is Project Ready, which provides academic support and encouragement for middle school and high school students. The division expanded the program in 2009–2010 to create the Middle School Transitions Project, which helps students in grades 5 through 8 make the jump from middle school to high school, and STEM, which works to provide urban students with the resources they need to excel in science, technology, engineering, and math (STEM).

120 Wall Street
New York, New York 10005
212-558-5300
www.nul.org

United Negro College Fund (UNCF)

The UNCF serves to enhance the quality of education by raising operating funds for its 39 member colleges and universities, providing financial assistance to deserving students, and increasing access to technology for students and faculty at historically black colleges and universities.

8260 Willow Oaks Corporate Drive
P.O. Box 10444
Fairfax, Virginia 22031-8044
800-331-2244 (toll-free)
www.uncf.org

STUDENT COUNSEL

QUESTION: How did you make the decision to attend a historically black college?

ANSWER: Selecting a college was one of the hardest decisions I've ever had to make. As a representative of the National Achievement Scholarship and a National History Day winner, I was offered scholarships to a number of colleges across the country, including many HBCUs. I tried to figure out which institution would be able to give me the most help in achieving my goals. I finally decided on Florida A&M University (FAMU) in my hometown of Tallahassee.

There are many pluses to attending college in my hometown. By living on campus, I have the freedom to make my own decisions and live as a young adult while being close to the loving support of my parents. Also, FAMU will help me succeed in my objective of obtaining a bachelor's degree in broadcast journalism. As I look back, I am glad that I, unlike some of my high school peers, did not rush to judgment during the process of choosing a college. I am very happy with my decision.

College student
Florida A&M University

American Indian Higher Education Consortium (AIHEC)

AIHEC's mission is to support the work of tribal colleges and the national movement for tribal self-determination through four objectives: maintain commonly held standards of quality in American Indian education; support the development of new tribally controlled colleges; promote and assist in the development of legislation to support American Indian higher education; and encourage greater participation by American Indians in the development of higher education policy.

121 Oronoco Street
Alexandria, Virginia 22314
703-838-0400
www.aihec.org

Gates Millennium Scholars (GMS)

GMS, funded by a grant from the Bill & Melinda Gates Foundation, was established in 1999 to provide outstanding African American, American Indian/Alaska Native, Asian Pacific Islander American, and Hispanic American students with an opportunity to complete an undergraduate college education in all discipline areas and a graduate education for those students pursuing studies in mathematics, science, engineering, education, or library science. The goal of GMS is to promote academic excellence and to provide an opportunity for thousands of outstanding students with significant financial need to reach their fullest potential.

P.O. Box 10500
Fairfax, Virginia 22031-8044
877-690-4677 (toll-free)
www.gmsp.org

Hispanic Association of Colleges & Universities (HACU)

HACU is a national association representing the accredited colleges and universities in the United States where Hispanic students constitute at least 25 percent of the total student enrollment. HACU's goal is to bring together colleges and

SHOULD YOU ATTEND A HISTORICALLY BLACK COLLEGE OR UNIVERSITY?

Choosing which college to attend is usually a difficult decision for anyone to make, but when an African American student considers attending a historically black college or university (HBCU), a whole other set of family and cultural issues are raised.

Many valid reasons favor one or the other. Some are obvious differences. Parents and their children have to be honest and take a long, hard look at students' needs and how the campus environment can fulfill them. The following are some questions to ask to help you decide:

Do I know what's really important to me?

Consider the reasons why you want a degree and what you want to achieve with it. Is the choice to attend an HBCU yours or your family's? Do you have a particular field of study you want to pursue? Sometimes students can get so caught up in applying to a particular institution that they don't realize it doesn't even offer their major.

How will this campus fit my plans for the future?

There's no substitute for doing your homework about the campuses you're seriously considering. Know the reputation of those campuses in the community and among employers and the general population. Find out about student retention, graduation, and placement rates.

Does this campus have the facilities and living conditions that suit my comfort level?

Finding a campus where you're comfortable is a big factor in choosing a college. What do you want in campus facilities and living conditions? For instance, if you currently attend a small private high school in a suburban setting, perhaps you wouldn't like living on a large urban campus with peers who don't mirror your background.

What level of support will I get on campus?

Students considering institutions where few people are like them should look at the available support systems and organizations that will be available to them. Parents need to feel comfortable with the contact person on campus.

When all the factors that determine the choice of a college are laid out, the bottom line is which institution best meets your needs. For some African American students, an HBCU is the best choice. For others, it's not. African American students reflect many backgrounds, and no single decision will be right for everyone.

universities, corporations, government agencies, and individuals to establish partnerships for promoting the developing Hispanic-serving colleges and universities; improving access to and the quality of postsecondary education for Hispanic students; and meeting the needs of business, industry, and government through the development and sharing of resources, information, and expertise.

8415 Datapoint Drive, Suite 400
San Antonio, Texas 78229
210-692-3805
www.hacu.net

Hispanic Scholarship Fund (HSF)

HSF is the nation's leading organization supporting Hispanic higher education. HSF was founded in 1975 with a vision to strengthen the country by advancing college education among Hispanic Americans. In support of its mission, HSF provides the Latino community with college scholarships and educational outreach support.

55 Second Street, Suite 1500
San Francisco, California 94105
877-473-4636 (toll-free)
www.hsf.net

LEAGUE Foundation

Since 1996, LEAGUE Foundation has awarded college scholarships totaling more than $132,000 to self-identified lesbian, gay, bisexual, or transgender (LGBT) U.S. high school students based on GPA, community service, and acceptance to an accredited U.S. college or university.

One AT&T Way, Room 4B214J
Bedminster, New Jersey 07921
571-354-4525
E-mail: info@leaguefoundation.org

STUDENTS WITH DISABILITIES GO TO COLLEGE

The Americans with Disabilities Act (ADA) requires educational institutions at all levels, public and private, to provide equal access to programs, services, and facilities. Schools must be accessible to students, as well as to employees and the public, regardless of any disability. To ensure such accessibility, they must follow specific requirements for new construction, alterations or renovations, academic programs, and institutional policies, practices, and procedures. Students with specific disabilities have the right to request and expect accommodations, including auxiliary aids and services that enable them to participate in and benefit from all programs and activities offered by or related to a school.

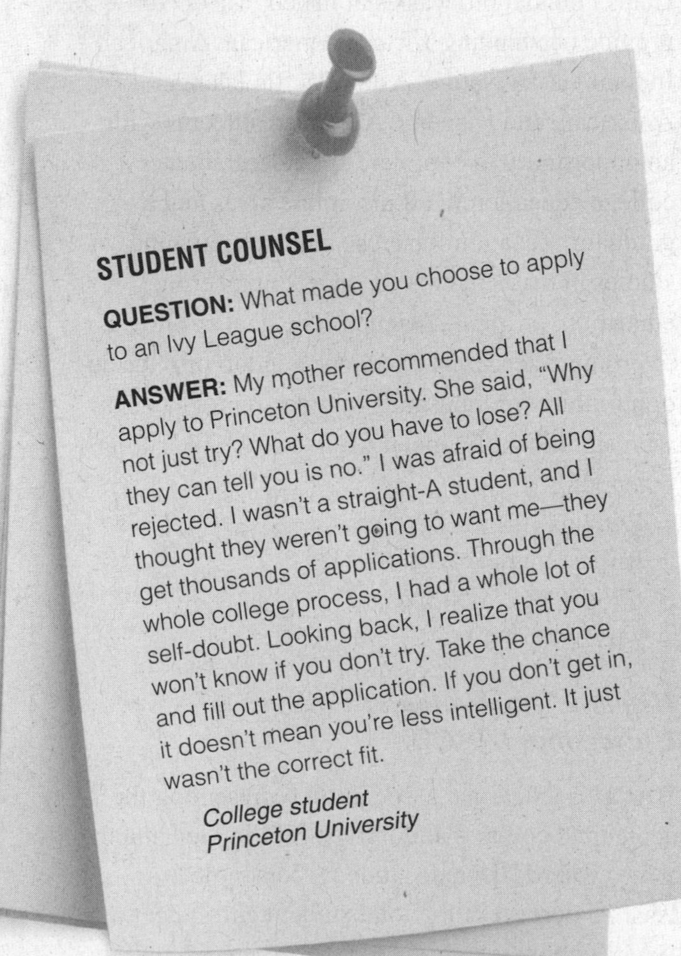

To comply with ADA requirements, many high schools and universities offer programs and information to answer questions for students with disabilities and to assist them both in selecting appropriate colleges and in attaining full inclusion once they enter college. And most colleges and universities have disabilities services offices to help students negotiate the system. When it comes time to apply to colleges, write to the ones that you're interested in to find out what kinds of programs they have in place. When it comes time to narrow down your choices, request a visit.

What Is Considered a Disability?

A person is considered to have a disability if he or she meets at least one of three conditions. The individual must

1. have a documented physical or mental impairment that substantially limits one or more major life activities, such as personal self-care, walking, seeing, hearing, speaking, breathing, learning, working, or performing manual tasks; or
2. have a record of such an impairment; or
3. be perceived as having such an impairment.

Physical disabilities include impairments of speech, vision, hearing, and mobility. Other disabilities, while less obvious, are similarly limiting; they include diabetes, asthma, multiple sclerosis, heart disease, cancer, mental illness, mental retardation, cerebral palsy, and learning disabilities.

Learning disabilities refer to an array of biological conditions that impede a person's ability to process and disseminate information. A learning disability is commonly recognized as a significant deficiency in one or more of the following areas: oral expression, listening comprehension, written expression, basic reading skills, reading comprehension, mathematical calculation, or problem solving. Individuals with learning disabilities also may have difficulty with sustained attention, time management, or social skills.

If you have a disability, you'll take the same steps to choose and apply to a college as other students, but you should also evaluate each college based on your special need(s). Get organized, and meet with campus specialists to discuss your specific requirements. Then, explore whether the programs, policies, procedures, and facilities meet your specific situation.

It is usually best to describe your disability in a letter attached to the application so the proper fit can be made between you and the school. You'll probably need to have your psychoeducational evaluation and testing record sent to the school. Some colleges help with schedules and offer transition courses, reduced course loads, extra access to professors, and special study areas to help address your needs.

Remember, admission to college is a realistic goal for any motivated student. If you invest the time and effort, you can make it happen.

STUDENT COUNSEL

The following quotes are from students who attend a college that offers services for learning disabled students.

"I have delayed development. I need help getting things done, and I need extra time for tests. As long as I'm able to go up to teachers and ask questions, I do well on tests."—*Anita*

"I have dyslexia. I thought the term 'disabilities services' was for people with visual and hearing impairments. But when I got here, I found it covered a variety of disabilities. It was like Christmas. You got everything you wanted and more."—*Debra*

"I am hard of hearing. I was always afraid I wouldn't be able to hear what [teachers] said. It's hard to read lips and listen at the same time. With note-takers, I still get what I need even if the teacher moves around. They want you to make it through."—*Jeannette*

DIRECTORY FOR STUDENTS WITH DISABILITIES

The following resources can help students, families, and schools with the legal requirements for accommodating disabilities. They can also link you with other groups and individuals that are knowledgeable in students' rights and the process of transition into postsecondary education.

Also, special interest, education, support, and advocacy organizations for persons with particular disabilities exist. Check with your counselor or contact one of the following organizations for information:

ACT ADMINISTRATION

http://www.act.org/aap/disab

Extended Time National Testing

ACT Registration Extended Time National Testing
301 ACT Drive
P.O. Box 4068
Iowa City, Iowa 52243-4068
319-337-1851

Special Testing

ACT Special Testing
301 ACT Drive
P.O. Box 4028
Iowa City, Iowa 52243-4028
319-337-1332

ASSOCIATION ON HIGHER EDUCATION AND DISABILITY (AHEAD)

107 Commerce Center Drive
Suite 204
Huntersville, North Carolina 28078
704-947-7779
www.ahead.org

ATTENTION DEFICIT DISORDER ASSOCIATION (ADDA)

P.O. Box 7557
Wilmington, Delaware 19803-9997
800-939-1019 (toll-free)
E-mail: info@add.org
www.add.org

CHILDREN AND ADULTS WITH ATTENTION-DEFICIT/HYPERACTIVITY DISORDER (CHADD)

8181 Professional Place
Suite 150
Landover, Maryland 20785
301-306-7070
www.chadd.org

COUNCIL FOR LEARNING DISABILITIES

11184 Antioch Road, Box 405
Overland Park, Kansas 66210
913-491-1011
www.cldinternational.org

HEATH RESOURCE CENTER ONLINE CLEARINGHOUSE ON POSTSECONDARY EDUCATION FOR INDIVIDUALS WITH DISABILITIES

HEATH Resource Center
The George Washington University
2134 G Street NW
Washington, DC 20052-0001
202-973-0904
www.heath.gwu.edu

THE INTERNATIONAL DYSLEXIA ASSOCIATION

40 York Road
Fourth Floor
Baltimore, Maryland 21204
410-296-0232
www.interdys.org

LEARNING DISABILITIES ASSOCIATION OF AMERICA (LDA)

4156 Library Road
Pittsburgh, Pennsylvania 15234-1349
412-341-1515
www.ldanatl.org

NATIONAL CENTER FOR LEARNING DISABILITIES (NCLD)

381 Park Avenue South
Suite 1401
New York, New York 10016
888-575-7373 (toll-free)
www.ncld.org

NATIONAL DISSEMINATION CENTER FOR CHILDREN WITH DISABILITIES (NICHCY)

1825 Connecticut Avenue NW
Suite 700
Washington, DC 20009
800-695-0285 (toll-free)
www.nichcy.org

RECORDING FOR THE BLIND & DYSLEXIC

20 Roszel Road
Princeton, New Jersey 08540
866-RFBD-585
www.rfbd.org

SAT SERVICES FOR STUDENTS WITH DISABILITIES (SSD)

College Board SSD Program
P.O. Box 8060
Mt. Vernon, Illinois 62864-0060
609-771-7137
www.collegeboard.com/ssd/student

TIPS FOR STUDENTS WITH DISABILITIES

- Document your disability with letters from your physician(s), therapist, case manager, school psychiatrist, and other service providers.
- Get letters of support from teachers, family, friends, and service providers that detail how you have succeeded despite your disability.
- Learn the federal laws that apply to students with disabilities.
- Research support groups for peer information and advocacy.
- Visit several campuses.
- Look into the services available, the pace of campus life, and the college's programs for students with disabilities.
- Ask about orientation programs, including specialized introductions for, or about, students with disabilities.
- Ask about flexible, individualized study plans.
- Ask if the school offers technology such as voice synthesizers, voice recognition, and/or visual learning equipment to its students.
- Ask about adapted intramural/social activities.
- Ask to talk with students who have similar disabilities to hear about their experiences on campus.
- Once you select a college, get a map of the campus and learn the entire layout.
- If you have a physical disability, make sure the buildings you need to be in are accessible to you. Even though they comply with the ADA, some aren't as accessible as others.
- Be realistic. If you use a wheelchair, for example, a school with an exceptionally hilly campus may not be your best choice, no matter what other accommodations it has.

CHAPTER 7

APPLYING TO COLLEGE

The big moment has arrived. It's time to make some decisions about where you want to apply.

Once your list is finalized, the worst part is filling out all the forms accurately and getting them in by the deadlines. Because requirements differ, you should check with all the colleges that you are interested in attending to find out what documentation is needed and when it is due.

WHAT SCHOOLS LOOK FOR IN PROSPECTIVE STUDENTS

As if you were sizing up the other team to plan your game strategy, you'll need to understand what admission committees want from *you* as you assemble all the pieces of your application.

Academic record: Admission representatives look at the breadth (how many), diversity (which ones), and difficulty (how challenging) of the courses on your transcript.

Grades: You should show consistency in your ability to work to your potential. If your grades are not initially good, colleges look to see that significant improvement has been made. Some colleges have minimum grade point averages that they are willing to accept.

Class rank: Colleges may consider the academic standing of a student in relation to the other members of his or her class. Are you in the top 25 percent of your class? Top half? Ask your counselor for your class rank.

Standardized test scores: Colleges look at test scores in terms of ranges. If your scores aren't high but you did well academically in high school, you shouldn't be discouraged. Admission does not rest on a set formula. Even at the most competitive schools, some students' test scores are lower than you would think.

Extracurricular activities: Colleges look for depth of involvement (variety and how long you participated), initiative (leadership), and creativity demonstrated in activities, service, or work.

PARENT PERSPECTIVE

QUESTION: How did your help your daughter with the college-selection process?

ANSWER: The key is to pace things out so that every college visit doesn't take place in the fall of your child's senior year, which is pretty late. Some kids want to start looking at schools in 9th grade; my daughter didn't feel ready until the spring of her junior year. As a parent, don't be afraid to ask questions to help your son or daughter figure out exactly what it is he or she wants to do and the kind of school she will feel most comfortable at. It's a big decision. Some parents hire a college consultant to help with the whole admissions process. My daughter and I looked in several college guidebooks and also on various Web sites. Then, when she had selected a few schools in the same geographical area, we planned a road trip to see the schools. That was the most important part of the process. At one school, my daughter determined half-way through the tour that the school was definitely not right for her. At another school, she knew it was a perfect fit—and she actually ended up at that school!"

Mother of college sophomore
Yardley, Pennsylvania

Recommendations: Most colleges require a recommendation from your high school guidance counselor. Some ask for references from teachers or other adults. If your counselor or teachers don't know you well, you should put together a student resume, or brag sheet, that outlines what you have done during your four years of high school. You'll find a worksheet that will help you put together your resume in this chapter.

College interview: An interview is required by most colleges with highly selective procedures. Refer back to "The College Interview" in the previous chapter.

ADMISSION PROCEDURES

Your first task in applying is to get application forms. That's easy. You can get them from your high school's guidance department, at college fairs, or by calling or writing to colleges and requesting applications. (See "Writing to a College for Information" in the previous chapter.) The trend, however, is leaning toward online applications, which are completed on the school's Web site. Admission information can be gathered from college representatives, catalogs, Web sites, and directories; alumni or students attending the college; and campus visits. Take a look at "Dos and Don'ts for Filling out Your Applications" (later in this chapter) for some guidelines.

Which Admission Option Is Best for You?

One of the first questions you'll be asked on applications for four-year colleges and universities is which admission option you want. What this means is whether you want to apply early action, early decision, deferred admission, and so on.

ADVICE FROM AN EDUCATIONAL CONSULTANT

Parents and teens should visit college campuses early and trust their gut feelings about whether the campus feels right. Above all, don't be blinded by name-brand colleges and the strong peer pressure that seems to steer your teen in the direction of prestigious colleges. Just as in shopping for clothing: Would you rather have a name brand or something that fits you well and makes you feel comfortable?

Ask your teen some questions. Do you really want to live in a pressure-cooker for the next four years? Some students thrive in a highly competitive environment, but many do not—even if they are excellent students. Before making a final decision, a teen should spend three or four days at the two colleges that interest him or her the most.

Senior year in high school is a time when teens go through many changes and experiment with many different roles. This can be bewildering to parents. Be patient. Realize that the time is equally bewildering to your son or daughter. Parents can be supportive and understanding, even though their teen may seem to be pushing them away. Offer guidance about choosing the right college, even though your teen might seem to be rejecting it. Teens hear everything, though they might not show it.

Educational consultant, family therapist, and parent
Agoura Hills, California

Four-year institutions generally offer the following admission options:

Early admission—A student of superior ability is admitted into college courses and programs before completing high school.

Early decision—A student declares a first-choice college, requests that the college decide on acceptance early (between November and January), and agrees to enroll if accepted. Students with a strong high school record who are sure they want to attend a certain school may want to consider early decision admission. (See "More on Early Decision")

Early action—This is similar to early decision, but if a student is accepted, he or she has until the regular admission deadline to decide whether to attend.

Early evaluation—A student can apply under early evaluation to find out if the chance of acceptance is good, fair, or poor. Applications are due before the regular admission deadline, and the student is given an opinion between January and March.

Regular admission—This is the most common option offered to students. A deadline is set for when all applications must be received, and all notifications are sent out at the same time.

Rolling admission—The college accepts students who meet the academic requirements on a first-come, first-served basis until it fills its freshman class. No strict application deadline is specified. Applications are reviewed and decisions are made immediately (usually within two to three weeks). This method is commonly used at large state universities, so students should apply early for the best chance of acceptance.

Open admission—Virtually all high school graduates are admitted, regardless of academic qualifications.

Deferred admission—An accepted student is allowed to postpone enrollment for a year. (See "The Gap-Year Option" at the end of this chapter.)

If you're going to a two-year college, these options also apply to you. Two-year colleges usually have an "open-door" admission policy, which means that high school graduates may enroll as long as space is available. Sometimes vocational/career colleges are somewhat selective, and competition for admission may be fairly intense for programs that are highly specialized.

More on Early Decision

Early decision is a legally binding agreement between you and the college. If the college accepts you, you pay a deposit within a short period of time and sign an agreement stating that you will not apply to other colleges. To keep students from backing out, some colleges mandate that applicants' high school counselors cannot send transcripts to other institutions.

In many ways, early decision is a win-win for both students and colleges. Students can relax and enjoy their senior year of high school without waiting to see if other colleges have accepted them. And colleges know early in the year which students are enrolled, and they can start planning the coming year.

STUDENT COUNSEL

QUESTION: What made you apply to college early decision?

ANSWER: I visited lots of schools in Pennsylvania, but the minute I walked on the campus of Gettysburg College, I knew I wanted to come here. I liked the way the campus was set up. It was small, and everything was together. The student-teacher ratio was low, and it had a good political science program. It had everything that I wanted.

But if you want to go early decision, you have to visit the schools to be able to compare and contrast the different campuses. Many of the schools will have the same things, like small class size. But the way you feel about the campus is the largest factor because that's where you will be living. I visited Gettysburg four times, so when I went early decision, I was confident about it. I realized it was a huge step and knew I had to be sure. But after visiting here so many times, I knew I'd be unhappy anywhere else.

Gettysburg College student
Gettysburg, Pennsylvania

When Is Early Decision the Right Decision?

For good and bad reasons, early decision is a growing trend, so why not just do it? Early decision is an excellent idea that comes with a warning. It's not a good idea unless you have done a thorough college search and know without a shred of doubt that this is the college for you. Don't go for early decision unless you've spent time on the campus and in classes and dorms, and you have a true sense of the academic and social climate of that college.

Early decision can get sticky if you change your mind. Parents of students who have signed agreements and then want to apply elsewhere get angry at high school counselors, saying they've taken away their rights to choose among colleges. They try to force them to send out transcripts even though their children have committed to one college. To guard against this scenario, some colleges ask parents and students to sign a statement signifying their understanding that early decision is a binding plan. Some high schools now have their own form for students and parents to sign acknowledging that they completely realize the nature of an early decision agreement.

The Financial Reason Against Early Decision

Another common argument against early decision is that if an institution has you locked in, it has no incentive to offer you the best financial package. The consensus seems to be that if you're looking to play the financial game, don't apply for early decision.

Some folks argue, however, that the best financial aid offers are usually made to attractive applicants. In general, if a student receives an early decision offer, he or she falls into that category and so would get "the sweetest" financial aid anyway. That doesn't mean that colleges aren't out there using financial incentives to get students to enroll. A strong candidate who applies to six or eight schools and gets admitted to all of them will look at how much money the colleges throw his or her way before making a decision.

Before You Decide...

If you're thinking about applying for early decision at a college, ask yourself these questions first. You'll be glad you did.

- Why am I applying early decision?
- Have I thoroughly researched several colleges, and do I know what my options are?
- Do I know why I'm going to college and what I want to accomplish there?
- Have I visited several schools, spent time in classes, stayed overnight, and talked to professors?
- Do the courses that the college offers match my goals?
- Am I absolutely convinced that one college clearly stands out above all others?

MORE MUMBO JUMBO

Besides confusing terms like deferred admission, early decision, and early evaluation, just discussed, you'll most likely stumble upon some additional terms that might bamboozle you. Here, we explain a few more.

Academic Calendar

Traditional semesters: Two equal periods of time during a school year.

Early semester: Two equal periods of time during a school year. The first semester is completed before the end of December.

Trimester: Calendar year divided into three equal periods of time. The third trimester replaces summer school.

Quarter: Four equal periods of time during a school year.

4-1-4: Two equal terms of about four months separated by a one-month term.

Accreditation

Accreditation is recognition of a college or university by a regional or national organization, which indicates that the institution has met its objectives and is maintaining prescribed educational standards. Colleges may be accredited by one of six regional associations of schools and colleges and by any one of the many national specialized accrediting bodies.

Specialized accreditation of individual programs is granted by national professional organizations. This is intended to ensure that specific programs meet or exceed minimum requirements established by the professional organization. States may require that students in some professions that grant licenses graduate from an accredited program as one qualification for licensure.

Accreditation is somewhat like receiving a pass/fail grade. It doesn't differentiate colleges and universities that excel from those that meet minimum requirements. Accreditation applies to all programs within an institution, but it does not mean that all programs are of equal quality within an institution. Accreditation does not guarantee transfer recognition by other colleges. Transfer decisions are made by individual institutions.

Affiliation

Not-for-profit colleges are classified into one of the following categories: state-assisted, private/independent, or private/church-supported. The institution's affiliation does not guarantee the quality or nature of the institution, and it may or may not have an effect on the religious life of students.

State-assisted colleges and universities and private/independent colleges do not have requirements related to the religious activity of their students. The influence of religion varies among private/church-supported colleges. At some, religious services or study are encouraged or required; at others, religious affiliation is less apparent.

Articulation Agreement

Articulation agreements facilitate the transfer of students and credits among state-assisted institutions of higher education by establishing transfer procedures and equitable treatment of all students in the system.

One type of articulation agreement links two or more colleges so that students can continue to make progress toward their degree, even if they must attend different schools at different times. For example, some states' community colleges have agreements with their state universities that permit graduates of college parallel programs to transfer with junior standing.

A second type of articulation agreement links secondary (high school) and postsecondary institutions to allow students to gain college credit for relevant vocational courses. This type of agreement saves students time and tuition in the pursuit of higher learning.

Because articulation agreements vary from school to school and from program to program, it is recommended that students check with their home institution and the institution they are interested in attending to fully understand the options available to them and each institution's specific requirements.

Cross-Registration

Cross-registration is a cooperative arrangement offered by many colleges and universities for the purpose of increasing the number and types of courses offered at any one institution. This arrangement allows students to cross-register for one or more courses at any participating host institution. While specific cross-registration program requirements may vary, typically a student can cross-register without having to pay the host institution additional tuition.

If your college participates in cross-registration, check with your home institution concerning any additional tuition costs and request a cross-registration form. Check with your adviser and registrar at your home institution to make sure that the course you plan to take is approved, and then contact the host institution for cross-registration instructions. Make sure that space is available in the course you want to take at the host institution, as some host institutions give their own students registration priority.

To participate in cross-registration, you may need to be a full-time student (some programs allow part-time student participation) in good academic and financial standing at your home institution. Check with both colleges well in advance for all of the specific requirements.

THE COMPLETE APPLICATION PACKAGE

Freshman applications can be filed any time after you have completed your junior year of high school. Colleges strongly recommend that students apply by April (at the latest) of their senior year to be considered for acceptance, scholarships, financial aid, and housing. College requirements may vary, so always read and comply with specific requirements. In general, admission officers are interested in the following basic materials:

- A completed and signed application and any required application fee.
- An official copy of your high school transcript, including your class ranking and grade point average. The transcript must include all work completed as of the date the application is submitted. Check with your guidance counselor for questions about these items. If you apply online, you must inform your guidance counselor and request that he or she send your transcript to the schools to which you are applying. Your application will not be processed without a transcript.
- An official record of your ACT and/or SAT scores.
- Other items that may be required include letters of recommendation, an essay, the secondary school report form and midyear school report (sent in by your guidance counselor after you fill out a portion of the form), and any financial aid forms required by the college.

Use the "College Application Checklist" to make sure you have what you need before you send everything off.

Filling out the Forms

Filling out college applications can seem like a daunting task, but the successful completion of this part of the process can be accomplished in six easy steps.

Step 1: Practice Copies

Make a photocopy of each application of each college to which you plan to apply. Since the presentation of your application may be considered an important aspect in the weighting for admission, you don't want to erase, cross out, or use white-out on your final application. Make all your mistakes on your copies. When you think you have it right, then transfer the information to your final original copy or go online to enter it on the college's electronic application. Remember, at the larger universities, the application packet may be the only part of you they see.

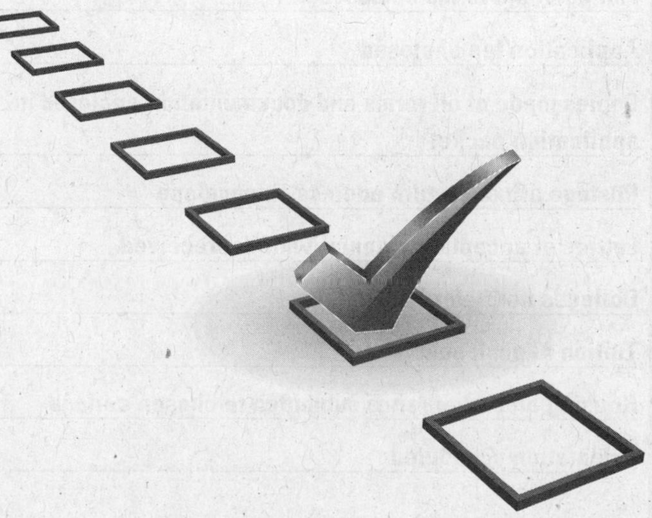

COLLEGE APPLICATION CHECKLIST

Keep track of your applications by inserting a check mark or the completion date in the appropriate column and row.

	College 1	College 2	College 3	College 4
Campus visit				
Campus interview				
Letters of recommendation				
NAME:				
Date requested				
Date followed-up				
NAME:				
Date requested				
Date followed-up				
NAME:				
Date requested				
Date followed-up				
Counselor recommendation form to counselor				
Secondary school report form to counselor				
Test scores requested				
Transcripts sent				
Application completed				
Essay completed				
All signatures collected				
Financial aid forms enclosed				
Application fee enclosed				
Copies made of all forms and documentation enclosed in application packet				
Postage affixed/return address on envelope				
Letters of acceptance/denial/wait list received				
Colleges notified of intent				
Tuition deposit sent				
Housing and other forms submitted to chosen college				
Orientation scheduled				

Step 2: Decide on Your Approach

What is it about your application that will grab the admission counselor's attention so that it will be pulled out of the sea of applications on his or her desk for consideration? Be animated and interesting in what you say. Be memorable in your approach to your application, but don't overdo it. You want the admission counselor to remember you, not your Spanish castle made of Popsicle sticks. Most important, be honest and don't exaggerate your academic and extracurricular activities. Approach this process with integrity every step of the way. First of all, it is the best way to end up in a college that is the right match for you. Second, if you are less than truthful, the college will eventually learn about it. How will they know? You have to supply support materials to accompany your application—things like transcripts and recommendations. If you tell one story and they tell another, the admission office will notice the disparity—trust us!

Step 3: Check the Deadlines

In September of your senior year, organize your applications in chronological order. Place the due dates for your final list of schools next to their names on your stretch, target, and safety list and on your "College Application Checklist." Work on materials with the earliest due date first.

Step 4: Check the Data on You

You need to make sure that the information you will be sending to support your applications is correct. The first thing to double-check is your transcript. This is an important piece because you must send a transcript with each application you send to colleges. Take a trip to the guidance office and ask for a "Transcript Request Form." Fill out the request for a formal transcript, indicating that you are requesting a copy for yourself and that you'll pick it up. Pay the fee if one is required.

When you get your transcript, look it over carefully. It will be several pages long and will include everything from the titles of all the courses that you have taken since the ninth grade to the final grade for each course and community service hours you have logged each year. Check the information carefully. It is understandable that with this much data, it is easy to make an input error. Because this information is vital to you and you are the best judge of accuracy, it is up to you to check it. Take any corrections or questions you have back to your guidance counselor to make the corrections. If it is a questionable grade, your counselor will help you find out what grade should have been posted on your transcript. Do whatever needs to be done to make sure your transcript has been corrected no later than October 1 of your senior year.

Step 5: List Your Activities

When you flip through your applications, you'll find a section on extracurricular activities. It is time to hit your computer again to prioritize your list of extracurricular activities and determine the best approach for presenting them to your colleges. Some students will prepare a resume and include this in every application they send. Other students will choose to develop an "Extracurricular, Academic, and Work Experience Addendum" and mark those specific sections of their application as "See attached Addendum."

If you are a powerhouse student with a great deal to say in this area, it will take time to prioritize your involvement in activities and word it succinctly yet interestingly. Your "Brag Sheet" will help (see "The Brag Sheet" later in this chapter). Put those activities that will have the strongest impact, show the most consistent involvement, and demonstrate your leadership abilities at the top of the list. This will take time, so plan accordingly. If you feel you have left out important information because the form limits you, include either an addendum or your resume as a backup.

DOS AND DON'TS FOR FILLING OUT YOUR APPLICATIONS

One of the most intimidating steps of applying for admission to college is filling out all the forms. This list of dos and don'ts will help you put your best foot forward on your college applications.

DO

- **Read applications and directions carefully.**
- **Make sure that everything that is supposed to be included is enclosed.**
- **Make copies of applications, and practice filling one out before you complete the original (if you're not using an online application).**
- **Start with the simple applications and then progress to the more complex ones.**
- **Type or neatly print your answers, and then proofread the applications and essays several times for accuracy. Also ask someone else to proofread them for you.**
- **If asked, describe how you can make a contribution to the schools to which you apply.**
- **Be truthful, and do not exaggerate your accomplishments.**
- **Keep a copy of all materials you submit to colleges.**
- **Be thorough and on time.**

DON'T

- **Write in script. If you don't have access to a computer, print neatly.**
- **Leave blank spaces. Missing information may cause your application to be sent back or delayed while admission officers wait for complete information.**
- **Be unclear. If the question calls for a specific answer, don't try to dodge it by being vague.**
- **Put it off!**

Step 6: Organize Your Other Data

What other information can you organize in advance of sitting down to fill out your applications?

The Personal Data Section

Most of this section is standard personal information that you won't have any difficulty responding to, but some items you'll need to think about. For example, you may find a question that asks, "What special college or division are you applying to?" Do you have a specific school in mind, such as the College of Engineering? If you are not sure about your major, ask yourself what interests you the most and then enter that college. Once you are in college and have a better sense of what you want to do, you can always change your major.

The application will provide an optional space to declare ethnicity. If you feel you would like to declare an area and that it would work to your advantage for admission, consider completing this section of the application.

You're also going to need your high school's College Entrance Examination Board (CEEB) number. That is the number you needed when you filled out your test packets. It is stamped on the front of your SAT and ACT packets, or, if you go to the guidance department, they'll tell you what it is.

The Standardized Testing Section

Applications ask you for your test dates and scores. Get them together accurately. All your College Board scores should be recorded with the latest test results you have received. Your latest ACT record will have only the current scores unless you asked for all past test results. If you have lost this information, call these organizations or go to your guidance department. Your counselor should have copies. Be sure the testing organizations are sending your official score reports to the schools to which you're applying. If you are planning to take one of these tests in the future, the colleges will want those dates, too; they will wait for those scores before making a decision. If you change your plans, write the admission office a note with the new dates or the reason for canceling.

The Senior Course Load Section

Colleges will request that you list your current senior schedule by semester. Set this information up in this order: List any AP or honors-level full-year courses first, as these will have the most impact. Then list other required full-year courses and then required semester courses, followed by electives. Make sure you list first-semester and second-semester courses appropriately. Don't forget to include physical education if you are taking it this year.

Writers for Your Letters of Recommendation

Most schools will require you to submit two or three letters of recommendation from adults who know you well.

Guidance Counselor Recommendations

Nearly all colleges require a letter of recommendation from the applicant's high school guidance counselor. Some counselors give students an essay question that they feel will give them the background they need to structure a recommendation. Other counselors canvass a wide array of individuals who know a student to gather a broader picture of the student in various settings. No one approach is better than the other. Find out which approach is used at your school. You'll probably get this information as a handout at one of those evening guidance programs or in a classroom presentation by your school's guidance department. If you're still not sure that you know what is expected of you or if the dog has eaten those papers, ask your guidance counselor what is due and by what date. Make sure that you complete the materials on time and that you set aside enough of your time to do them justice.

Teacher Recommendations

In addition to the recommendation from your counselor, colleges may request additional recommendations from your teachers. Known as formal recommendations, these are sent directly to the colleges by your subject teachers. Most colleges require at least one formal recommendation in addition to the counselor's recommendation. However, many competitive institutions require two, if not three, academic recommendations. Follow a school's directions regarding the exact number. A good rule of thumb is to have recommendations from teachers in two subject areas.

Approach your recommendation writers personally to request that they write for you. If they agree, provide them with a copy of your Brag Sheet. On the other hand, you may be met with a polite refusal on the order of "I'm sorry, but I'm unable to write for you. I've been approached by so many seniors already that it would be difficult for me to accomplish your recommendation by your due dates." This teacher may really be overburdened with requests for recommendations, especially if this is a senior English teacher, or the teacher may be giving you a signal that someone else may be able to write a stronger piece for you. Either way, it's best to just accept the refusal politely, and seek another recommendation writer.

How do you decide whom to ask? The following are some questions to help you select your writers:

- How well does the teacher know you?
- Has the teacher taught you for more than one course? Has he or she watched your talents and skills develop?
- Has the teacher sponsored an extracurricular activity in which you made a contribution?
- Do you get along with the teacher?
- Does the college/university indicate that a recommendation is required or recommended from a particular subject-area instructor?
- If you declare an intended major, can you obtain a recommendation from a teacher in that subject area?

THE BRAG SHEET

At the beginning of this chapter, we described how a student resume can help your guidance counselors and teachers write their letters of recommendation for you. Putting together a list of your accomplishments will also help you organize all of the information you will need to include when you fill out your college applications.

ACADEMICS

GPA (Grade Point Average) ______

THE HONORS COURSES I HAVE TAKEN ARE:

English ______

History ______

Math ______

Science ______

Language ______

Electives ______

THE AP COURSES I HAVE TAKEN ARE:

English ______

History ______

Math ______

Science ______

Language ______

Electives ______

STANDARDIZED TEST SCORES

PSAT ______

1st SAT ______

2nd SAT ______

ACT ______

SAT SUBJECT TESTS

Test 1 ______ **Score** ______

Test 2 ______ **Score** ______

Test 3 ______ **Score** ______

SPECIAL TALENTS

I have received the following academic awards: ______

I have performed in these theatrical productions: ______

I lettered in the following sports: ______

I have played on the following traveling teams: ______

I am a member of the following musical groups: ______

EXTRACURRICULAR ACTIVITIES

I participate on a regular basis in the following extracurricular activities: ______

I have held the following offices: ______

I have established the following extracurricular organizations: ______

I have held the following after-school and/or summer jobs: ______

GOALS

I plan to major in the following area in college: ______

Other Recommendation Writers

Consider getting recommendations from your employer, your rabbi or pastor, the director of the summer camp where you worked for the last two summers, and so on—but only if these additional letters are going to reveal information about you that will have a profound impact on the way a college will view your candidacy. Otherwise, you run the risk of overloading your application with too much paper.

FROM THE GUIDANCE OFFICE

Essays are so important to the college application. Students focus more on grades than anything else. They think grades are the be-all and end-all and that an SAT score will get them in. For most selective schools, that's just one piece of the pie. Many of the schools in the upper 20 percent of competitive schools consider the essay more heavily. Essays show whether the student is a thinker, is creative, and is analytical. They're looking for the type of personality that can shine rather than one that simply can spit out names and dates. When everyone has high SATs in a pool of applicants, the essay is what makes one student stand out over another.

Counselor
MacArthur High School
San Antonio, Texas

Writing the Application Essay

Application essays show how you think and how you write. They also reveal additional information about you that is not in your other application material. Not all colleges require essays, and those that do often have a preferred topic. Make sure you write about the topic that is specified and keep to the length of pages or words. If the essay asks for 300 words, don't submit 50 or 500. The following are some examples of essay topics:

Tell us about yourself. Describe your personality and a special accomplishment. Illustrate the unique aspects of who you are, what you do, and what you want out of life. Share an experience that made an impact on you, or write about something you have learned from your parents.

Tell us about an academic or extracurricular interest or idea. Show how a book, experience, quotation, or idea reflects or shapes your outlook and aspirations.

Tell us why you want to come to our college. Explain why your goals and interests match the programs and offerings of that particular school. This question requires some research about the school. Be specific.

Show us an imaginative side of your personality. This question demands originality but is a great opportunity to show off your skills as a writer.

Start writing your thoughts and impressions well before the essay is due. Think about how you have changed over the years so that if and when it comes time to write about yourself, you'll have plenty of information. Write about something that means a lot to you, and support your thoughts with reasons and examples. Then explain why you care about your topic.

The essay should not be a summary of your high school career. Describe yourself as others see you, and use a natural, conversational style. Use an experience to set the scene in which you illustrate something about yourself. For example, you might discuss how having a disabled relative helped you appreciate life's simple pleasures. Or you may use your athletic experiences to tell how you learned the value of teamwork. The essay is your chance to tell something positive or enriching about yourself, so highlight an experience that will make the reader interested in you.

Outline in the essay what you have to offer the college. Explain why you want to attend the institution and how your abilities and goals match the strengths and offerings at the university. Write, rewrite, and edit. Do not try to dash off an essay in one sitting. The essay will improve with time and thought. Proofread and concentrate on spelling, punctuation, and content. Have someone else take a look at your essay. Keep copies to save after mailing the original.

Admission officers look for the person inside the essay. They seek students with a breadth of knowledge and experiences, someone with depth and perspective. Inner strength and commitment are admired, too. Not everyone is a winner all the time. The essay is a tool you can use to develop your competitive edge. Your essay should explain why you should be admitted over other applicants.

As a final word, write the essay from the heart. It should have life but not be contrived or one-dimensional. Avoid telling them what they want to hear; instead, be yourself.

SPECIAL INFORMATION FOR ATHLETES

If you weren't a planner before, but you want to play sports while in college or go to college on an athletic scholarship, you'd better become a planner now. You need to know about regulations and conditions ahead of time so that you don't miss out on possible opportunities.

First, consider whether you have what it takes to play college sports. It's a tough question to ask, but it's a necessary one. In general, playing college

SAMPLE APPLICATION ESSAY

Here is one student's college application essay. She answered the question, "Indicate a person who has had a significant influence on you, and describe that influence."

Mrs. Morrone did not become my guidance counselor until my sophomore year of high school. During my first meeting with her, I sat across from her in an uncomfortable vinyl chair and refused to meet her eyes as I told her about my long and painful shyness, how I detested oral reports, and how I feared raising my hand in class or being called on to answer a question—all because I didn't want to be the center of attention.

She did not offer me advice right away. Instead, she asked me more about myself—my family, my friends, what kinds of music, books, and movies I liked. We talked easily, like old friends, and it was not long before I began to look forward to our weekly meetings. Her office was one of the few places where I felt like I could be myself and let my personality shine through, where I knew that I was accepted and liked unconditionally.

In November of that year, the drama club announced auditions for the spring play, The Glass Menagerie. I had studied it in English class and it was one of my favorites; not surprisingly, I identified strongly with the timid Laura. I talked with Mrs. Morrone about the play and how much I liked theater. At one point I sighed, "I'd love to play Laura."

"Why don't you try out for the show?" Mrs. Morrone suggested.

The very idea of performing, onstage, in a spotlight, in front of dozens of people frightened me. She did not press the matter, but at the end of the session she encouraged me to bring a copy of the play to our next few meetings and read some of the character's lines, "just for fun." I did, and found myself gradually transforming into Laura as I recited her lines with increasing intensity.

After a couple of these amateur performances, she told me that I was genuinely good as Laura, and she would love to see me at least audition for the part. "I would never force you to do it," she said, "but I would hate to see you waste your potential." I insisted that I was too frightened, but she promised that she would come and watch my audition. She told me to pretend she was the only person in the audience.

A week later, I did read for the part of Laura. Mrs. Morrone beamed with pride in the back of the auditorium. I discovered that I truly enjoyed acting; slipping into another character cracked the shell that I had built around myself. I did not get the part, but I had found a passion that enriched my life in immeasurable ways. I owe Mrs. Morrone so much for putting me on the path to becoming a professional actress and for helping me to finally conquer my shyness. Without her quiet support and strength, none of this would have come to pass.

sports requires basic skills and natural ability, a solid knowledge of the sport, overall body strength, speed, and sound academics. Today's athletes are stronger and faster because of improved methods of training and conditioning. They are coached in skills and techniques, and they begin training in their sport at an early age. Remember, your talents will be compared with those from across the United States and around the world. (You might want to fill out the "Athletic Resume."

Second, know the background. Most college athletic programs are regulated by the National Collegiate Athletic Association (NCAA), an organization that has established rules on eligibility, recruiting, and financial aid. The NCAA has three membership divisions: Division I, Division II, and Division III. Institutions are members of one or another division according to the size and scope of their athletic programs and whether they provide athletic scholarships.

If you plan to enroll in college as a freshman and you wish to participate in Division I or Division II athletics, you must be certified by the NCAA Eligibility Center (http://web1.ncaa.org/ECWR2/NCAA_EMS/NCAA.html). The Center was established as a separate organization by the NCAA member institutions to ensure consistent interpretation of NCAA eligibility requirements for all prospective student athletes at all member institutions.

You should start the certification process when you are a junior in high school. Check with your counselor to make sure you are taking a core curriculum that meets NCAA requirements. Also, register to take the ACT or SAT as a junior. Submit your Student Release Form (available in your guidance counseling office) to the Center by the beginning of your senior year.

FROM THE GUIDANCE OFFICE

Some athletes think that their athletic ability alone will get them a scholarship and do not believe that their academics must be acceptable. The NCAA Division I or II schools cannot offer scholarships if the student has not met the academic standards required by the school for admission. Our counselors start reminding students in the freshman year and every year after that the courses they take do make a difference in how colleges view their transcripts. Students can't start preparing in their senior year of high school.

Guidance Counselor
Sterling High School
Baytown, Texas

Initial Eligibility of Freshman Athletes for Divisions I and II

Students who plan to participate in NCAA Divisions I or II college sports must obtain the Student Release Form from their high school, complete it, and send it to the NCAA Eligibility Center. This form authorizes high schools to release student transcripts, including test scores, proof of grades, and other academic information, to the Center. It also authorizes the Center to release this information to the colleges that request it. The form and corresponding fee must be received before any documents will be processed. (Fee waivers are available in some instances. Check with your counselor for fee waiver information.)

Students must also make sure that the Center receives ACT and/or SAT score reports. Students can have score reports sent directly to the Center by entering a specific code (9999) printed in the ACT and SAT registration packets.

Once a year, high schools will send an updated list of approved core courses, which lists each course offering that meets NCAA core course requirements. The Center personnel will validate the form. Thereafter, the Center will determine each student's initial eligibility. Collegiate institutions will request information from the Center on the initial eligibility of prospective student athletes. The Center will make a certification decision and report it directly to the institution.

Additional information about the Center can be found in the *Guide for the College-Bound Student-Athlete*, published by the NCAA. To get a copy of this guide, visit the NCAA Web site at www.ncaa.org.

National Association of Intercollegiate Athletics (NAIA) Regulations

The National Association of Intercollegiate Athletics (NAIA) has different eligibility requirements for student athletes. To be eligible to participate in intercollegiate athletics as an incoming freshman, you must have two of the following three requirements:

1. Minimum overall high school grade point average of 2.0 on a 4.0 scale
2. Composite score of 18 or higher on the ACT or a total score of 860 or higher on the SAT Critical Reading and Math sections
3. Final class rank in the top-half of your high school graduating class

Student athletes must also have on file at the college an official ACT or SAT score report from the appropriate national testing center. Results reported on the student's high school transcript are not acceptable. Students must request that their test scores be forwarded to the college's admission office.

ATHLETIC RESUME

Name ____________________

Address ____________________

____

High school address and phone number

____

____

____

GPA ____________________

Class rank ____________________

ACT or SAT scores (or when you plan to take them) ____________________

____

Coach's name ____________________

Height/weight ____________________

Foot speed (by specific event) ____________________

Position played ____________________

Weight classification ____________________

Athletic records held ____________________

____

All-state teams ____________________

Special awards ____________________

Off-season accomplishments ____________________

Weightlifting exercises ____________________

Vertical jumps ____________________

Push-ups ____________________

Bench jumps ____________________

Shuttle run ____________________

Leadership characteristics ____________________

Outstanding capabilities ____________________

Citizenship ____________________

Former successful athletes from your high school

____

Alumni parents/relatives ____________________

Include the following with your resume:

- **Team schedule with dates and times**
- **Footage with jersey number identified**
- **Newspaper clippings about you and/or your team**

If you have additional questions about NAIA eligibility, contact them at the following location:

NAIA
1200 Grand Boulevard
Kansas City, Missouri 64106
816-595-8000
www.naia.org

AUDITIONS AND PORTFOLIOS

If you decide to study the arts, such as theater, music, or fine arts, you may be required to audition or show your portfolio to admission personnel. The following tips will help you showcase your talents and skills when preparing for an audition or portfolio review.

Music Auditions

High school students who wish to pursue a degree in music, whether vocal or instrumental, typically must audition. If you're a singer, prepare at least two pieces in contrasting styles. One should be in a foreign language, if possible. Choose from operatic, show music, or art song repertoires, and make sure you memorize each piece. If you're an instrumentalist or pianist, be prepared to play scales and arpeggios, at least one etude or technical study, and a solo work. Instrumental audition pieces need not be memorized. In either field, you may be required to sight-read.

When performing music that is sight-read, you should take time to look over the piece and make certain of the key and time signatures before proceeding with the audition. If you're a singer, you should bring a familiar accompanist to the audition.

"My advice is to ask for help from teachers, try to acquire audition information up front, and know more than is required for the audition," says one student. "It is also a good idea to select your audition time and date early."

"Try to perform your solo in front of as many people as you can as many times as possible," says another student. "You may also want to try to get involved in a high school performance."

Programs differ, so students are encouraged to call the college and ask for audition information. In general, music departments seek students who demonstrate technical competence and performance achievement.

Music program admission varies in degree of competitiveness, so you should audition at a minimum of three colleges and a maximum of five to amplify your opportunity. The degree of competitiveness also varies by instrument, especially if a renowned musician teaches a certain instrument. Some colleges offer a second audition if you think you did not audition to your potential. Ideally, you'll be accepted into the music program of your choice, but keep in mind that it's possible to not be accepted. You must then make the decision to either pursue a music program at another college or consider another major at that college.

Dance Auditions

At many four-year colleges, an open class is held the day before auditions. A performance piece that combines improvisation, ballet, modern, and rhythm is taught and then students are expected to perform the piece at auditions. Professors look for coordination, technique, rhythm, degree of movement, and body structure. The dance faculty members also assess your ability to learn and your potential to complete the curriculum. Dance programs vary, so it's a good idea to check with the college of your choice for specific information.

Art Portfolios

A portfolio is simply a collection of your best pieces of artwork. A well-developed portfolio can help you gain acceptance into a prestigious art college and increase your chances of being awarded a scholarship in national portfolio competitions. The pieces you select to put in your portfolio should demonstrate your interest and aptitude for a serious education in the arts and should show diversity in technique and variety in subject matter. You may show work in any medium (oils, photography, watercolors, pastels, etc.) and in either black-and-white or color. Your portfolio can include classroom assignments as well as independent projects. You can also include your sketchbook.

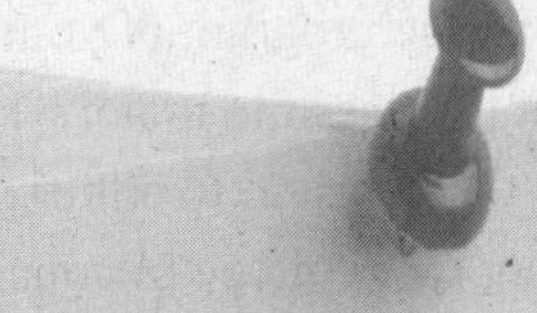

STUDENT COUNSEL

QUESTION: What is it like going to an art school?

ANSWER: Going to an art school is not your normal college experience. You totally immerse yourself in an art and commit all your time to it. It's intense and can be stressful. The teachers are great. Most are working professionals. The student body is impressive. I have people in my class who are 35 and have gone to a regular college.

Coming from high school, it's hard to get into an art school. You're at a disadvantage because you haven't worked. I suggest going to the portfolio days in high school where schools will evaluate your portfolio and you can get an idea of where you want to go. Since my sophomore year in high school, I kept in touch with the admissions person I talked to at portfolio day. She followed me along and saw my interest.

Art Center College of Design student
Pasadena, California

Specialized art colleges request that you submit an average of ten pieces of art, but remember that quality is more important than quantity. The admission office staff will review your artwork and transcripts to assess your skill and potential for success. Some schools have you present your portfolio in person; however, others allow students to mail artwork if distance is an issue. In terms of art portfolios, the only formula for success is hard work. In addition, remember that a "perfect portfolio" doesn't exist, and no specific style or direction will help you achieve one.

Tips for Pulling Your Portfolio Together:

- Try to make your portfolio as clean and organized as possible.
- It is important to protect your work, but make sure the package you select is easy to handle and does not interfere with the viewing of the artwork.
- Drawings that have been rolled up are difficult for the jurors to handle and view. You may shrink-wrap the pieces, but it is not required.
- Avoid loose sheets of paper between pieces. Always spray fixative on any pieces that could smudge.
- If you choose to mount or mat your work (not required), use only neutral gray tones, black, or white.
- Slides should be presented in a standard 8 × 11 plastic slide sleeve.
- Label each piece with your name, address, and high school.
- Check with each school to see if they accept media presentations. Ask which software format they can accommodate.

Theater Auditions

Most liberal arts colleges do not require students to audition to be accepted into the theater department unless they offer a Bachelor of Fine Arts (B.F.A.)

degree in theater. You should apply to the college of your choice prior to scheduling an audition. You should also consider spending a full day on campus so that you may talk with theater faculty members and students, attend classes, meet with your admission counselor, and tour the facilities.

Although each college and university has different requirements, you should prepare two contrasting monologues taken from plays of your choice if you're auditioning for a B.F.A. acting program. Musical theater requirements generally consist of one up-tempo musical selection and one ballad, as well as one monologue from a play or musical of your choice. The total of all your pieces should not exceed 5 minutes. Music for the accompanist, a resume of your theater experience, and a photo are also required.

Tips to Get You Through an Audition Successfully:

- Choose material suitable for your age.
- If you choose your monologue from a book of monologues, you should read the entire play and be familiar with the context of your selection.
- Select a monologue that allows you to speak directly to another person; you should play only one character.
- Memorize your selection.
- Avoid using characterization or style, as they tend to trap you rather than tapping deeper into inner resources.

THE GAP-YEAR OPTION

What is a gap year? The term "gap year" originated in the United Kingdom and usually refers to time taken between high school and college—or while in college—to travel, do service work, and explore areas of interest. It is a long-standing tradition for British students. In the United States, the gap-year option is a more recent phenomenon. The first independent gap-year counseling service, the Center for Interim Programs, appeared in 1980. At that time, taking a structured break between high school and college was highly unusual. Since then, the gap year has been steadily gaining popularity and acceptance by students, parents, guidance counselors, and colleges alike. (Check out the Top 10 Reasons For Taking a Gap Year.)

How Does the Gap Year Work?

Most students interested in a gap year apply to colleges in their senior year and then request a year's deferral once accepted. Aside from state universities that may not offer the option of a deferred year, colleges are usually willing to defer a student because they realize that an extra year of maturity and life experience often translates into an overall better student. Other students wait to apply to college until halfway through their gap year when they have a better idea of where they want to go and what they want to study.

What Is a Successful Gap-Year Experience?

The best gap-year experiences usually involve several programs in different areas of interest with at least one based outside the United States. Good structure and planning are key components for a successful year. The following is just one example:

June–August. Work a job at home to help pay for expenses.

September–December. Cultural study program teaching in schools in Costa Rica for three months with 12 other students and 2 leaders (Spanish fluency and teaching experience as primary benefits).

December. Home for holiday break (and working on college applications).

January–March. Internship in politics, photojournalism, radio stations, marketing, computers, or teaching in cities in another part of your state or the United States (experience in potential career interest as primary benefit).

April–May. Short, intensive workshops in filmmaking or learning how to run a recording studio, or outdoor work in conservation or national parks in Australia or the United States.

June–August. Some free travel and/or working a job again at home.

It is important to know that you can tailor a year to match your particular interests, whether those interests are outdoor education, conservation work, kids, social-service work, animals, healing arts/medicine, studio arts, language study, cultural immersion, professional internships, and so on.

A MESSAGE FOR PARENTS

I suspect that most parents value any process that fosters independence and happy self-confidence. If the process can guide their young adult toward a meaningful and fulfilling career, there is even greater incentive to take part. A well-constructed gap year can [help with] all of this–and the invaluable benefit of a life enriched by varied experience and the inspiration to continue to create such a life.

Holly Bull, President, Center for Interim Programs Excerpted from "The Possibilities of the Gap Year," The Chronicle of Higher Education, *July 7, 2006.*

How to Plan the Best Gap Year

A variety of resources are available to assist students and parents in planning a fulfilling gap year. These resources range from books on the topic to independent gap-year counselors to the Internet. Preparation and thorough research definitely add to the success of a gap-year experience.

Useful Books

Some of these books include sample student scenarios and programs:

The Gap-Year Advantage: Helping Your Child Benefit from Time Off Before or During College by Karl Haigler and Rae Nelson

Taking Time Off by Colin Hall and Ron Lieber

The Teenage Liberation Handbook: How to Quit School and Get a Real Life and Education by Grace Llewellyn

Success Without College: College May Not Be Right for Your Child, or Right Just Now by Linda Lee

Gap-Year Counseling Organizations

Working with a gap-year consultant can save research time and can help weed out potentially poor program options.

The Center for Interim Programs (www.interimprograms.com)

LEAPNOW (www.leapnow.org)

Taking Off (www.takingoff.net)

Where You Headed? (www.timeoutassociates.com)

TOP 10 REASONS FOR TAKING A GAP YEAR

10 Experience an easier transition from college to the work world.

9 Determine your college focus and avoid changing majors and incurring additional costs.

8 Improve your chances for college acceptance.

7 Increase your level of self-confidence and maturity from independent travel and real-world experience.

6 Gain practical skills and work experience (resume-building before college or seeking a job).

5 Follow up on interests and enhance prospective studies.

4 Choose and create your life for a year.

3 Find your passion or determine what is not of interest in you.

2 K–12 years of schooling = potential burnout.

1 It is harder to take this kind of time when you are older!

CHAPTER 8

FINANCIAL AID DOLLARS AND SENSE

Getting financial aid can be intimidating—but don't let that stop you.

Finding the money you need to attend a two- or four-year institution or vocational/career college is a challenge, but you can do it if you devise a strategy well before you actually start applying to college. Financial aid comes from many different sources. You'll find lots of help in this guide in locating those sources and obtaining advice. Financial aid is available to help meet both direct educational costs (tuition, fees, books) and personal living expenses (food, housing, transportation).

Times have changed to favor the student in the financial aid process. Because the pool of potential traditional college students is somewhat limited, colleges and universities are competing to attract the top students to their school. In fact, some colleges and universities use financial aid not only as a method to help students fund their college education but also as a marketing and recruitment tool. This puts students and families at an advantage, one that should be recognized and used for bargaining power.

It used to be that colleges and universities offered need-based and merit-based financial aid to only needy and/or academically exceptional students. Now some schools offer what might be called incentive or tuition discount aid to encourage students to choose them over another college. This aid, which is not necessarily based on need or merit, is aimed at students who meet the standards of the college but who wouldn't necessarily qualify for traditional kinds of aid.

PROJECTED COLLEGE EXPENSES

The following chart estimates the cost of one year of college education, including tuition, fees, and room and board. Estimates are based on a 6 percent annual increase.

SCHOOL YEAR	PUBLIC 4-YEAR (in-state students)	PRIVATE 4-YEAR (nonprofit)
2009–10	$15,212	$35,464
2010–11	16,140	36,993
2011–12	17,000	39,000
2015–16	21,400	49,200

Source: The College Entrance Examination Board, "Trends in College Pricing, 2010"

A BIRD'S-EYE VIEW OF FINANCIAL AID

You and your family should be assertive in negotiating financial aid packages. It used to be that there was no room for such negotiation, but in today's environment, it is wise to be a comparison shopper. Families should wait until they've received all of their financial offers and then talk to their first-choice college to see if the college can match the better offers from other colleges.

To be eligible to receive federal/state financial aid, students must maintain satisfactory academic progress toward a degree or certificate. This criterion is established by each college or university. Students also need a valid social security number, and all male students must register for selective service on their eighteenth birthday.

You apply for financial aid during your senior year. Every school requires the Free Application for Federal Student Aid (FAFSA), which cannot be filed until after January 1 of your senior year. Your application will be processed in about four weeks if you use the paper application or about one week if you apply online at www.fafsa.ed.gov. You'll then receive a Student Aid Report (SAR), which will report the information from the FAFSA and show your calculated Expected Family Contribution (EFC—the number used in determining your eligibility for federal student aid). Each school you listed on the application, as well as your state of legal residence, will also receive your FAFSA information. If you are applying to higher-cost colleges or some scholarship programs, you also may have to file the CSS/Financial Aid PROFILE® application. This should be completed in September or October of your senior year. More information on the PROFILE is available from your high school guidance office or online at www.collegeboard.org. The PROFILE application requires a fee.

FINANCIAL AID GLOSSARY

ASSETS: The amount a family has in savings and investments. This includes savings and checking accounts, a business, a farm or other real estate, and stocks, bonds, and trust funds. Cars are not considered assets, nor are possessions such as stamp collections or jewelry. The net value of the principal home is counted as an asset by some colleges in determining their own awards but is not included in the calculation for eligibility for federal funds.

CITIZENSHIP/ELIGIBILITY FOR AID: To be eligible to receive federally funded college aid, a student must be one of the following:

1. A U.S. citizen;
2. A U.S. national (includes natives of American Samoa or Swain's Island);
3. A U.S. permanent resident with an I-551 Permanent Resident Card or I-551C Alien Registration Receipt Card
4. A holder of an I-94 (Arrival-Departure Record) from U.S. Citizenship and Immigration Services (USCIS) showing one of the following designations:
   - "Refugee"
   - "Asylum Granted"
   - "Cuban/Haitian Entrant, Status Pending"
   - "Conditional Entrant" (valid if issued before April 1, 1980)
   - "Victims of human trafficking, T-visa" (T-2, T-3, or T-4, etc.) holder
   - "Parolee" (You must be paroled into the United States for at least one year and you must be able to provide evidence from the USCIS that you are in the United States for other than a temporary purpose and that you intend to become a U.S. citizen or permanent resident.)

Individuals in the United States with only a Notice of Approval to Apply for Permanent Residence (I-171 or I-464), individuals with F1 or F2 student visas or J1 or J2 exchange visitor visas, and individuals with G series visas cannot get federal aid.

COOPERATIVE EDUCATION: A program offered by many colleges in which students alternate periods of enrollment with periods of employment, usually paid, and that can lengthen the usual baccalaureate program to five years.

EXPECTED FAMILY CONTRIBUTION (EFC): A figure determined by a congressionally mandated formula that indicates how much of a family's resources should be considered "available" for college expenses. Factors such as taxable and nontaxable income and the value of family assets are taken into account to determine a family's financial strength. Allowances for maintaining a family and future financial needs are then taken into consideration before determining how much a family should be able to put toward the cost of college.

INDEPENDENT STUDENT: A student who reports only his or her own income and assets (and that of a spouse, if relevant) when applying for federal financial aid. Students are automatically considered independent at 24 years of age. Students who are under age 24 will be considered independent if they are

- married as of the date of filing the FAFSA.
- provide more than half the support of a legal dependent other than a spouse.
- a veteran of the U.S. Armed Forces.
- an orphan or ward of the court.
- classified as independent by a college's financial aid administrator because of other unusual circumstances.
- a graduate or professional student.

MERIT-BASED AID: Any form of financial aid awarded on the basis of personal achievement or individual characteristics without reference to financial need.

You must reapply for federal aid every year. Also, if you decide to transfer to another school, your aid doesn't necessarily go with you. You'll need to check with your new school to find out what steps you must take to continue receiving aid. You should plan any transfer at least three months in advance.

Once you've decided on the schools where you want to apply, talk to the financial aid officers of those schools. When it comes to understanding your financial aid options, the best place to get information is from the source. That personal contact can lead you to substantial amounts of financial aid.

If you qualify for admission, don't let the sticker price of the college or program scare you away, because you may get enough financial assistance to pay for the education you want. Don't rule out a private institution until you have received its financial aid package. Private colleges, to attract students from all income levels, offer significant amounts of financial aid. Public-supported institutions tend to offer less financial aid because the lower tuition acts as a form of assistance. In addition, students attending school in their home state often have more aid possibilities than if they

COLLEGE FUNDS AVAILABLE Use this chart to estimate resources that will be available for college expenses. Check your progress at the end of your sophomore and junior years to see if your plans for seeking financial aid need to be revised. **YOUR RESOURCES**	**Estimated amount available**	**Actual amount: 11th grade**	**Actual amount: 12th grade**
Savings and other assets			
Summer earnings			
Part-time work during school year			
Miscellaneous			
PARENTS' RESOURCES			
From their current income			
From college savings			
Miscellaneous (insurance, annuities, stocks, trusts, home equity, property assets)			
TOTAL			

Source: American College Testing Program

attend an out-of-state college. Use the "College Funds Available" chart to determine how much you and your family can contribute to your education and the "College Cost Comparison Worksheet" to figure out which schools best suit you financially.

TYPES OF FINANCIAL AID

Be sure that you understand the differences between the types of financial aid so you are fully prepared to apply for each. One or more of these financial resources may make it possible to pursue the education you want.

Grants

Grants usually go to students with financial need. But the term is also used for athletics (Division I only), academics, demographics, and special talents. Grants do not have to be repaid.

Scholarships

Scholarships, also called "merit aid," are awarded for academic excellence or other special talents or abilities. Repayment is not required.

Loans

Student loans, which have very favorable terms and conditions, are sponsored by the federal government, state governments, and through commercial lending institutions. The Financial Aid Office is the best source of information on student loans. Loans must be repaid, generally after you graduate or leave school.

Federal Work-Study

Federal work-study (FWS) is a federally sponsored program that enables colleges to hire students for employment. If eligible, students work a limited number of hours throughout the school year. Many colleges use their own funds to hire students to work in the many departments and offices on campus. If you do not receive an FWS award, you should contact the Student Employment Office or the Financial Aid Office to help locate nonfederal work-study positions that may be available.

Other Sources

The federal government is the single largest source of financial aid for students, making more than an estimated $94 billion available in loans, grants, and other aid to millions of students. In addition, a number of sources of financial aid are available to students from state governments, private lenders, foundations, and private sources, and the colleges and universities themselves.

FEDERAL GRANTS

The federal government offers a number of educational grants. Let's take a peek.

Teacher Education Assistance for College and Higher Education (TEACH) Grant

In 2007, Congress created the TEACH Grant Program, which is available to students who plan to pursue a career in teaching at a public or private school that serves low-income families. The grant provides up to $4,000 per year to students who meet this criterion. Recipients of the TEACH Grant must work full-time for at least four school years, within an eight-year period, in a high-need field. High-need fields include the following:

- Bilingual education
- English-language acquisition
- Foreign language
- Mathematics
- Reading specialist
- Science
- Special education
- Other areas listed in the Department of Education's Annual Teacher Shortage Area Nationwide Listing (This list can be accessed at www.ed.gov/about/offices/list/ope/pol/tsa.doc.)

If a recipient fails to meet these conditions, the grant will be converted to a Federal Direct Unsubsidized Stafford Loan, which must be repaid with interest accruing from the date the TEACH Grant was disbursed. For a list of schools serving low-income students go to www.tcli.ed.gov/CBSWebApp/tcli/TCLIPubSchoolSearch.jsp. Colleges need to participate in this program, so you should contact schools directly for more information about this grant.

Federal Pell Grant

The Federal Pell Grant is the largest grant program in the nation; it awarded more than 8 million grants in 2010. This grant is intended to be the base or starting point of assistance for lower-income families. Eligibility for a Federal Pell Grant depends on the EFC, or Expected Family Contribution. (See the "Financial Aid Glossary" for a description of commonly used terms.) The actual Pell Grant award amounts depend on how much funding is appropriated by Congress each year. The maximum individual grant for the 2010–11 school year was $5,550. How much you receive depends not only on your EFC, but also on your cost of attendance and whether you're a full-time or part-time student.

Federal Supplemental Educational Opportunity Grant (FSEOG)

As its name implies, the Federal Supplemental Educational Opportunity Grant (FSEOG) provides additional need-based federal grant money to supplement the Federal Pell Grant. Each participating college is given funds to award to especially needy students. The maximum award is $4,000 per year, but the amount a student receives depends on the college's policy, the availability of FSEOG funds, the total cost of education, and the amount of other aid awarded.

COLLEGE COST COMPARISON WORKSHEET

Chart your course to see which college or university best fits your financial resources. Your totals in expenses and funds available should be the same amount. If not, you have a funding gap, meaning that you have more expenses than funds available.

	College 1	College 2	College 3	College 4
EXPENSES				
Tuition and fees	$	$	$	$
Books and supplies	$	$	$	$
Room and board	$	$	$	$
Transportation	$	$	$	$
Miscellaneous	$	$	$	$
TOTAL	$	$	$	$
FUNDS AVAILABLE				
Student and parent contributions	$	$	$	$
Grants	$	$	$	$
Scholarships	$	$	$	$
Work-study	$	$	$	$
TOTAL	$	$	$	$
Funding gap	$	$	$	$

Iraq and Afghanistan Service Grant

A student who is not eligible for the Federal Pell Grant may be eligible for the Iraq and Afghanistan Service Grant if his or her parent or guardian died during service in Iraq or Afghanistan after September 11, 2001. The student must be under 24 years old and have been enrolled in college when his or her parent or guardian died. The amount of the grant is equal to the maximum amount a Federal Pell Grant would award.

FINANCIAL AID ADVICE

Students and their parents need to remember to get their financial application filed early enough so that if they run into problems, they can be corrected. Parents often make mistakes, such as not answering the question about the amount of taxes paid the previous year. A lot of parents think that if they didn't send a check to the IRS, they didn't pay taxes. Something as simple as that causes a lot of problems. If their financial information is recorded incorrectly, it can really mess them up. They should read all the information on the financial aid form, and if they have questions, they should ask someone. Speaking from my experience, if you can't get in touch with the college your child is thinking of attending, you may want to call a financial aid specialist at your local college. Any time an application doesn't go through the system smoothly, it can cause major problems.

Now that you can apply online, the applications are much simpler and are worded in layman's terms. If applicants miss filling in some information, that will trigger a warning that they omitted something.

Financial Aid Officer
Lee College
Baytown, Texas

FEDERAL SCHOLARSHIPS

The following scholarships are available through the federal government.

ROTC Scholarships

The Armed Forces (Army, Air Force, Navy, Marines) may offer up to a four-year scholarship that pays full-college tuition plus a monthly allowance; however, these scholarships are very competitive and are based on GPA, class rank, ACT or SAT scores, and physical qualifications. Apply as soon as possible before December 1 of your senior year. Contact the headquarters of each of the Armed Forces for more information: Army, 800-USAROTC; Air Force, 800-423-USAF; Navy, 800-USANAVY; Marines, 800-MARINES (all numbers are toll-free).

Scholarships from Federal Agencies

Federal agencies—such as the Central Intelligence Agency (CIA), National Aeronautics and Space Administration (NASA), Department of Agriculture, and Office of Naval Research—offer an annual stipend as well as a scholarship. In return, the student must work for the agency for a certain number of years or else repay all the financial support. See your counselor for more information.

Robert C. Byrd Honors Scholarship

To qualify for this state-administered scholarship, you must demonstrate outstanding academic achievement and excellence in high school as indicated by class rank, high school grades, test scores, and leadership activities. Award amounts of $1,500 are renewable for four years. Contact your high school counselor for application information. Deadlines may vary per state, so also contact your state's Department of Education.

FEDERAL LOANS

The following are methods through which you may borrow money from the federal government.

Federal Perkins Loan

This loan provides low-interest (5 percent) aid for students with exceptional financial need. The Federal Perkins Loans are made through the college's Financial Aid Office—that is, the college is the lender. For undergraduate study, you may borrow a maximum of $5,500 per year for up to five years of undergraduate study and may take up to ten years to repay the loan, beginning nine months after you graduate, leave school, or drop below half-time status. No interest accrues while you are in school and, under certain conditions (e.g., if you teach in a low-income area, work in law enforcement, are a full-time nurse or medical technician, or serve as a Peace Corps or VISTA volunteer), some or all of your loans may be either partially paid or cancelled in full. Payments also can be deferred under certain conditions, such as unemployment.

Direct Stafford Loan

Direct Stafford Loans come from the U.S. Department of Education and are available to help cover the costs of higher education. Two types of Direct Stafford Loans exist: subsidized and unsubsidized. Subsidized loans are for those who have financial needs and unsubsidized loans are available to everyone. In addition, interest on a subsidized loan does not begin to accrue until the student is no longer in school, while the interest on an unsubsidized loan begins to accrue upon disbursement of funds.

Your year in school, your tax status, and other factors determine the maximum amount of money you are eligible to receive. The following chart lists the maximum amounts available for subsidized and unsubsidized loans.

Year	Dependent Undergraduate Student (except students whose parents are able to obtain PLUS Loans)	Independent Undergraduate Student (and dependent students whose parents are unable to obtain PLUS Loans)	Graduate and Professional Degree Student
First Year	$5,500—No more than $3,500 of this amount may be in subsidized loans.	$9,500—No more than $3,500 of this amount may be in subsidized loans.	$20,500—No more than $8,500 of this amount may be in subsidized loans.
Second Year	$6,500—No more than $4,500 of this amount may be in subsidized loans.	$10,500—No more than $4,500 of this amount may be in subsidized loans.	
Third and Beyond (each year)	$7,500—No more than $5,500 of this amount may be in subsidized loans.	$12,500—No more than $5,500 of this amount may be in subsidized loans.	
Maximum Total Debt from Stafford Loans When You Graduate (aggregate loan limits)	$31,000—No more than $23,000 of this amount may be in subsidized loans.	$57,500—No more than $23,000 of this amount may be in subsidized loans.	$138,500—No more than $65,500 of this amount may be in subsidized loans. The graduate debt limit includes Stafford Loans received for undergraduate study.

Source: Student Aid on the Web, http://studentaid.ed.gov

Funds are disbursed through individual schools in at least two installments. A small percentage of the loan amount will be deducted for a loan fee. From July 1, 2010 to July 30, 2011, the fee was 1 percent of the loan amount. Academic and tuition fees are then paid out and any remaining funds are given to the student.

Direct PLUS Loans for Parents and Graduate/Professional Students

Direct PLUS Loans are for parents of dependent students and graduate/professional students and are designed to help families with cash-flow problems. No needs test is required to qualify, and the loans are available under the Federal Direct Loan Program. Direct PLUS Loans have a fixed interest rate of 7.9 percent. Parents or graduate/professional students can borrow up to the cost of the education less other financial aid received. The repayment period begins once the loan is fully disbursed, and the first payment due date will be within sixty days of the repayment period begin date. Up to a 4 percent fee may be charged for these loans and deducted from the loan proceeds. A credit check will be performed, and the borrower must have no adverse credit to qualify for a Direct PLUS Loan.

Nursing Student Loan Program

These loans are awarded to nursing students with demonstrated financial need. This loan may not exceed $3,300 unless a student is in his or her last two years of the program. Then, the loan may not

FINANCIAL AID RESOURCES

You can use these numbers for direct access to federal and state agencies and processing services.

FEDERAL STUDENT AID INFORMATION CENTER

Provides duplicate student aid reports and aid applications to students. Also answers questions on student aid, mails Department of Education publications, makes corrections to applications, and verifies college federal aid participation. Call 800-4-Fed-Aid (toll-free) or visit their Web site at www.studentaid.ed.gov.

VETERANS BENEFITS ADMINISTRATION (VBA)

Provides dependent education assistance for children of disabled veterans. College-bound students should call the VBA to determine whether or not they qualify for assistance, what the benefits are, and if a parent's disability qualifies them for benefits. Call 888-442-4551 (toll-free) or visit their Web site at www.gibill.va.gov.

ACT FINANCIAL AID NEED ESTIMATOR (FANE)

Mails financial tabloids to students, provides information on filling out financial aid forms, and estimates financial aid amounts. Also mails financial need estimator forms. Forms are also accessible online. Go to www.act.org\fane or call 319-337-1000.

COLLEGE SCHOLARSHIP SERVICE (PROFILE®)

Provides free applications and registration forms for federal student aid. Helps students fill out applications. Call 305-829-9793 or visit http://profileonline.collegeboard.com.

COLLEGE FOR TEXANS

Here is everything a Texan needs to know about preparing for, applying for, and paying for college or technical school. It's all in one up-to-date, easy-to-navigate site as big as the state itself. And remember $4 billion is available every year to help Texans attend college. Go to www.collegefortexans.com for more information.

exceed $5,200—not to exceed $17,000 overall. Contact your college's Financial Aid Office for deadline and other information.

OTHER FEDERAL PROGRAMS

The following programs offer alternative ways to earn money for college.

Federal Work-Study

The Federal Work-Study (FWS) program provides both on- and off-campus jobs to students who have financial need. Funding for this program is from federal grants to the institutions, plus a partial match from the employer. Students work on an hourly basis and are paid at least the minimum wage. Students are allowed to work up to the amount of the grant authorized by the college. Contact the Financial Aid Office for more information.

AmeriCorps

AmeriCorps engages 70,000 Americans in intensive service to meet community needs in education, the environment, public safety, homeland security, and other areas. Members serve with national nonprofit organizations like Habitat for Humanity, the American Red Cross, and Teach For America, as well as with hundreds of smaller community organizations, both secular and faith-based. Other members serve with AmeriCorps NCCC (National Civilian Community Corps), a team-based residential program for adults ages 18 to 24, or in low-income communities with AmeriCorps VISTA (Volunteers in Service to America). In exchange for a year of service, AmeriCorps members earn a Segal AmeriCorps Education Award of $4,725 to pay for college, graduate school, or to pay back qualified student loans. Members who serve part-time receive a partial award. Some AmeriCorps members may also receive a modest living allowance during their term of service. You should speak to your college's

Financial Aid Office for more details about this program and any other initiatives available to students. For details on AmeriCorps, visit http://www.americorps.gov/about/overview/index.asp.

FROM THE GUIDANCE OFFICE

Parents and students ask what college is going to cost and how they will pay for it. I tell them to start early and keep looking. Don't discount a school because of cost. Private schools have a higher price tag, but they do have financial aid packages that are bigger than you might expect.

Kids need some help to initiate searches for scholarships. Each year, we have a group of students who start early and get their applications in and recommendations written. Then there's the group of procrastinators who miss out on opportunities of getting into the college of their choice—and the scholarships they need. It can be a big disappointment.

Counselor
East Richland High School
Olney, Illinois

THINKING AHEAD TO PAYING BACK YOUR STUDENT LOAN

More than ever before, loans have become an important part of financial assistance. The majority of students find that they must borrow money to finance their education. If you accept a loan, you are incurring a financial obligation. You'll have to repay the loan in full, along with all of the interest and any additional fees (collection, legal, etc.). Since you'll be making payments to satisfy the loan obligation, carefully consider the burden your loan amount will impose on you after you leave college. Defaulting on a student loan can jeopardize your financial future. Borrow intelligently.

Repaying Your Loans

Upon graduating from college, dropping below half-time enrollment status, or leaving school, loan borrowers receive a six-month grace period before they must start repaying their loans. Federal Perkins Loan holders receive a nine-month grace period. Normal loan repayment terms are ten to twenty-five years and depend on the loan repayment plan you choose. The following are some repayment options available to borrowers of federally guaranteed student loans:

The Standard Repayment Plan requires fixed monthly payments (at least $50) over a period of up to ten years. The length of the repayment period depends on the loan amount. This plan usually results in the lowest total interest paid because the repayment period is shorter than under the other plans.

The Extended Repayment Plan allows loan repayment to be extended up to twenty-five years. The borrower must have more than $30,000 outstanding in Federal Direct Loan debt. Borrowers may opt to pay a fixed amount each month or make graduated payments that start out low and increase every two years. Because the monthly payments are typically less than they are with the standard repayment plan, this plan may make repayment more manageable; however, borrowers usually will pay more interest because the repayment period is longer.

The Graduated Repayment Plan allows payments to start out low and increase every two years for up to ten years. This option works well for those who expect their income to steadily increase over time. Although your monthly payment will gradually increase, no single payment may be more than three times the amount of any other payment. The repayment period is ten years.

The Income-Based Repayment Plan has a monthly payment capped at an amount that is intended to be affordable based on income and family size. The monthly payment may be adjusted once each year, and the repayment period may exceed ten years. To be eligible for this plan, payment under the standard ten-year repayment plan must exceed the monthly income-based repayment amount. Under income-based repayment, you may be eligible to have the outstanding balance of your loans cancelled after a certain amount of time. In addition, public service workers making payments under an income-based repayment plan for ten years may have their balances cancelled.

The Income Contingent Repayment Plan in the Federal Direct Loan Program bases monthly payments on adjusted gross income (AGI), family size, and the total amount borrowed. As your income rises or falls each year, monthly payments will be adjusted accordingly. The required monthly payment will not exceed 20 percent of the borrower's discretionary income as calculated under a published formula. Borrowers have up to twenty-five years to repay; after that time, any unpaid amount will be discharged, and borrowers must pay taxes on the amount discharged. In other words, if the federal government forgives the balance of a loan, the amount is considered to be part of the borrower's income for that year.

FAMILIES' GUIDE TO TAX CUTS FOR EDUCATION

Many tax benefits for adults who want to return to school and for parents who are sending or planning to send their children to college are now available. These tax cuts effectively make the first two years of college universally available, and they give many more working Americans the financial means to go back to school if they want to choose a new career or upgrade their skills. Millions of families are eligible for the American Opportunity Tax Credit (formerly Hope Scholarship Tax Credit) and Lifetime Learning Tax Credit, as well as the taxable income deduction allowed for tuition and fees.

American Opportunity Tax Credit

The American Opportunity Tax Credit helps to reduce the cost of higher education by reducing the amount of income tax you have to pay. In 2010, the maximum credit was $2,500 for qualified education expenses paid for each eligible student. Qualified expenses include tuition and fees required for enrollment. The credit is limited to families with modified adjusted gross income (MAGI) of $90,000 or less if single head of household or qualifying widow(er) or $180,000 or less if married and filing jointly. Forty percent of the American Opportunity Tax Credit may be refundable, which means that if the refundable portion of the credit is more than your tax, you'll receive the excess as a refund.

The American Opportunity Tax Credit is available only for the first four years of postsecondary education and only for four tax years per eligible student, including any prior years in which the Hope Credit was claimed. To be eligible, a student must be working toward an undergraduate degree or some other recognized education credential and must be enrolled at least half-time for at least one academic period that begins during the tax year.

CHECKLIST FOR SENIORS

Applying for financial aid can become confusing if you don't record what you've done and when. Use this chart to keep track of important information. Remember to keep copies of everything!

COLLEGE APPLICATIONS	COLLEGE 1	COLLEGE 2	COLLEGE 3	COLLEGE 4
Application deadline				
Date sent				
Official transcript sent				
Letters of recommendation sent				
SAT/ACT scores sent				
Acceptance received				
COLLEGE FINANCIAL AID AND SCHOLARSHIP APPLICATIONS				
Application deadline				
Date sent				
Acceptance received				
FREE APPLICATION FOR FEDERAL STUDENT AID (FAFSA) AND/OR PROFILE®				
Form required				
Date sent				
School's priority deadline				
PROFILE® ACKNOWLEDGMENT (if filed)				
Date received				
Correct (Y/N)				
Date changes made, if needed				
Date changes were submitted				
STUDENT AID REPORT				
Date received				
Correct (Y/N)				
Date changes made, if needed				
Date changes were submitted				
Date sent to colleges				
FINANCIAL AWARD LETTERS				
Date received				
Accepted (Y/N)				

Source: The Dayton-Montgomery County Scholarship Program

The Lifetime Learning Tax Credit

This tax credit is targeted at adults who want to go back to school, change careers, or take a course or two to upgrade their skills and to college juniors, seniors, graduate students, and professional-degree students. In 2010, the maximum credit was $2,000 per return for tuition and required fees paid for all eligible students. Just like the American Opportunity Tax Credit, the Lifetime Learning Tax Credit is available for qualified expenses. It is limited to families with modified adjusted gross income of $60,000 or less if single head of household or qualifying widow(er) and $120,000 or less if married and filing jointly. The Lifetime Learning Tax Credit is nonrefundable, which means that if the credit is more than your tax, you won't receive the excess as a refund.

The Lifetime Learning Tax Credit is available for all years of postsecondary education, including courses to further or improve job skills, for an unlimited number of years. To be eligible, students do not need to be working toward a degree or another recognized education credential, but they must have been enrolled in one or more courses during the tax year. Families will be able to claim the Lifetime Learning Tax Credit for some members of their family and the American Opportunity Tax Credit for others who qualify in the same year.

Student Loan Interest Deduction

Even if taxpayers do not itemize their deductions, borrowers can deduct up to $2,500 of interest paid on student loans each year. Unlike a credit, which reduces the amount of income tax you may have to pay, a deduction reduces the amount of income subject to tax.

APPLYING FOR FINANCIAL AID

Applying for financial aid is a process that can be made easier when you take it step by step.

1 **You must complete the Free Application for Federal Student Aid (FAFSA) to be considered for federal financial aid.** Pick up the FAFSA from your high school guidance counselor, college Financial Aid Office, or the Department of Education's Web site at www.fafsa.ed.gov. The FAFSA can be filed after January 1 of the year you will be attending school. Submit the form as soon as possible but never before the first of the year. If you need to estimate income tax information, it is easily amended later in the year.

2 **Apply for any state grants.** Most states use the FAFSA for determining state aid, but be sure to check out the specific requirements with your state's Higher Education Assistance agency. Your high school guidance office can answer most questions about state aid programs.

3 **Some schools (usually higher-cost private colleges) require an additional form known as the CSS/Financial Aid PROFILE®.** This application is needed for institutional grants and scholarships controlled by the school. Check to see if the schools you are applying to require the PROFILE form. The form should be completed in September or October of your senior year. Additional information is available from your high school guidance office or online through the College Board at www.collegeboard.com. A fee is associated with this form. Some schools may require an institutional aid application. This is usually found with the admission application. Contact each college you are considering to be sure you have filed the required forms.

4 **Complete all required financial aid application forms on time.** These deadlines are usually before March 15, but check to be sure. Financial aid funds are limited, and schools usually do not waver on their deadlines. Check and double-check all application dates to be sure you are filing on time.

5 **Make sure your family completes the required forms during your senior year of high school.**

6 **Always apply for grants and scholarships along with applying for student loans.** Grants and scholarships are essentially free money. Loans must be repaid with interest.

Use the "Checklist for Seniors" to keep track of the financial aid application process.

NATIONAL, STATEWIDE, AND LOCAL SCHOLARSHIPS

Without a doubt, the best source for up-to-date information on private scholarships is the Internet, which has a variety of excellent Web sites to explore. Watch out for scholarship scams, however; these scams ask you to either pay for a scholarship search by an independent organization or pay a "processing fee" to a particular organization to receive its scholarship. (Find out more about scholarship scams later in this chapter.)

State and Local Scholarships

The following are some excellent resources for seeking financial assistance.

- Your guidance counselor
- A high school teacher or coach
- Your high school and elementary school PTA (yes, many elementary school PTAs award scholarships to alumni)
- Your local library
- College admission office
- Your parent's alma mater
- Your employer
- Your parent's employer
- Professional and social organizations in your community
- The local Financial Aid Office of a college in your area
- Your state's Higher Education Assistance Agency
- Veterans' organizations, such as the American Legion and the VFW

SCHOLARSHIPS FOR MINORITY STUDENTS

The following is just a sample of the many scholarships available to minority students.

Bureau of Indian Education
1849 C Street NW/Mail Stop 3609 MIB
Washington, D.C. 20240
202-208-6123
www.bie.edu

The Gates Millennium Scholars
P.O. Box 10500
Fairfax, Virginia 22031-8044
877-690-4677
www.gmsp.org

Hispanic Scholarship Fund
55 Second Street, Suite 1500
San Francisco, California 94105
877-473-4636
www.hsf.net

National Merit Scholarship Corporation
1560 Sherman Avenue, Suite 200
Evanston, Illinois 60201-4897
847-866-5100
www.nationalmerit.org

National Association of Multicultural Engineering Program Advocates (NAMEPA) National Scholarship
341 N. Maitland Avenue, Suite 130
Maitland, Florida 32751
407-647-8839
www.namepa.org

Jackie Robinson Foundation
One Hudson Square
75 Varick Street, 2nd Floor
New York, New York 10013-1917
212-290-8600
www.jackierobinson.org

APPLYING FOR SCHOLARSHIPS

Use the following tips to help make your scholarship hunt successful.

- **Start early.** Your freshman year is not too early to plan for scholarships by choosing extracurricular activities that will highlight your strengths and getting involved in your church and community—all things that are important to those who make scholarship decisions.
- **Search for scholarships.** The best source of scholarships can be found on the Internet. Many great, free Web sites are available, and you should also check www.finaid.org and http://studentaid.ed.gov. Scholarship information is also available at your local library.
- **Apply, apply, apply.** One student applied for nearly sixty scholarships and was fortunate enough to win seven. "Imagine if I'd applied for five and only gotten one," she says.
- **Plan ahead.** It takes time to get transcripts and letters of recommendation. Letters from people who know you well are more effective than letters from prestigious names who don't know you.
- **Be organized.** In the homes of scholarship winners, you can often find a file box where all relevant information is stored. This method allows you to review deadlines and requirements every so often. Computerizing the information, if possible, allows you to change and update information quickly.
- **Follow directions.** Make sure that you don't disqualify yourself by filling out forms incorrectly, missing a deadline, or failing to supply important information. Type your applications, if possible, and have someone proofread them.

WHAT YOU NEED TO KNOW ABOUT ATHLETIC SCHOLARSHIPS

Whether you're male or female or interested in baseball, basketball, crew, cross-country, fencing, field hockey, football, golf, gymnastics, lacrosse, sailing, skiing, soccer, softball, swimming and diving, tennis, track and field, volleyball, or wrestling, scholarship dollars may be available for you. But here's that word again—planning. You must plan ahead if you want to get your tuition paid in return for your competitive abilities.

At the beginning of your junior year, ask your guidance counselor to help you make sure that you take the required number and mix of academic courses and to inform you of the SAT and ACT score minimums that must be met to play college sports. Also ask your counselor about academic requirements, because you must be certified by the NCAA Eligibility Center, and this process must be started by the end of your junior year.

But before you do all that, think. Do you want and need an athletic scholarship? Certainly, it is prestigious to receive an athletic scholarship, but some athletes compare having an athletic scholarship to having a job at which you are expected to perform. Meetings, training sessions, practices, games, and (don't forget!) studying take away from social and leisure time. Also, with very few full-ride scholarships available, you'll most likely receive a partial scholarship or a one-year renewable contract. If your scholarship is not renewed, you may be left scrambling for financial aid. So ask yourself if you are ready for the demands and roles associated with accepting an athletic scholarship.

If you decide that you want an athletic scholarship, you need to market yourself to beat the stiff competition. Think of yourself as a newly designed sports car, and you're selling your speed, look, and all those other goodies to a waiting public. The point is that you're going to have to sell, or market, your abilities to college recruiters. You're the product, and

TYPES OF ATHLETIC SCHOLARSHIPS

Colleges and universities offer two basic types of athletic scholarships: the institutional grant, which is an agreement between the athlete and the college, and the conference grant, which also binds the college to the athlete. The difference is that the athlete who signs an institutional grant can change his or her mind and sign with another team. The athlete who signs a conference contract cannot renegotiate another contract with a school that honors conference grants. Here are the various ways that a scholarship may be offered:

Full four-year. Also known as full ride, these scholarships pay for room, board, tuition, and books. Due to the high cost of awarding scholarships, this type of grant is being discouraged by conferences around the country in favor of the one-year renewable contract or the partial scholarship.

Full one-year renewable contract. This type of scholarship, which has basically replaced the four-year grant, is automatically renewed at the end of each school year for four years if the conditions of the contract are met. The recruiter will probably tell you in good faith that the intent is to offer a four-year scholarship, but he is legally only allowed to offer you a one-year grant. You must ask the recruiter as well as other players what the record has been of renewing scholarships for athletes who comply athletically, academically, and socially. Remember—no athlete can receive more than a full scholarship.

One-year trial grant (full or partial). A verbal agreement between you and the institution that at the end of the year, your renewal will be dependent upon your academic and athletic performance.

Partial scholarship. The partial grant is any part of the total cost of college. You may be offered room and board but not tuition and books, or you may be offered just tuition. The possibility exists for you to negotiate to a full scholarship after you complete your freshman year.

Waiver of out-of-state fees. This award is for out-of-state students to attend the college or university at the same fee as an in-state student.

the college recruiter is the buyer. What makes you stand out from the rest?

College recruiters look for a combination of the following attributes when awarding athletic scholarships: academic excellence, a desire to win, self-motivation, ability to perform as a team player, willingness to help others, cooperation with coaching staff, attitude in practice, attitude in games/matches, toughness, strength, optimal height and weight, and excellence.

To successfully sell your skills to a college or university, you'll need to take three main steps:

1. Locate the colleges and universities that offer scholarships in your sport.
2. Contact the institution in a formal manner.
3. Follow up on each lead.

Finding and Getting Athletic Scholarships

The following four steps can help you snag that scholarship:

1. **Contact the school formally.** Once you make a list of schools in which you are interested, get the names of the head coaches and write letters to the top twenty schools on your list. Then compile a factual resume of your athletic and academic accomplishments. Put together 10 to 15 minutes of video highlights of your athletic performance (with your jersey number noted), get letters of recommendation from your high school coach and your off-season coach, and include a season schedule.
2. **Ace the interview.** When you meet a recruiter or coach, be certain to exhibit self-confidence with a firm handshake and by maintaining eye contact. In addition, make sure that you are well groomed. According to recruiters, the most effective attitude is quiet confidence, respect, sincerity, and enthusiasm.
3. **Ask good questions.** Don't be afraid to probe the recruiter by getting answers to the following questions: Do I qualify athletically and academically? If I am recruited, what would the parameters of the scholarship be? For what position am I being considered?

It's okay to ask the recruiter to declare what level of interest he or she has in you.

4 **Follow up.** Persistence pays off when it comes to seeking an athletic scholarship, and timing can be everything. The following are four good times when a follow-up letter from your coach or a personal letter from you is extremely effective: prior to your senior season, during or just after the senior season, just prior to or after announced conference-affiliated signing dates or national association signing dates, and mid to late summer, in case other scholarship offers have been withdrawn or declined.

To sum up, you know yourself better than anyone else, so you must look at your skills—both athletic and academic—objectively. Evaluate the skills you need to improve, and keep the desire to improve alive in your heart. Develop your leadership skills, and keep striving for excellence with your individual achievements. Keep your mind open as to what school you want to attend, and keep plugging away, even when you are tired, sore, and unsure. After all, athletes are trained to be winners!

WINNING THE SCHOLARSHIP WITH A WINNING ESSAY

Who knew it was going to be this hard?

You've already dealt with SO much: the SAT and ACT, doing community service, excelling in those tough AP classes, and convincing your parents that you will be fine attending a college 1,500 miles from home. And now, in front of you, is an application for a scholarship, with a required essay—approximately 500 words that could greatly ease the financial burden of your college education.

Is It Really That Easy?

Much as you may feel like saying, "C'mon, I'm worth it—just give me the scholarship money," we all know it just doesn't work like that. Why? Because lots of students are worth it, and lots of students are special, just like you. And where does that leave a scholarship selection committee in deciding to whom their money should be awarded? Yes, now you are catching on—those scholarship essays will be scrutinized greatly by the scholarship committee.

So, first and foremost, look at your scholarship essay as the way you can make it SO EASY for the scholarship-awarding committees to do their job! It's almost like a partnership—you show them (in 500 words, more or less) why *you* are the most worthy recipient, and they say, "Yes, you're right. Here is a scholarship for you." And everyone wins! Easy, right?

Sorry, It Really Isn't That Easy!

What? You are still sitting there in front of a blank computer screen with nary a thought or sentence? Understood. It's really not that easy. That, too, is part of the point.

No doubt that your GPA, SAT scores, volunteer efforts, leadership roles, and community service are immensely important, but, again, you must remember that, during the process of selecting an award recipient, pretty much all the applicants are going to be stellar on some level. So, as the scholarship-awarding committee members look for a reason to select *you* over everyone else, they use your essay to see what really sets you apart from the crowd.

Your scholarship essay serves many purposes. It shows the scholarship-awarding committee that you are able to

- Effectively communicate through the written word

- Substantiate your merit and unique qualities
- Follow directions and adhere to guidelines

A winning scholarship essay can mean up to tens of thousands of dollars for your college education, so let's get started on putting that money in your hands.

Effective Written Communication

Be Passionate

Let's face it—you have already written lots of essays. And, it's likely that most were probably about topics that were as interesting to you as watching paint dry, right? But you plowed through them and even managed to get some good grades along the way. You may think about just "plowing through" your scholarship essay the same way—mustering up the same amount of excitement you feel when you have to watch old home movies of your Aunt Monica on her summer camping trips. And that would be a huge mistake.

An important common feature of all winning essays is that they are written on subjects about which the author is truly passionate. Think about it—it actually takes a good bit of effort to fake passion for a subject. But when you are genuinely enthusiastic about something, the words and thoughts flow much more easily and your passion and energy naturally shine through in your writing. Therefore, when you are choosing your scholarship essay topic, be sure it is something you truly care about and can show your affinity for—keeping both you and your reader interested and intrigued.

Be Positive

You've probably heard the expression: "If you don't have anything nice to say, don't say anything at all." Try to steer clear of essays that are too critical, pessimistic, or antagonistic. This doesn't mean that your essay shouldn't acknowledge a serious problem nor does it mean that everything has to have a happy ending. But it does mean that you should avoid focusing on the negative. If you are writing about a problem, then offer solutions. If your story doesn't have a happy ending, then write about what you learned from the experience and how you would do things differently if faced with a similar situation in the future. Your optimism is what makes the scholarship-awarding committee excited about giving you money to pursue your dreams. Use positive language and be proud to share information about yourself and your accomplishments. Everyone likes an uplifting story, and even scholarship judges want to feel your enthusiasm and zest for life.

Be Clear and Concise

Don't fall into the common essay-writing trap of using general statements instead of specific ones. All scholarship judges read at least one essay that starts with "Education is the key to success." And that means nothing to them. What does mean something is writing about how your tenth grade English teacher opened your eyes to the understated beauty and simplicity of haiku, how you learned that less can be more, and how that then translated into your donating some of your old video games to a homeless shelter where you now volunteer once a month. That's powerful stuff! It's a very real story, one that clearly correlates education to a successful outcome. Focusing on a specific and concise example from your life helps readers relate to you and your experiences. It also guarantees you bonus points for originality!

Edit and Proofread and Then Edit and Proofread Again

There is an old saying: "Behind every good writer is an even better editor." Find people (friends, siblings, coaches, teachers, guidance counselors) to read your essay, provide feedback on how to make it better, and edit it for silly, sloppy mistakes. Some people will read your essay and find issues with your grammar. Others will read your essay and point out how one paragraph doesn't make sense in relation to another paragraph. Some people will tell you how to give more examples to better make your point. All of those people are giving you great information, and you need to take it all in and use it to your advantage! However, don't be overwhelmed by it, and don't let it become all about what everyone else thinks. It's *your* essay and *your* thoughts—the goal of editing and proofreading is to clean up the rough edges and make the entire essay shine!

When you do get to that magical point where you think you're done, just put the essay aside for a few days. Come back to it with an open mind, and read, edit, and proofread it one last time. Check it one last time for spelling and grammar fumbles. Check the essay one last time for clarity and readability (reading it out loud helps!). Check it one last time to ensure it effectively communicates why you are absolutely the winning scholarship candidate.

Your Unique Qualities

It's one thing to help out at the local library a few hours a week; it's a completely different thing if you took it upon yourself to suggest, recruit, organize, and lead a fundraising campaign to buy ten new laptops for kids to use at the library.

And don't simply rattle off all your different group memberships. Write about things you did that demonstrate leadership and initiative within those groups. For example, did you recruit new members, offer to head up a committee, find a way for the local news station to cover your event, or reach out to another organization to collaborate on an activity? Think about *your* unique qualities and how you use them to bring about change.

A Slice of Your Life

While one goal of your essay is surely to explain why you should win the scholarship money, an equally important goal is to reveal something about you, something that makes it easy to see why you should win. Notice we said to reveal "something" about you and not "everything" about you. Most likely, the rest of the scholarship application gathers quite a bit of information about you. The essay is where you need to hone in on just one aspect of your unique talents, one aspect of an experience, and one aspect of reaching a goal. It's not about listing all your accomplishments in your essay (again, you probably did that on the application). It's about sharing a slice of your life—telling your story and offering details about what makes YOU memorable.

Your Accomplishments, Loud and Proud

Your extracurricular activities illustrate your personal priorities and let the scholarship selection committee know what's important to you. Being able to elaborate on your accomplishments and awards within those activities certainly bolsters your chances of winning the scholarship. Again, though, be careful to not just repeat what is already on the application itself. Use your essay to focus on a specific accomplishment (or activity, talent, or award) of which you are most proud.

Did your community suffer through severe flooding last spring? Did you organize a clothing drive for neighbors who were in need? How did that make you feel? What feedback did you get? How did it inspire your desire to become a climatologist?

Were school budget cuts going to mean the disbanding of some after-school clubs? Did you work with teachers and parents to write a proposal to present to the school board, addressing how new funds could be raised in order to save the clubs? How did that make you feel? What feedback did you get? How did it inspire you to start a writing lab for middle school students?

You have done great things—think about that one special accomplishment and paint the picture of how it has made you wiser, stronger, or more compassionate to the world around you. Share the details!

But Don't Go Overboard

A five-hanky story may translate into an Oscar®-worthy movie, but rarely does it translate into winning a scholarship. If your main reason for applying for the scholarship is that you feel you deserve the money because of how much suffering you have been through, you need a better reason. Scholarship selection committees are not really interested in awarding money to people *with* problems; they want to award money to people who *solve* problems. While it's just fine to write about why you need the scholarship money to continue your education, it's not fine for your essay to simply be a laundry list of family tragedies and hardships.

So, instead of presenting a sob story, present how you have succeeded and what you have accomplished despite the hardships and challenges you faced. Keep in mind that everyone has faced difficulties. What's different and individual to you is how YOU faced your difficulties and overcame them. That is what makes your essay significant and memorable.

Following Directions

Does Your Essay Really Answer the Question?

Have you ever been asked one question but felt like there was another question that was really being asked? Maybe your dad said something like, "Tell me about your new friend Logan." But what he really meant to ask you was, "Tell me about your new friend Logan. Do his lip rings and tattoos mean he's involved in things I don't want you involved in?"

The goal of every scholarship judge is to determine the best applicant out of a pool of applicants who are all rather similar. Pay attention and you'll find that the essay question is an alternate way for you to answer the real question the scholarship-awarding committee wants to ask. For instance, an organization giving an award to students who plan to study business might ask, "Why do you want to study business?" But their real underlying question is, "Why are you the best future business person to whom we should give our money?" If there is a scholarship for students who want to become doctors, you can bet that 99 percent of the students applying want to become doctors. If you apply for that scholarship with an essay that delves into your lifelong desire to be a potter, well, that doesn't make you unique—it simply makes you unqualified for that opportunity. Be sure to connect your personal skills, characteristics, and experiences with the objectives of the scholarship and its awarding organization.

Does Your Essay Theme Tie In?

Let's say that you are applying for an award based on community service, and on the application, you list all the community service groups you belong to and all the awards you have won. But in your essay, you write about how homeless people should find a job instead of sitting on street corners begging for money. Yes, everyone is entitled to his or her opinion, but you'd have to agree that there is some sort of disconnect between your application and your essay. No doubt you would probably make the scholarship-awarding committee wonder the same thing.

So how do you ensure your essay doesn't create a conflicting message? You need to examine the theme of your essay and how it relates both to your application and the reason the scholarship exists in the first place. If the scholarship-funding organization seeks to give money to someone who wants a career in public relations, and your essay focuses on how you are not really a "people person," well, you can see how that sends a mixed message to the reader.

Think about it this way: The theme of your essay should naturally flow around the overarching purpose or goal of the organization awarding the scholarship money. Once you have clarified this nugget, you can easily see if and how your words tie in to the organization's vision of who should win their scholarship.

Three More Pieces of Advice

1. Follow the essay length guidelines closely. You certainly don't want your essay disqualified simply because it was too long or too short.
2. The deadline is the deadline. A day late and you could certainly be more than a dollar short in terms of the award money. Your application and essay must arrive by the due date—if not, it's late, and most likely, it will not be considered. Begin the essay-writing process well in advance of the scholarship deadline. Writing and editing and rewriting takes time, so you should probably allow yourself at least two weeks to write your scholarship essay.
3. Finally, tell the truth. No need to say anything further on that, right? Right!

MYTHS ABOUT SCHOLARSHIPS AND FINANCIAL AID

The scholarship and financial aid game is highly misunderstood by many high school students. And high school guidance counselors often lack the time to fully investigate scholarship opportunities and inform students about them. The myths and misconceptions persist while the truth about scholarships remains hidden, the glittering prizes and benefits unknown to many teenagers.

Myth 1: Scholarships are rare, elusive awards won only by valedictorians, geniuses, and brainiacs.

The truth is that with proper advice and strategies, private scholarships are very much within the grasp of high school students who possess talent and ability in almost any given field. Thousands of high school students like you compete and win.

Myth 2: My chances of being admitted to a college are reduced if I apply for financial aid.

The truth is that most colleges have a policy of "need-blind" admission, which means that a student's financial need is not taken into account in the admission decision. A few colleges, however, do consider ability to pay before deciding whether to admit a student. A few more look at ability to pay of those whom they placed on a waiting list to get in or those students who applied late. Some colleges will mention this in their literature, but others may not. In making decisions about the college application and financing process, however, families should apply for financial aid if the student needs the aid to attend college.

Myth 3: All merit scholarships are based on a student's academic record.

The truth is that many of the best opportunities are in areas such as writing, public speaking, leadership, science, community service, music and the arts, foreign languages, and vocational-technical skills. So that means you don't always have to have a 3.99 GPA to win if you excel in a certain area.

Myth 4: You have to be a member of a minority group to get a scholarship.

The truth is that some scholarships are targeted toward women and minority students. Other scholarships require membership in a specific national club or student organization (such as 4-H or the National Honor Society), which makes these scholarships just as exclusive. Most scholarship opportunities, however, are not exclusive to any one segment of the population.

Myth 5: If you have need for and receive financial aid, it's useless to win a scholarship from some outside organization because the college will just take away the aid that the organization offered.

It's true that if you receive need-based aid, you can't receive more than the total cost of attendance (including room and board, books, and other expenses, not just tuition). If the financial aid that you've been awarded meets the total cost and you win an outside scholarship, colleges have to reduce something. But usually they reduce the loan or work-study portion of your financial aid award before touching the grant portion that they've awarded you. This means that you won't have to borrow or earn so much at a job. Also, most colleges don't meet your full financial need when you qualify for need-based financial aid. So, if you do win an outside scholarship, chances are that your other aid will not be taken away or reduced.

SCHOLARSHIP SCAMS

Although most scholarship sponsors and most scholarship search services are legitimate, schemes that pose as either legitimate scholarship search services or scholarship sponsors have cheated thousands of families.

These fraudulent businesses advertise in campus newspapers, distribute flyers, mail letters and postcards, provide toll-free phone numbers, and have sites on the Web. The most obvious frauds operate as scholarship search services or scholarship clearinghouses. Another, quieter segment sets up as a scholarship sponsor, pockets the money from the fees and charges that are paid by thousands of hopeful scholarship seekers, and returns little, if anything, in proportion to the amount it collects. A few of these frauds inflict great harm by gaining access to individuals' credit or checking accounts with the intent to extort funds.

The Federal Trade Commission (FTC), in Washington, D.C., has a campaign called Project $cholar$cam to confront this type of fraudulent activity (http://www.ftc.gov/bcp/edu/microsites/scholarship/index.shtml). Legitimate services do exist; however, a scholarship search service cannot truthfully guarantee that a student will receive a scholarship, and students almost always will fare as well or better by doing their own homework using a reliable scholarship information source than by wasting money and time with a search service that promises a scholarship.

The FTC warns you to be alert for these six warning signs of a scam:

1. **"This scholarship is guaranteed or your money back."** No service can guarantee that it will get you a grant or scholarship. Refund guarantees often have impossible conditions attached. Review a service's refund policies in writing before you pay a fee.

2 **"The scholarship service will do all the work."** Unfortunately, nobody else can fill out the personal information forms, write the essays, and supply the references that many scholarships may require.

3 **"The scholarship will cost some money."** Be wary of any charges related to scholarship information services or individual scholarship applications, especially in significant amounts. Before you send money to apply for a scholarship, investigate the sponsor.

4 **"You can't get this information anywhere else."** Scholarship directories from Peterson's and other publishers are available in bookstores, your local public library, and high school guidance offices; they're also available as eBooks.

5 **"You are a finalist"** or **"You have been selected by a national foundation to receive a scholarship."** Most legitimate scholarship programs almost never seek out particular applicants. Most scholarship sponsors will contact you only in response to an inquiry because they generally lack the budget to do anything more than this. If you think a real possibility exists that you may have been selected to receive a scholarship, investigate before you send any money, to be sure that the sponsor or program is legitimate.

6 **"The scholarship service needs your credit card or checking account number in advance."** NEVER provide your credit card or bank account number on the telephone to the representative of an organization that you do not know. Get information in writing first.

In addition to the FTC's six signs, here are some other points to keep in mind when considering a scholarship program:

- Fraudulent scholarship operations often use official-sounding names, containing words such as *federal*, *national*, *administration*, *division*, *federation*, and *foundation*. Their names are often a slight variant of the name of a legitimate government or private organization. Do not be fooled by a name that seems reputable or official, an official-looking seal, or a Washington, D.C., address.
- If you win a scholarship, you'll receive written official notification by mail, not by phone. If the sponsor calls to inform you, it will follow up with a letter in the mail. If a request for money is made by phone, the operation is probably fraudulent.
- Be wary if an organization's address is a box number or a residential address. If a bona fide scholarship program uses a post office box number, it usually will include a street address and telephone number on its stationery.
- Beware of telephone numbers with a 900 area code. These may charge you a fee of several dollars a minute for a call that could be a long recording that provides only a list of addresses or names.
- Watch for scholarships that ask you to "act now." A dishonest operation may put pressure on an applicant by saying that awards are on a "first-come, first-served" basis. Some scholarship programs will give preference to earlier qualified applications. However, if you are told, especially on the telephone, that you must respond quickly but that you won't hear about the results for several months, there may be a problem.

- Be wary of endorsements. Fraudulent operations will claim endorsements by groups with names similar to well-known private or government organizations. The Better Business Bureau (BBB) and government agencies do not endorse businesses.
- Don't pay money for a scholarship to an organization that you've never heard of before or whose legitimacy you can't verify. If you have already paid money to such an organization and find reason to doubt its authenticity, call your bank to stop payment on your check, if possible, or call your credit card company and report that you think you were the victim of consumer fraud.

To find out how to recognize, report, and stop a scholarship scam, write to the Federal Trade Commission's Consumer Response Center at 600 Pennsylvania Avenue, NW, Washington, D.C. 20580. On the Web, go to www.ftc.gov, or call 877-FTC-HELP (toll-free).

You can also check with the Better Business Bureau (BBB), which is an organization that maintains files of businesses about which it has received complaints. You should call both your local BBB office and the BBB office in the area of the organization in question; each local BBB has different records. Call 703-276-0100 to get the phone number of your local BBB, or look online at www.bbb.org for a directory of local BBBs and downloadable BBB complaint forms.

FINANCIAL AID ON THE WEB

A number of good financial aid resources exist on the Web. It is quick and simple to access general financial aid information, links to relevant Web sites, loan information, employment and career information, advice, scholarship search services, interactive worksheets, forms, and free Expected Family Contribution (EFC) calculators. Also visit the Web sites of individual colleges to find more school-specific financial aid information.

FAFSA Online

The Free Application for Federal Student Aid (FAFSA) can be filed on the Web at www.fafsa.ed.gov. You can download a worksheet from this Web site, since the questions are formatted differently from the paper application. FAFSA on the Web is a much quicker process and helps eliminate errors. To file electronically, the student and one parent will need an electronic signature Personal Identification Number (PIN). To get a PIN, go to www.pin.ed.gov. The PIN will be sent to you within 24 hours.

Nelnet, Inc.

Nelnet is one of the leading education planning and finance companies in the United States and is focused on providing quality college planning and financing products and services to students and schools nationwide. Nelnet offers a broad range of financial services and technology-based products, including student loan origination, loan consolidation guarantee servicing, and software solutions. Visit the Web site at www.nelnet.com.

The Education Resources Institute (TERI)

TERI is a private, not-for-profit organization that was founded to help middle-income Americans afford a college education. This site contains a database describing programs that aim to increase college attendance from underrepresented groups. (The target population includes students from low-income families and those who are the first in their family to pursue postsecondary education.) Visit TERI's Web site at www.teri.org.

FinAid

FinAid was established in 1994 as a public service. The Web site offers numerous links to valuable financial aid information, including scholarship search engines. FinAid has earned a stellar reputation in the educational community for its informative and objective data to help students finance their education. You can find the site at www.finaid.org.

Mapping Your Future®

Mapping Your Future® is a public-service, nonprofit organization offering college, career, financial aid, and financial literacy information and services. Its goal is to help individuals achieve lifelong success by empowering students, families, and schools with free, Web-based information and services. You can find this site at www.mappingyourfuture.org.

Student Financial Assistance Information, U.S. Department of Education

This site takes you to some of the major publications on student aid, including the latest edition of *Funding Education Beyond High School: The Guide to Federal Student Aid*. Visit http://studentaid.ed.gov/students/publications/student_guide/index.html

CHAPTER 9

WHAT TO EXPECT IN COLLEGE

If you were going on a long trip, wouldn't you want to know what to expect once you reached your destination? The same should hold true for college.

No one can fill in all the details of what you'll find once you begin college. However, here's some information about a few of the bigger questions you might have, such as how to choose your classes or major and how you can make the most of your life outside the classroom.

CHOOSING YOUR CLASSES

College is designed to give you freedom, but, at the same time, it teaches you responsibility. You'll probably have more free time than in high school, but you'll also have more class material to master. Your parents may entrust you with more money, but it is up to you to make sure there's enough money in your bank account when school fees are due. The same principle applies to your class schedule: You'll have more decision-making power than ever before, but you also need to know and meet the requirements for graduation.

To guide you through the maze of requirements, you'll have an adviser. This person, typically a faculty member, will help you select classes that meet your interests and graduation requirements. During your first year or two at college, you and your adviser will choose classes that meet general education requirements and select electives, or nonrequired classes, that pique your interests. Early on, it is a good idea to take a lot of general education classes. They are meant to expose you to new ideas and help you explore possible majors. Once you have selected a major, you'll have an adviser for that particular area of study. This person will help you understand and meet the requirements for that major.

In addition to talking to your adviser, talk to other students who have already taken a class you're interested in and who really enjoyed how a professor taught the class. Then try to get into that professor's class when registering. Remember, a dynamic professor can make a dry subject engaging. A boring professor can make an engaging subject dry.

As you move through college, you'll notice that focusing on the professor is more important than focusing on the course title. Class titles can be cleverly crafted. They can sound captivating. However, the advice above still holds true: "Pop Culture and Icons" could turn out to be awful, and "Beowulf and Old English" could be a blast.

When you plan your schedule, watch how many heavy reading classes you take in one semester. You don't want to live in the library or the dorm study lounge. In general, the humanities, such as history, English, philosophy, and theology, involve a lot of reading. Math and science classes involve less reading; they focus more on solving problems.

Finally, don't be afraid to schedule a fun class. Even the most intense program of study will let you take a few electives. So take a deep breath, dig in, and explore!

CHOOSING YOUR MAJOR

You can choose from hundreds of majors—from accounting to zoology—but which is right for you? Should you choose something traditional or select a major from an emerging area? Perhaps you already know what career you want, so you can work backward to decide which major will best help you achieve your goals.

If you know what you want to do early in life, you'll have more time to plan your high school curriculum, extracurricular activities, jobs, and community service to coincide with your college major. Your college selection process may also focus upon the schools that provide strong academic programs in a certain major.

Where Do I Begin?

Choosing a major usually starts with an assessment of your career interests. If you took the self-assessment inventory in Chapter 2, you should have a clearer understanding of your interests, talents, values, and goals. With that in mind, you can review possible majors and try several on for size. Picture yourself taking classes, writing papers, making presentations, conducting research, or working in a related field. Talk to people you know who work in your fields of interest, and see if you like what you hear. Also, try reading the classified ads in your local newspaper. What jobs sound interesting to you? Which ones pay the salary that you'd like to make? What level of education is required in the ads you find interesting? Select a few jobs that you think you'd like and then consult the following list of majors to see which major(s) coincide. If your area of interest does not appear here, talk to your counselor or teacher about where to find information on that particular subject.

Majors and Related Careers

Agriculture

Many agriculture majors apply their knowledge directly on farms and ranches. Others work in industry (food, farm equipment, and agricultural supply companies), federal agencies (primarily in the Departments of Agriculture and the Interior), and state and local farm and agricultural agencies. Jobs might be in research and lab work, marketing and sales, advertising and public relations, or journalism and radio/TV (for farm communications media). Agriculture majors also pursue further training in biological sciences, animal health, veterinary medicine, agribusiness management, vocational agriculture education, nutrition and dietetics, and rural sociology.

Architecture

Architecture and related design fields focus on the built environment as distinct from the natural environment of the agriculturist or the conservationist. Career possibilities include drafting, design, and project administration in architectural engineering, landscape design, interior design, industrial design, planning, real estate, and construction firms; government agencies involved in construction, housing, highways, and parks and recreation; and government and nonprofit organizations interested in historic or architectural preservation.

Area/Ethnic Studies

The research, writing, analysis, critical-thinking, and cultural awareness skills acquired by area/ethnic studies majors, combined with the expertise gained in a particular area, make this group of majors valuable in a number of professions. Majors find positions in administration, education, public relations, and communications in such organizations as cultural, government, international, and (ethnic) community agencies; international trade (import-export); social service agencies; and the communications industry (journalism, radio, and TV). These studies also provide a good background for further training in law, business management, public administration, education, social work, museum and library work, and international relations.

Art

Art majors most often use their training to become practicing artists, though the settings in which they work vary. Aside from the most obvious art-related career—that of the self-employed artist or craftsperson—many fields require the skills of a visual artist. These include advertising; public relations; publishing; journalism; museum work; television, movies, and theater; community and social service agencies concerned with education, recreation, and entertainment; and teaching. A background in art is also useful if a student wishes to pursue art therapy, arts or museum administration, or library work.

Biological Sciences

The biological sciences include the study of living organisms from the level of molecules to that of populations. Majors find jobs in industry; government agencies; technical writing, editing, or illustrating; science reporting; secondary school teaching (which usually requires education courses); and research and laboratory analysis and testing. Biological sciences are also a sound foundation for further study in medicine, psychology, health and hospital administration, and biologically oriented engineering.

Business

Business majors comprise all the basic business disciplines. At the undergraduate level, students can major in a general business administration program or specialize in a particular area, such as marketing or accounting. These studies lead not only to positions in business and industry but also to management positions in other sectors. Management-related studies include the general management areas (accounting, finance, marketing, and management) as well as special studies related to a particular type of organization or industry. Management-related majors may be offered in a business school or in a department dealing with the area in which the management skills are to be applied. Careers can be found throughout the business world.

Communication

Jobs in communication range from reporting (news and special features), copywriting, technical writing, copyediting, and programming to advertising, public relations, media sales, and market research. Such positions can be found at newspapers, radio and TV stations, publishing houses (book and magazine), advertising agencies, corporate communications departments, government agencies, universities, and firms that specialize in educational and training materials.

Computer, Information, and Library Sciences

Computer and information science and systems majors stress the theoretical aspects of the computer and emphasize mathematical and scientific disciplines. Data processing, programming, and computer technology programs tend to be more practical; they are more oriented toward business than to scientific applications and to working directly with the computer or with peripheral equipment. Career possibilities for computer and information science majors include data processing, programming, and systems development or maintenance in almost any setting: business and industry, banking and finance, government, colleges and universities, libraries, software firms, service bureaus, computer manufacturers, publishing, and communications.

Library science gives preprofessional background in library work and provides valuable knowledge of research sources, indexing, abstracting, computer technology, and media technology, which is useful for further study in any professional field. In most cases, a master's degree in library science is necessary to obtain a job as a librarian. Library science majors find positions in public, school, college, corporate, and government libraries and research centers; book publishing (especially reference books); database and information retrieval services; and communications (especially audiovisual media).

STUDENT COUNSEL

QUESTION: Why did you choose a seven-year premed program instead of a traditional four-year college program?

ANSWER: I'm one of those people who knew what I wanted to do since I was very little, so that made choosing easier. If I was not 100 percent sure that I wanted to go into medicine, I would not be in this seven-year program. For students who are interested but not really sure that they want to go into medicine, they should pick a school they will enjoy, get a good education, and then worry about medical school. That way, if they decide in their junior year that medicine is not for them, they have options.

Premed student
Boston University
Boston, Massachusetts

Education

Positions as teachers in public elementary and secondary schools, private day and boarding schools, religious and parochial schools, vocational schools, and proprietary schools are the jobs most often filled by education majors. However, teaching positions also exist in noneducational institutions, such as museums, historical societies, prisons, hospitals, and nursing homes; jobs are also available as educators and trainers in government and industry. Administrative (nonteaching) positions in employee relations and personnel, public relations, marketing and sales, educational publishing, TV and film media, test-development firms, and government and community social service agencies also tap the skills and interests of education majors.

STUDENT COUNSEL

QUESTION: What advice do you have for any high school students who are considering going into engineering?

ANSWER: In high school, take AP courses in a lot of different areas. That gives you an idea of what those subjects will be like in college. I knew I was good at science and math but didn't know which direction would really interest me. I took an AP English course and didn't do so well. Then I took a chemistry course and knew I could see myself digging deeper. An AP course will give you an idea if that subject is something you want to pursue as a major.

Most engineering majors don't have to decide on what engineering discipline they want until their sophomore year. As a freshman, you can take courses and not really know what type of engineering your want. I took an introduction to engineering course, and it convinced me that this is what I want to do. Your freshman year will give you a flavor for different engineering majors, so you don't end up in your junior year and realize you don't like that major.

Chemical Engineering student
Cornell University
Ithaca, New York

Engineering and Science Technology

Engineering and science technology majors prepare students for practical design and production work rather than for jobs that require more theoretical, scientific, and mathematical knowledge. Engineers work in a variety of fields, including aeronautics, bioengineering, geology, nuclear engineering, and quality control and safety. Industry, research labs, and government agencies where technology plays a key role, such as in manufacturing, electronics, construction communications, transportation, and utilities, hire engineering as well as engineering technology and science technology graduates regularly. Work may be in technical activities (research, development, design, production, testing, scientific programming, or systems analysis) or in nontechnical areas where a technical degree is needed, such as marketing, sales, or administration.

Family and Consumer Sciences and Social Services

Family and consumer sciences encompasses many different fields—basic studies in foods and textiles as well as consumer economics and leisure studies—that overlap with aspects of agriculture, social science, and education. Jobs can be found in government and community agencies (especially those in education, health, housing, or human services), nursing homes, child-care centers, journalism, radio/TV, educational media, and publishing. Types of work also include marketing, sales, and customer service in consumer-related industries, such as food processing and packaging, appliance manufacturing, utilities, textiles, and secondary school home economics teaching (which usually requires education courses).

Majors in social services find administrative positions in government and community health, welfare, and social service agencies, such as hospitals, clinics, YMCAs and YWCAs, recreation commissions, welfare agencies, and employment services. See the "Law and Legal Studies" section for information on more law-related social services.

Foreign Language and Literature

Knowledge of foreign languages and cultures is increasingly recognized as important in today's international world. Language majors possess skills that are used in organizations with international dealings as well as in career fields and geographic areas where languages other than English are prominent. Career possibilities include positions with business firms with international subsidiaries; import-export firms; international banking; travel agencies; airlines; tourist services; government and international agencies dealing with international affairs, foreign trade, diplomacy, customs, or immigration; secondary school foreign language teaching and bilingual education (which usually require education courses); freelance translating and interpreting (high level of skill necessary); foreign language publishing; and computer programming (especially for linguistics majors).

Health Professions

Health professions majors, while having a scientific core, are more focused on applying the results of scientific investigation than on the scientific disciplines themselves. Allied health majors prepare graduates to assist health professionals in providing diagnostics, therapeutics, and rehabilitation. Medical science majors, such as optometry, pharmacy, and the premedical profession sequences, are, for the most part, preprofessional studies that comprise the scientific disciplines necessary for admission to graduate or professional school in the health or medical fields. Health service and technology majors prepare students for positions in the health fields that primarily involve services to patients or working with complex machinery and materials. Medical technologies cover a wide range of fields, such as cytotechnology, biomedical technologies, and operating-room technology.

Administrative, professional, or research assistant positions in hospitals, occupational health units in industry, health agencies, community and school health departments, government agencies (environmental protection, public health), and international health organizations are available to majors in health fields, as are jobs in marketing and sales of health-related products and services, health education (with education courses), advertising and public relations, journalism and publishing, and technical writing.

Humanities (Miscellaneous)

The majors that constitute the humanities (sometimes called "letters") are the most general and widely applicable and the least vocationally oriented of the liberal arts. They are essentially studies of the ideas and concerns of humankind. These include classics, history of philosophy, history of science, linguistics, and medieval studies. Career possibilities for humanities majors can be found in business firms, government and community agencies, advertising and public relations, marketing and sales, publishing, journalism and radio/TV, secondary school teaching in English and literature (which usually requires education courses), freelance writing and editing, and computer programming (especially for those with a background in logic or linguistics).

Law and Legal Studies

Students of legal studies can use their knowledge of law and government in fields involving the making, breaking, and enforcement of laws; the crimes, trials, and punishment of law breakers; and the running of all branches of government at local, state, and federal levels. Graduates find positions of all types in law firms, legal departments of other organizations, the court or prison system, government agencies (such as law enforcement agencies or offices of state and federal attorneys general), and police departments.

Mathematics and Physical Sciences

Mathematics is the science of numbers and the abstract formulation of their operations. Physical sciences involve the study of the laws and structures of physical matter. The quantitative skills that are acquired through the study of science and mathematics are especially useful for computer-related careers. Career possibilities include positions in industry (manufacturing and processing companies, electronics firms, defense contractors, consulting firms); government agencies (defense, environmental protection, law enforcement); scientific/technical writing, editing, or illustrating; journalism (science reporting); secondary school teaching (usually requiring education courses); research and laboratory analysis and testing; statistical analysis; computer programming, systems analysis; surveying and mapping; weather forecasting; and technical sales.

Natural Resources

A major in the natural resources field prepares students for work in areas as generalized as environmental conservation and as specialized as groundwater contamination. Jobs are available in industry (food, energy, natural resources, and pulp and paper companies), consulting firms, state and federal government agencies (primarily the Departments of Agriculture and the Interior and the Environmental Protection Agency), and public and private conservation agencies. See the "Agriculture" and "Biological Sciences" sections for more information on natural resources–related fields.

Psychology

Psychology involves the study of behavior and can range from the biological to the sociological. Students can study individual behavior, usually that of humans, or the behavior of crowds. Students of psychology do not always go into the obvious clinical fields, the fields in which psychologists work with patients. Certain areas of psychology, such as industrial/organizational, experimental, and social, are not clinically oriented. Psychology and counseling careers can be in government (such as mental health agencies), schools, hospitals, clinics, private practice, industry, test-development firms, social work, and personnel. The careers listed in the "Social Sciences" section are also pursued by psychology and counseling majors.

Religion

Religion majors are usually seen as preprofessional studies for those who are interested in entering the ministry. Career possibilities for religion also include casework, youth counseling, administration work in community and social service organizations, teaching in religious educational institutions, and writing for religious and lay publications. Religious studies also prepare students for the kinds of jobs other humanities majors often pursue.

Social Sciences

Social sciences majors study people in relation to their society. Thus, students majoring in social science can apply their education to a wide range of occupations that deal with social issues and activities. Career opportunities are varied. People with degrees in the social sciences find careers in government, business, community agencies (serving children, youth, and senior citizens), advertising and public relations, marketing and sales, secondary school social studies teaching (with education courses), casework, law enforcement, parks and recreation, museum work (especially for anthropology, archaeology, geography, and history majors), preservation (especially for anthropology, archaeology, geography, and history majors), banking and finance (especially for economics majors), market and survey research, statistical analysis, publishing, fund-raising and development, and political campaigning.

MAKING THAT MAJOR DECISION: REAL-LIFE ADVICE FROM COLLEGE SENIORS

Somewhere between her junior and senior year in high school, Karen got the psychology bug. When choosing a major in college, she knew just what she wanted. Justin, on the other hand, did a complete 180. He thought he'd study physics, then veered toward philosophy. It wasn't until he took survey courses in literature that he found where his heart really lay, and now he's graduating with a degree in English.

You might find yourself at either end of this spectrum when choosing a major. Either you'll know just what you want or you'll try on a number of different hats before finally settling on one. To give you a taste of what it could be like for you, meet four college seniors who have been through the trials and errors of choosing their majors. Hopefully you'll pick up some pointers from them or at least find out that you don't have to worry so much about what your major will be.

From Grove City College, a liberal arts school in Pennsylvania, meet Karen , who will graduate with a degree in psychology, and English major Justin. From Michigan State University, meet computer engineering major Seth, and Kim, who is finishing up a zoology degree. Here's what they had to say.

HOW THEY CHOSE THEIR MAJORS

Karen: During high school, I volunteered at a retirement center, and my supervisor gave me a lot of exposure to applied psychology. After my freshman year in college, I talked to people who were using a psychology degree. You put in a lot of work for a degree and can wonder if it's worth all the work. It helps to talk to someone who has gone through it so you can see if that's what you want to be doing when you graduate.

Justin: I wasn't sure about what my major would be. One professor told me to take survey courses to see if I was interested in the subject. I took English literature, math, psychology, and philosophy. I liked English the best and did well in it. The next semester, I took two English courses and decided to switch my major. My professors told me not to worry about choosing a major. They said to get my feet wet and we'll talk about your major in two years. I decided that if they're not worried about a major, I wouldn't be either, but I still had it on my mind. I was around older students who were thinking about their careers, so I talked to them about the jobs they had lined up.

Seth: I liked computers in high school. In college, I started out in computer science but got sick of coding. My interest in computers made me pick computer science right off the bat. I didn't know about computer engineering until I got to college.

Kim: I wanted to be a veterinarian but after two years decided that I didn't want to go to school for that long. I was still interested in animals and had two options. One was in animal science, which is working more with farm animals, or going into zoology. I decided to concentrate on zoo and aquarium science. Besides being a vet, the closest interaction with animals would be being a zookeeper.

THE ELECTIVES THEY TOOK AND WHY

Karen: My adviser told me to take different classes, so I took philosophy, art, religion, and extra psychology classes that weren't required.

Justin: I was planning to do a double major, but my professors said to take what interested me. English majors have lots of freedom to take different courses, unlike science majors.

Seth: Because I'm in computer engineering, I don't get to take a lot of electives. I am taking a swimming class right now and took a critical incident analysis class where we looked at major accidents. I wanted something that wasn't computer engineering–related but extremely technical.

Kim: I took a kinesiology class, which was pretty much an aerobics class. I needed to work out and figured I could get credit for it. I also took sign language because I'm interested in it.

WHAT THEY'RE GOING TO DO WITH THEIR DEGREES

Karen: I want to go to graduate school and hopefully get some experience working with kids.

Justin: I'm applying to graduate school in English literature and cultural studies. I want to do research and become a college professor.

Seth: I'm going to work for the defense department. It's not the highest offer I've gotten, but it will be the most fun, which is more important to me than the money.

Kim: My goals have changed again. I don't plan on using my degree. I just got married a year ago, and my husband and I want to go into full-time ministry. I'll work for a while, and then we'll go overseas.

THE CHANGES THEY WOULD MAKE IN THE CLASSES THEY TOOK IF THEY COULD

Karen: There are classes I wouldn't necessarily take again. But even though I didn't learn as much as I wanted to, it was worth it. I learned how to work and how to organize my efforts.

Justin: I should have worried less about choosing a major when I first started college. I didn't have the perspective as to how much time I had to choose.

Seth: I have friends who would change the order in which they took their humanities classes. I was lucky enough to think ahead and spread those classes out over the entire time. Most [engineering] students take them their freshman year to get them all out of the way. Later on, they're locked in the engineering building all day. Because I didn't, it was nice for me to get my mind off engineering.

Kim: Something I can't change are the labs. They require a lot of work, and you only get one credit for 3 hours. Some labs take a lot of work outside of class hours. I had a comparative anatomy lab, which kept me busy over entire weekends. I suggest you don't take a lot of classes that require labs all at once.

THEIR ADVICE FOR YOU

Karen: You don't have to know what you want to do with the rest of your life when you get to college. Most people don't even stay with the major they first choose. Colleges recognize that you will see things you may have not considered at first. Some high school students say they won't go to college unless they know what they want to do.

Justin: If it's possible, take a little of this and a little of that. If you're an engineering student, you'll have it all planned out [for you], but if you're a liberal arts major and are not sure, you probably can take something from each department.

Seth: If possible, take AP exams in high school. You'll be able to make a decision about a major. Freshmen who think they want to do engineering suffer through math and physics classes. Then by their sophomore or junior year, they realize they don't want to be engineers. If they'd taken AP classes, they'd know by their freshman year.

Kim: When I changed my major, I was worried that I might have spent a year in classes that wouldn't count toward my new major. But you shouldn't be scared to change majors because if you stick with something you don't like, you'll have to go back and take other classes anyway.

Though these four seniors arrived at a decision about which major they wanted in different ways, they had similar things to say;

- **It's okay to change your mind about what you want out of college.**
- **To find out which major you might want, start with what you like to do.**
- **Talk to professionals who have jobs in the fields that interest you.**
- **Ask your professors about what kinds of jobs you could get with the degree you're considering.**
- **Talk to seniors who will be graduating with a degree in the major you're considering.**
- **Take electives in areas that interest you, even though they may have nothing to do with your major.**
- **College is a time to explore many different options, so take advantage of the opportunity.**

Technologies

Technology majors, along with trade fields, are most often offered as two-year programs. Majors in technology fields prepare students directly for jobs; however, positions are in practical design and production work rather than in areas that require more theoretical, scientific, and mathematical knowledge. Engineering technologies prepare students with the basic training in specific fields (e.g., electronics, mechanics, or chemistry) that are necessary to become technicians on the support staffs of engineers. Other technology majors center more on maintenance and repair. Work may be in technical activities, such as production or testing, or in nontechnical areas where a technical degree is needed, such as marketing, sales, or administration. Industries, research labs, and government agencies in which technology plays a key role—such as in manufacturing, electronics, construction, communications, transportation, and utilities—hire technology graduates regularly.

Still Unsure?

Relax! You don't have to know what you want to major in before you enroll in college. More than half of all freshmen are undecided when they start school and prefer to get a feel for what's available at college before making a decision. Most four-year colleges don't require students to formally declare a major until the end of their sophomore year or beginning of their junior year. Part of the experience of college is being exposed to new subjects and new ideas. Chances are your high school never offered anthropology. Or marine biology. Or applied mathematics. So take these classes and follow your interests. While you're fulfilling your general course requirements, you might stumble upon a major that appeals to you, or maybe you'll discover a new interest while you're volunteering or participating in other extracurricular activities. Talking to other students might lead to new options you'll want to explore.

Can I Change My Major If I Change My Mind?

Choosing a major does not set your future in stone, nor does it necessarily disrupt your life if you need to change your major. However, choosing a major sooner rather than later has its advantages. If you wait too long to choose, you may have to take additional classes to satisfy the requirements, which may cost you additional time and money.

THE OTHER SIDE OF COLLEGE: HAVING FUN!

College is more than writing papers, reading books, and sitting through lectures. Your social life plays an integral part in your college experience.

Meeting New People

The easiest time to meet new people is at the beginning of something new. New situations shake people up and make them feel just uncomfortable enough to take the risk of extending their hand in friendship. Fortunately for you, college is filled with new experiences, such as the first weeks of being the newest students. This can be quickly followed by becoming a new member of a club or activity. And with each passing semester, you'll be in new classes with new teachers and new faces. College should be a time of constantly challenging and expanding yourself, so never feel that it is too late to meet new people.

But just how do you take that first step in forming a relationship? It's surprisingly easy. Be open to the opportunities of meeting new people and having new experiences. Join clubs and activities. Investigate rock-climbing. Try ballet. Write for the school paper. But most of all—get involved.

Campus Activities

College life will place a lot of demands on you. Your classes will be challenging. Your professors will expect more from you. You'll have to budget and manage your own money. But college life has a plus side that you probably haven't thought of yet: college students do have free time.

The average student spends about 3 hours a day in class. Add to this the time you'll need to spend studying, eating, and socializing, and you'll still have time to spare. One of the best ways to use this time is to participate in campus activities.

Intramural Sports

Intramurals are sports played for competition between members of the same campus community. They provide competition and a sense of belonging without the same level of intensity in practice schedules. Anyone can join an intramural sport. Dormitories, sororities, or fraternities often form teams that play sports such as soccer, volleyball, basketball, flag football, baseball, and softball. Individual intramural sports such as swimming, golf, wrestling, and diving are also available. If you want to get involved, just stop by the intramural office. Usually it is located near the student government office.

Student Government

Student government will be set up in a way that is probably similar to your high school. Students form committees and run for office. However, student government in college has more power than in high school. The officers address all of their class's concerns directly to the president of the college or university and the board of trustees. Most student governments have a branch responsible for student activities that brings in big-name entertainers and controversial speakers. You may want to get involved to see how these contacts are made and appearances are negotiated.

Community Service

Another aspect of student life is volunteering, commonly called community service. Many colleges offer a range of opportunities. Some allow you to simply commit an afternoon to a cause, such as passing out food at a food bank. Others require an ongoing commitment. For example, you might decide to help an adult learn to read every Thursday at 4 p.m. for three months. Some colleges will link a service commitment with class credit. This will enhance your learning, giving you some real-world experience. Be sure to stop by your community service office and see what is available.

Clubs

Most college campuses have a variety of clubs spanning just about every topic you can imagine. Amnesty International regularly meets on most campuses to write letters to help free prisoners in foreign lands. Most college majors band together in a club to discuss their common interests and career potential. Other clubs are based on the use of certain computer software or engage in outdoor activities such as sailing or downhill skiing. The list is endless. If you cannot find a club for your interest, consider starting one of your own. Stop by the student government office to see what rules you'll need to follow. You'll also need to find a location to hold meetings and post signs to advertise your club. When you hold your first meeting, you'll probably be surprised at how many people are willing to take a chance and try a new club.

Greek Life

A major misconception of Greek life (sororities and fraternities) is that it only revolves around wild parties and alcohol. In fact, the vast majority of fraternities and sororities focus on instilling values of scholarship, friendship, leadership, and service in their members. (From this point forward, we will refer to both fraternities and sororities as fraternities.)

Scholarship. A fraternity experience helps you make the academic transition from high school to college. Although the classes taken in high school are challenging, they'll be even harder in college. Fraternities almost always require members to meet certain academic standards. Many hold mandatory study times, keep old class notes and exams on file for study purposes, and make personal tutors available. Members of a fraternity have a natural vested interest in seeing that other members succeed academically, so older members often assist younger members with their studies.

Friendship. Social life is an important component of Greek life. Social functions offer an excellent opportunity for freshmen to become better acquainted with others in the chapter. From Halloween parties to formal dances, members have numerous chances to develop poise and confidence. By participating in these functions, students enrich friendships and build memories that will last a lifetime. Remember, social functions aren't only parties; they can include such activities as intramural sports and homecoming.

Leadership. Because fraternities are self-governing organizations, leadership opportunities abound. Students are given hands-on experience in leading committees, managing budgets, and interacting with faculty members and administrators. Most houses have as many as ten officers, along with an array of committee members. By becoming actively involved in leadership roles, students gain valuable experience that is essential for a successful career. Interestingly, although Greeks represent less than 10 percent of most undergraduate student populations, they often hold the majority of leadership positions on campus.

Service. According to the North American Interfraternity Conference, fraternities are increasingly involved in philanthropies and hands-on service projects. Helping less fortunate people is a major focus of Greek life. This can vary from work with Easter Seals, blood drives, and food pantry collections to community upkeep, such as picking up trash, painting houses, or cleaning up area parks. Greeks also get involved in projects with organizations such as Habitat for Humanity, the American Heart Association, and Children's Miracle Network. By being involved in philanthropic projects, students not only raise money for worthwhile causes but also gain a deeper insight into themselves and their responsibility to the community.

ROOMMATES

When you arrive on campus, you'll face a daunting task: to live peacefully with a stranger for the rest of the academic year.

To make this task easier, most schools use some type of room-assignment survey. This can make roommate matches more successful. For example, two people who prefer to stay up late and play guitar can be matched, while two people who prefer to rise at dawn and hit the track can be a pair. Such differences are easy to ask about on a survey and easy for students to report. However, surveys cannot ask everything, and chances are pretty good that something about your roommate is going to get on your nerves.

To avoid conflict, plan ahead. When you first meet, work out some ground rules. Most schools have roommates write a contract together and sign it during the first week of school. Ground rules help eliminate conflict from the start by allowing each person to know what is expected. You should consider the following areas: privacy, quiet time, chores, and borrowing.

When considering privacy, think about how much time alone you need each day and how you and your roommate will arrange for private time. Class schedules usually give you some alone time. Be aware of this; if your class is cancelled, consider going for a cup of coffee or a browse in the bookstore instead of immediately rushing back to your room. Privacy also relates to giving your roommate space when he or she has had a bad day or just needs time to think. Set up clear hours for quiet time. Your dorm may already have some quiet hours established. You can choose to simply reiterate those or add additional time. Just be clear.

Two other potentially stormy issues are chores and borrowing. If cleaning chores need to be shared, make a schedule and stick to it. No one appreciates a sink full of dirty dishes or a dingy shower. Remember the golden rule: do your chores as you wish your roommate would. When it comes to borrowing, it's important to set up clear rules. The safest bet is to not allow it; but if you do, limit when, for how long, and what will be done in case of damage.

Another issue many students confront is whether to live with a best friend from high school who is attending the same college. Generally, this is a bad idea for several reasons. First, you may think you know your best friend inside and out, but you may be surprised by his or her personal living habits. Nothing will reveal the annoying routines of your friend like the closeness of a dorm room. Plus, personalities can change rapidly in college. Once you are away from home, you may be surprised at how you or your friend transforms from shy and introverted to late-night partygoer. This can cause conflict. A final downfall is that the two of you will stick together like glue in the first few weeks and miss out on opportunities to meet other people.

Armed with this information, you should have a smooth year with your new roommate. But just in case you are the exception, most colleges do allow students who absolutely cannot get along to move. Prior to moving, each student must usually go through a dispute-resolution process. This typically involves your resident adviser (RA), you, and your roommate trying to work through your problems in a structured way.

Living with a roommate can be challenging at times, but the ultimate rewards—meeting someone new, encountering new ideas, and learning how to compromise—will serve you well later in life. Enjoy your roommate and all the experiences you'll have, both good and bad, for they are all part of the college experience.

COMMUTING FROM HOME

For some students, home during the college years is the same house in which they grew up. Whether you are in this situation because you can't afford to live on campus or because you'd just rather live at home with your family, some basic guidelines will keep you connected with campus life.

STUDENT COUNSEL

QUESTION: How did you and your first roommate get along?

ANSWER: I was really lucky. My roommate became my best friend. But, to tell you the truth, I didn't really think that was going to happen. When I got her name, I quickly went on Facebook®. I looked at her profile pictures, and I was sure that we would have nothing in common. I was positive that we'd just sort of coexist in our room and that we'd probably go our separate ways as soon as we could. Was I ever wrong! On the first night in our room, we just chatted and chatted, and we discovered that we had so much in common. We spent a lot of time during orientation together, and we quickly became the closest of friends. As a matter of fact, some people thought we'd been friends forever. They couldn't believe that we'd just met! We're going to be juniors, and we're still rooming together and still great friends. I couldn't imagine my college life without her.

Penn State student
University Park, Pennsylvania

By all means, do not just go straight home after class. Spend some of your free time at school. Most schools have a student union or a coffee shop where students gather and socialize. Make it a point to go there and talk to people between classes. Also, get involved in extracurricular activities, and visit classmates in the dorms.

If you drive to school, find other students who want to carpool. Most schools have a commuters' office or club that will give you a list of people who live near you. Sharing a car ride will give you time to talk and form a relationship with someone else who knows about the challenges of commuting.

Commuters' clubs also sponsor a variety of activities throughout the year—give them a try! Be sure also to consider the variety of activities open to all members of the student body, ranging from student government to community service to intramural sports. You may find this takes a bit more effort on your part, but the payoff in the close friendships you'll form will more than make up for it.

WHAT IF YOU DON'T LIKE THE COLLEGE YOU PICK?

In the best of all worlds, you compile a list of colleges, find the most compatible one, and are accepted. You have a great time, learn a lot, graduate, and head off to a budding career. You may find, however, that the college you chose isn't the best of all worlds. Imagine these scenarios:

- Halfway through your first semester of college, you come to the distressing conclusion that you can't stand being there for whatever reason. The courses don't match your interests. The campus is out in the boonies, and you don't ever want to see another cow. The selection of extracurricular activities doesn't cut it.
- You have methodically planned to go to a community college for two years and move to a four-year college to complete your degree. Transferring takes you nearer to your goal.
- You thought you wanted to major in art, but by the end of the first semester, you find yourself more interested in British literature. Things get confusing, so you drop out of college to sort out your thoughts, and now you want to drop back in, hoping to rescue some of those credits.

HOMESICKNESS

Homesickness in its most basic form is a longing for the stuff of home: your parents, friends, bedroom, school, and all of the other familiar people and objects that make you comfortable. But on another level, homesickness is a longing to go back in time. Moving away to college forces you to take on new responsibilities and begin to act like an adult. This can be scary.

While this condition is often described as a "sickness," no pill will provide a quick fix. Instead, you need to acknowledge that your feelings are a normal reaction to a significant change in your life. Allow yourself to feel the sadness of moving on in life and be open to conversations about it that may crop up in your dorm or among your new friends. After all, everyone is dealing with this issue. Then, make an effort to create a new home and a new life on campus. Create new habits and routines so that this once-strange place becomes familiar. Join activities and engage in campus life. This will help you to create a feeling of belonging that will ultimately be the key to overcoming homesickness.

- You didn't do that well in high school—socializing got in the way of studying. But you've wised up, have gotten serious about your future, and two years of community college have brightened your prospects of transferring to a four-year institution.

Circumstances shift, people change, and, realistically speaking, it's not all that uncommon to transfer. Many people do. The reasons why students transfer run the gamut, as do the institutional policies that govern them. Among the most common transfers are students who move from a two-year to a four-year university.

If your plan is to attend a two-year college with the ultimate goal of transferring to a four-year school, you'll be pleased to know that the increased importance of the community college route to a bachelor's degree is recognized by all segments of higher education. As a result, many two-year schools have revised their course outlines and established new courses in order to comply with the programs and curricular offerings of the universities. Institutional improvements to make transferring easier have also proliferated at both the two- and four-year levels. The generous transfer policies of the Pennsylvania, New York, and Florida state university systems, among others, reflect this attitude; these systems accept all credits from students who have graduated from accredited community colleges.

If you are interested in moving from a two-year college to a four-year school, the sooner you make up your mind that you are going to make the switch, the better position you will be in to transfer successfully (that is, without having wasted valuable time and credits). The ideal point at which to make such a decision is before you register for classes at your two year school; a counselor can help you plan your course work with an eye toward fulfilling the requirements needed for your major course of study.

Naturally, it is not always possible to plan your transferring strategy that far in advance, but keep in mind that the key to a successful transfer is preparation, and preparation takes time—time to think through your objectives and time to plan the right classes to take.

Here are some commonly asked questions by transferring students—and their answers:

QUESTION: Do students who go directly from high school to a four-year college do better academically than transfer students from community colleges?

ANSWER: On the contrary: some institutions report that transfers from two-year schools who persevere until graduation do better than those who started as freshmen in a four-year college.

QUESTION: Why is it so important that my two-year college be accredited?

ANSWER: Four-year colleges and universities accept transfer credits only from schools formally recognized by a regional, national, or professional educational agency. This accreditation signifies that an institution or program of study meets or exceeds a minimum level of educational quality necessary for meeting stated educational objectives.

QUESTION: What do I need to do to transfer?

ANSWER: First, send for your high school and college transcripts. Having chosen the school you wish to transfer to, check its admission requirements against your transcripts. If you find that you are admissible, file an application as early as possible before the deadline. Part of the process will be asking your former schools to send official transcripts to the admission office—not the copies you used in determining your admissibility.

Plan your transfer program with the head of your new department as soon as you have decided to transfer. Determine the recommended general education pattern and necessary preparation for your major. At your present school, take the courses you will need to meet transfer requirements for the new school.

QUESTION: What qualifies me for admission as a transfer student?

ANSWER: Admission requirements for most four-year institutions vary. Depending on the reputation or popularity of the school and program you wish to enter, requirements may be quite selective and competitive. Usually, you will need to show satisfactory test scores, an academic record up to a certain standard, and completion of specific subject matter.

Transfer students can be eligible to enter a four-year school in a number of ways: by having been eligible for admission directly upon graduation from high school, by making up shortcomings in grades (or in subject matter not covered in high school) at a community college, or by satisfactory completion of necessary courses or credit hours at another postsecondary institution. Ordinarily, students coming from a community college or from another four-year institution must meet or exceed the receiving institution's standards for freshmen and show appropriate college-level course work taken since high school. Students who did not graduate from high school can present proof of proficiency through results on the General Educational Development (GED) test.

QUESTION: Is it possible to transfer courses from several different institutions?

ANSWER: Institutions ordinarily accept the courses that they consider transferable, regardless of the number of accredited schools involved. However, there is the danger of exceeding the maximum number of credit hours that can be transferred from all other schools or earned through credit by examination, extension courses, or correspondence courses. The limit placed on transfer credits varies from school to school, so read the catalog carefully to avoid taking courses you won't be able to use. To avoid duplicating courses, keep attendance at different campuses to a minimum.

QUESTION: Which is more important for transfer—my grade point average or my course completion pattern?

ANSWER: Some schools believe that your past grades indicate academic potential and overshadow prior preparation for a specific degree program. Others require completion of certain introductory courses before transfer to prepare you for upper-division work in your major. In any case, appropriate course selection will cut down the time to graduation and increase your chances of making a successful transfer.

CHAPTER 10

OTHER OPTIONS AFTER HIGH SCHOOL

Years ago, most people went directly to work after high school. Today, most people first go to school for more training, but many do not go to traditional four-year colleges.

There are numerous reasons why many high school graduates do not continue their education at a four-year college, but instead pursue further education elsewhere. This chapter tells you about the various options that are available after high school.

WHO IS ON THE TRADITIONAL 4-YEAR COLLEGE PATH?

According to statistics from the U.S. Census Bureau and the U.S. National Center for Education Statistics,[1] of the 3,151,000 students aged 16 to 24 who graduated from high school or received a GED in 2008, approximately 69 percent enrolled in college. About 40 percent of the students in this age group enrolled at four-year colleges.[2] Not all of those students will go on to complete a degree, and those who do may not end up using the degree they earned in their future employment. But an important question remains: Why aren't the remaining 60 percent of students choosing traditional four-year colleges?

The reasons are as varied as the students. Life events can often interfere with plans to attend college. Responsibilities to a family may materialize that make it impossible to delay earning an income for four years. One may have to work and go to school. And traditional colleges demand certain conventions, behaviors, and attitudes that don't fit every kind of person. Some people need a lot of physical activity to feel satisfied, while others just aren't interested in spending day after day sitting, reading, memorizing, and analyzing. Years of strict time management and postponed rewards are more than they can stand.

If any of these reasons rings true with you, rest assured that you have many postsecondary options available to you, all of which not only will allow you to pursue further education but also will train you for a career. Let's take a look at some of the educational directions you can follow.

[1]http://www.census.gov/compendia/statab/2011/tables/11s0272.pdf
[2]http://www.census.gov/compendia/statab/2011/tables/11s0279.pdf

DISTANCE LEARNING

As a future college student, can you picture yourself in any of these scenarios?

- **You need some information, but the only place to find it is at a big state university.** Trouble is that it's hundreds of miles away. No problem. You simply go to your local community college and link up electronically with that university. Voilà! The resources are right there for you.
- **That ten-page paper is due in a few days, but you still have some last-minute questions to ask the professor before you turn it in and you won't see the professor until after the paper is due.** Not to worry. Since you have the professor's e-mail address, just like all the other students in the class, you simply e-mail your question to her. She replies. You get your answer, finish the paper, and even turn it in electronically.
- **After graduating from high school, you can't go to college right away, but your employer has a connection with a college that offers courses via the Internet.** During your lunch hours, you log in to a class and get college credit.

Not too long ago, if you'd offered these scenarios to high school graduates as real possibilities, they would have thought you were a sci-fi freak. Distance education usually meant getting courses via snail mail or watching a course on TV or on videotape. Well, today you are in the right place at the right time. Distance education is a reality for countless high school graduates.

What distance education now means is that you can access educational programs and do not have to physically be in a classroom on a campus. Through such technologies as cable or satellite television, DVDs, CDs, fax, high-speed Internet services, computer conferencing and videoconferencing, and other means of electronic delivery, the classroom comes to you—sometimes even if you're sitting in your bedroom in your pajamas at 2 in the morning.

Distance learning expands the reach of the classroom by using various technologies to deliver university resources to off-campus sites, transmitting college courses into the workplace, and enabling you to view class lectures in the comfort of your home.

Where and How Can I Take Distance Learning Courses?

New, cheaper telecommunications technology is getting better all the time, and there is a growing demand for education by individuals who can't afford either the time or money to be a full-time, on-campus student. To fill that demand, educational networks also are growing and changing how and when you can access college courses.

Most states have established new distance learning systems to advance the delivery of instruction to schools, postsecondary institutions, and state government agencies. Colleges and universities are collaborating with commercial telecommunication entities to provide education to far-flung student constituencies. Professions such as law, medicine, and accounting, as well as knowledge-based industries, are utilizing telecommunications networks for the transmission of customized higher education programs to working professionals, technicians, and managers.

Ways in Which Distance Learning May Be Offered

- **Credit courses.** In general, if these credit courses are completed successfully, they can be applied toward a degree.
- **Noncredit courses and courses offered for professional certification.** These programs can help you acquire specialized knowledge in a concentrated, time-efficient manner and stay on top of the latest developments in your field. They provide a flexible way for you to prepare for a new career or study for professional licensure and certification. Many of these university programs are created in cooperation with professional and trade associations so that courses are based on real-life work force needs, and the practical skills learned are immediately applicable in the field.

How Distance Learning Works

Enrolling in a distance learning course may simply involve filling out a registration form, making sure that you have access to the equipment needed, and paying the tuition and fees. In this case, your application may be accepted without entrance examinations or proof of prior educational experience.

Other courses may involve educational prerequisites and access to equipment not found in all geographic locations. Some institutions offer detailed information about individual courses, such as a course outline, upon request. If you have access to the Internet and simply wish to review course descriptions, you may be able to peruse an institution's course catalog electronically by accessing the institution's home page on the Web.

Time Requirements

Some courses allow you to enroll at your convenience and work at your own pace. Others closely adhere to a traditional classroom schedule. Specific policies and time limitations pertaining to withdrawals, refunds, transfers, and renewal periods can be found in the institutional catalog.

Admission to a Degree Program

If you plan to enter a degree program, you should consult the academic advising department of the institution of your choice to learn about entrance requirements and application procedures. You may find it necessary to develop a portfolio of your past experiences and accomplishments that may have resulted in college-level learning.

How Do I Communicate with My Instructor?

Student-faculty exchanges occur using electronic communication (through fax and e-mail). Many institutions offer their distance learning students access to toll-free numbers so students can talk to their professors or teaching assistants without incurring any long-distance charges.

Responses to your instructor's comments on your lessons, requests for clarification of comments, and all other exchanges between you and your instructor will take time. Interaction with your instructor—whether by computer, phone, or letter—is important, and you must be willing to take the initiative.

What Else Does Distance Learning Offer?

Distance learning comes in a variety of colors and flavors. Along with traditional college degrees, you can earn professional certification or continuing education units (CEUs) in a particular field.

College Degrees

You can earn degrees at a distance at the associate, baccalaureate, and graduate levels. Two-year community college students are able to earn baccalaureate degrees—without relocating—by transferring to distance learning programs offered by four-year universities. Corporations are forming partnerships with universities to bring college courses to worksites and encourage employees to continue their education. Distance learning is especially popular among people who want to earn their degree part-time while continuing to work full-time. Although on-campus residencies are sometimes required for certain distance learning degree programs, they generally can be completed while employees are on short-term leave or vacation.

Professional Certification

Certificate programs often focus on employment specializations, such as hazardous waste management or electronic publishing, and can be helpful to those seeking to advance or change careers. Also, many states mandate continuing education for professionals such as teachers, nursing home administrators, or accountants. Distance learning offers a convenient way for many individuals to meet professional certification requirements. Health care, engineering, and education are just a few of the many professions that take advantage of distance learning to help their professionals maintain certification.

Many colleges offer a sequence of distance learning courses in a specific field of a profession. For instance, within the engineering profession, certificate programs in computer-integrated manufacturing, systems engineering, test and evaluation, waste management education, and research consortium are offered via distance learning.

Business offerings include distance learning certification in information technology, total quality management, and health services management.

Within the field of education, you'll find distance learning certificate programs in areas such as early reading instruction and special education for the learning handicapped.

Continuing Education Units (CEUs)

If you choose to take a course on a noncredit basis, you may be able to earn continuing education units (CEUs). The CEU system is a nationally recognized system to provide a standardized measure for accumulating, transferring, and recognizing participation in continuing education programs. One CEU is defined as 10 contact hours of participation in an organized continuing education experience under responsible sponsorship, capable direction, and qualified instruction.

COMMUNITY COLLEGES

Two-year colleges or community colleges are often called "the people's colleges." With their open-door policies (admission is open to individuals with a high school diploma or its equivalent), community colleges provide access to higher education for millions of Americans who might otherwise be excluded. Community college students are diverse, of all ages, races, and economic backgrounds. While many community college students enroll full-time, an equally large number attend on a part-time basis so they can fulfill employment and family commitments as they advance their education.

Community colleges are also referred to as either technical or junior colleges, and they may either be under public or independent control. What unites all two-year colleges is that they are regionally accredited, postsecondary institutions, whose highest credential awarded is the associate degree. With few exceptions, community colleges offer a comprehensive curriculum, which includes transfer, technical, and continuing education programs.

Important Factors in a Community College Education

The student who attends a community college can count on receiving high-quality instruction in a supportive learning community. This setting frees the student to pursue his or her own goals, nurture special talents, explore new fields of learning, and develop the capacity for lifelong learning.

From the student's perspective, these characteristics capture the essence of community colleges:

- They are community-based institutions that work in close partnership with high schools, community groups, and employers in extending high-quality programs at convenient times and places.
- Community colleges are cost effective. Annual tuition and fees at public community colleges average approximately half those at public four-year colleges and less than 15 percent of private four-year institutions. In addition, since most community colleges are generally close to their students' homes, these students can also save a significant amount of money on the room, board, and transportation expenses traditionally associated with a college education.
- They provide a caring environment, with faculty members who are expert instructors, known for excellent teaching and for meeting students at the point of their individual needs, regardless of age, sex, race, current job status, or previous academic preparation. Community colleges join a strong curriculum with a broad range of counseling and career services that are intended to assist students in making the most of their educational opportunities.
- Many offer comprehensive programs, including transfer curriculums in liberal arts programs, such as chemistry, psychology, and business management, which lead directly to a baccalaureate degree and career programs that prepare students for employment or assist those already employed in upgrading their skills. For those students who need to strengthen their academic skills, community colleges also offer a wide range of developmental programs in mathematics, languages, and learning skills, designed to prepare the student for success in college studies.

Getting to Know Your Two-Year College

The best way to learn about your college is to visit in person. During a campus visit, be prepared to ask a lot of questions. Talk to students, faculty members, administrators, and counselors about the college and its programs, particularly those in which you have a special interest. Ask about available certificates and associate degrees. Don't be shy. Do what you can to dig below the surface. Ask college officials about the transfer rate to four-year colleges. If a college emphasizes student services, find out what particular assistance is offered, such as educational or career guidance. Colleges are eager to provide you with the information you need to make informed decisions.

The Money Factor

For many students, the decision to attend a community college is often based on financial factors. If you aren't sure what you want to do or what talents you have, community colleges allow you the freedom to explore different career interests at a low cost. For those students who can't afford the cost of university tuition, community colleges offer a way for them to take care of their basic classes before transferring to a four-year institution. Many two-year colleges offer you instruction in your own home through cable television or public broadcast stations or through home study courses that can save both time and money. Look into all your options, and be sure to add up all the costs of attending various colleges before deciding which is best for you.

Working and Going to School

Over the past decades, a steadily growing number of students have chosen to attend community colleges while they fulfill family and employment responsibilities. Many two-year college students maintain full-time or part-time employment while they earn their degrees. To enable these students to balance the demands of home, work, and school, most community colleges offer classes at night and on weekends.

For the full-time student, the usual length of time it takes to obtain an associate degree is two years. However, your length of study will depend on the course load you take: the fewer credits you earn each term, the longer it will take you to earn a degree. To assist you in moving more quickly toward your degree, many community colleges now award credit through examination or for equivalent knowledge gained through relevant life experiences. Be certain to find out the credit options that are available to you at the college in which you are interested. You may discover that it will take less time to earn a degree than you first thought.

Preparation for Transfer

Studies have repeatedly shown that students who first attend a community college and then transfer to a four-year college or university do at least as well academically as the students who entered the four-year institutions as freshmen. Most community colleges have agreements with nearby four-year institutions to make transfer of credits easier. If you are thinking of transferring, be sure to meet with a counselor or faculty adviser before choosing your courses. You'll want to map out a course of study with transfer in mind. Make sure you also find out the credit-transfer requirements of the four-year institution you might want to attend.

New Career Opportunities

Community colleges realize that many entering students are not sure about the field in which they want to focus their studies or the career they would like to pursue. Community colleges have the resources to help students identify areas of career interest and to set challenging occupational goals.

Once a career goal is set, you can be confident that a community college will provide job-relevant, high-quality occupational and technical education. About half of the students who take courses for credit at community colleges do so to prepare for employment or to acquire or upgrade skills for their current job. Especially helpful in charting a career path is the assistance of a counselor or a faculty adviser, who can discuss job opportunities in your chosen field and help you map out your course of study.

In addition, since community colleges have close ties to their communities, they are in constant contact with leaders in business, industry, organized labor, and public life. Community colleges work with these individuals and their organizations to prepare students for direct entry into the world of work. For example, some community colleges have established partnerships with local businesses and industries to offer specialized training programs. Some also provide the academic portion of apprenticeship training, while others offer extensive job-shadowing and cooperative education opportunities. Be sure to examine all of the career-preparation opportunities offered by the community colleges in which you are interested.

Community Colleges and the New Green Economy

As the United States transforms its economy into a "green" one, community colleges are leading the way—filling the need for educated technicians whose skills can cross industry lines as well as the need for technicians who are able to learn new skills as technologies evolve.

Community colleges are training workers to work in fields such as renewable energy, energy efficiency, wind energy, green building, and sustainability. The programs are as diverse as the campuses housing them.

At one community college in New Mexico, there are state-of-the-art facilities for research and for training qualified technicians in wind energy technology. The college offers associate degrees in this field, meeting the fast-growing demand for "windsmiths" in the western part of the country.

Another community college in Massachusetts has become one of the nation's leading colleges in promoting and integrating sustainability and green practices throughout all campus operations and technical training programs. Its wind technician program is considered a state model for community-based clean energy workforce development and education. This community college has awarded hundreds of degrees in coastal management, solar technology, wastewater, and studies for other green careers.

In the Renewable Energies and Sustainable Living program at one Michigan community college, students gain field experience refurbishing public buildings with renewable materials, performing energy audits for the government, and working with small businesses and hospitals to reduce waste and pollution. At another Michigan community college, the new Wind Turbine Training Program has more applicants than spaces, and students are being hired BEFORE they even graduate.

An Oregon community college now offers training programs for the windpower generation industry. It offers a one-year certificate and a two-year Associate of Applied Science (A.A.S.) degree in renewable energy technology. The Renewable Energy Technology program was designed in collaboration with industry partners from the wind energy industry and the power generation industry. Students are prepared for employment in a broad range of industries, including hydro-generation, wind-generation, automated manufacturing, engineering technology, and solar array technology.

In North Carolina, one community college has been leading the way in "green" programs for more than a decade. It was the first community college in the nation to offer an Associate in Applied Science degree in sustainable agriculture and the first in that state to offer an associate degree in biofuels. It also offers an associate degree in sustainable technology, a natural chef culinary arts program, and an ecotourism certificate program.

It's clear that there are many exciting "green" programs at community colleges throughout the United States. If any of these options sound interesting to you, take a look at the vast array of programs offered at a community college near you.

VOCATIONAL/CAREER COLLEGES

Career education is important for every employcc as tcchnology continues to change. From the largest employers, such as the U.S. military, defense contractors, aviation, and health care, down to the company with one and two employees, issues of keeping up with technology and producing goods and services cheaper, faster, and at less cost requires—indeed demands—a skilled, world-class workforce. In good or bad economic times, you'll always have a distinct advantage if you have a demonstrable skill and can be immediately productive while continuing to learn and improve. If you know how to use technology, work collaboratively, and find creative solutions, you'll always be in demand.

Career colleges offer scores of opportunities to learn the technical skills required by many of today and tomorrow's top jobs. This is especially true in the areas of computer and information technology, health care, and hospitality (culinary arts, travel and tourism, and hotel and motel management). Career colleges range in size from those with a handful of students to universities with thousands enrolled. They are located in every state in the nation and share one common objective—to prepare students for a successful career in the world of work through a focused, intensive curriculum.

America's career colleges are privately owned and operated by for-profit companies. Instead of using tax support to operate, career colleges pay taxes. Because career colleges are businesses, they must be responsive to the workforce needs of their communities or they will cease to exist.

Generally, career colleges prepare you for a specific career. Some will require you to take academic courses such as English or history. Others will relate every class you take to a specific job, such as computer-aided drafting or interior design. Some focus specifically on business or technical fields. The negative side to this kind of education is that if you haven't carefully researched what you want to do, you could waste a lot of time and money. Unlike community colleges, where you can find yourself and take courses in several areas, these schools don't allow much room for exploring alternative career options.

So how do you find the right career college for you? Having a general idea what you want to do is a good place to start. You don't need to know the fine details of your goals, but you should have a broad idea, such as a career in allied health or business or computing.

After you've crossed that hurdle, the rest is easy. Since professional training is the main purpose of career colleges, its graduates are the best measure of a school's success. Who hires the graduates? How do their jobs relate to the education they received? In addition to focusing on the needs of their students, career colleges also want to ensure they meet the needs of the employers who are hiring their graduates. Career colleges should be able to provide that data to prospective students.

Checking the credentials of a career college is one of the most important steps you should take in your career college search. Though not every career college has to be accredited, it is a sign that the college has gone through a process that ensures quality. It also means that students can qualify for federal grant and loan programs. Furthermore, you should see if the college has met the standards of professional training organizations. In fields such as court reporting and health-related professions, those criteria are paramount.

WHAT TO LOOK FOR IN A CAREER COLLEGE

A tour of the college is a must! While visiting the campus, do the following:

- **Get a full explanation of the curriculum, including finding out how you will be trained.**
- **Take a physical tour of the classrooms and laboratories and look for cleanliness, modern equipment/computers, and size of classes. Observe the activity in classes: Are students engaged in class, and are lectures dynamic?**
- **Ask about employment opportunities after graduation. What are the placement rates (most current) and list of employers? Inquire about specific placement assistance: resume preparation, job leads, etc. Look for "success stories" on bulletin boards, placement boards, and newsletters.**
- **Find out about tuition and other costs associated with the program. Ask about the financial aid assistance provided to students.**
- **Find out if an externship is part of the training program. How are externships assigned? Does the student have any input as to externship assignment?**
- **Ask if national certification and registration in your chosen field is available upon graduation.**
- **Inquire about the college's accreditation and certification.**
- **Also find out the associations and organizations to which the college belongs. Ask what awards or honors the college has had bestowed.**
- **Ask if the college utilizes an advisory board to develop employer relationships.**
- **Ask about the rules and regulations. What GPA must be maintained? What is the attendance policy? What are grounds for termination? What is the refund policy if the student drops out or is terminated? Is there a dress code? What are the holidays of the college?**

Source: Arizona College of Allied Health, Phoenix, Arizona

FINANCIAL AID OPTIONS FOR CAREER AND COMMUNITY COLLEGES

The financial aid process is basically the same for students attending a community college, a career college, or a technical institute as it is for students attending a four-year college. However, a few details can make the difference between only scraping by and getting the maximum amount of financial aid.

The federal government is still your best source of financial aid. Most community colleges and career and technical schools participate in federal financial aid programs. To get detailed information about federal financial aid programs and how to apply for them, read through Chapter 8: "Financial Aid Dollars and Sense."

Don't overlook scholarships. What many two-year students don't realize is that they could be eligible for scholarships. Regrettably, many make the assumption that scholarships are only for very smart students attending prestigious universities. You'd be surprised to learn how many community and career colleges offer scholarships. It's critical to talk to the financial aid officer of each school you plan to attend to find out what scholarships may be available.

Two-year students should find out how their state of residence can help them pay for tuition. Every state in the union has some level of state financial aid that goes to community college students. The amounts are dependent on which state you live in, and most aid is in the form of grants.

APPRENTICESHIPS

Some students like working with their hands and have the skill, patience, and temperament to become expert mechanics, carpenters, or electronics repair technicians. If you think you'd enjoy a profession like this and feel that college training isn't for you, then you might want to think about a job that

SNAPSHOT OF TWO CAREER COLLEGE STUDENTS

Katrina
Network Systems Administration
Silicon Valley College
Fremont, California

ABOUT KATRINA

Right after high school, Katrina headed for junior college, but she felt like she was spinning her wheels. She wanted something that was goal-oriented. Community college offered too many options. She needed to be focused in one direction.

At first, Katrina thought she would become a physical therapist. Then she realized how much schooling she would need to begin working. Turning to the computer field, she saw some definite benefits. For one, she had messed around with them in high school. She could get a degree and get out in two years. She saw that computer careers are big and getting bigger. Plus, there weren't a lot of women in that field, which signaled more potential for her. But before she switched schools, she visited the career college, talked to students, and sat in on lectures. She really liked the way the teachers related to their students. Along with her technical classes, she's taken algebra, psychology, English composition, and management communication.

WHAT I LIKE ABOUT BEING A CAREER STUDENT

"Career colleges are for fast-track-oriented students who want to get out in the work field and still feel that they have an appropriate education."

Nicholas
Automotive Techniques Management
Education America/Vale Technical Institute
Blairsville, Pennsylvania

ABOUT NICHOLAS

Nicholas has completely repainted his 1988 Mercury Topaz, redone all the brakes, put in a brand-new exhaust system, and fixed lots of smaller stuff here and there. But he says that nothing compares to the completely totaled cars some of his classmates haul into the school. Talk about hands-on—they're able to completely restore them while going through the program.

Nicholas didn't always have gasoline running through his veins. In fact, he just recently discovered how much he likes automotives. After graduating from high school, he went to a community college, and after one semester, he left to work at a personal care home. Standing over a sink of dirty dishes made him realize he wanted more than just a job. He started thinking about what he wanted to do and visited a few schools and the body shop where his brother worked. Where others saw twisted car frames, Nicholas saw opportunity and enrolled in the program.

WHAT I LIKE ABOUT BEING A CAREER STUDENT

"I compare career college to a magnifying glass that takes the sun and focuses it. You learn just what you need to learn."

requires apprenticeship training. If you're looking for a soft job, forget it. An apprenticeship is no snap. It demands hard work and has tough competition, so you've got to have the will to see it through.

An apprenticeship is a program formally agreed upon between a worker and an employer where the employee learns a skilled trade through classroom work and on-the-job training. Apprenticeship programs vary in length, pay, and intensity among the various trades. A person completing an apprenticeship program generally becomes a journeyperson (skilled craftsperson) in that trade.

The advantages of apprenticeships are numerous. First and foremost, an apprenticeship leads to a lasting lifetime skill. As a highly trained worker, you can take your skill anywhere you decide to go. The more creative, exciting, and challenging jobs are put in the hands of the fully skilled worker, the all-around person who knows his or her trade inside out.

Skilled workers advance much faster than those who are semi-skilled or whose skills are not broad enough to equip them to assume additional responsibilities in a career. Those who complete an apprenticeship also have acquired the skills and judgment that are necessary to start their own businesses if they choose.

What to Do If You're Interested in an Apprenticeship

If you want to begin an apprenticeship, you have to be at least 16 years old, and you must fill out an application for employment. These applications may be available year-round or only at certain times during the year, depending on the trade in which you're interested.

Federal regulations prohibit anyone under the age of 16 from being considered for an apprenticeship. Some programs require a high school degree or certain course work. Other requirements may include passing certain aptitude tests, proof of physical ability to perform the duties of the trade, and possession of a valid driver's license.

Once you have met the basic program entrance requirements, you'll be interviewed and awarded points on your interest in the trade, your attitude toward work in general, and personal traits, such as appearance, sincerity, character, and habits. Openings are awarded to those who have achieved the most points.

Because an apprentice must be trained in an area where work actually exists and where a certain pay scale is guaranteed upon completion of the program, the wait for application acceptance may be pretty long in areas of low employment. This standard works to your advantage, however. Just think: You wouldn't want to spend one to six years of your life learning a job where no work exists or where the wage is the same as, or just a little above, that of an unskilled or semi-skilled laborer.

If you're considering an apprenticeship, the best sources of assistance and information are vocational or career counselors, local state employment security agencies, field offices of state apprenticeship agencies, and regional offices of the Employment and Training Administration's Office of Apprenticeship (OA). Apprenticeships are usually registered with the OA or a state apprenticeship council. Some apprenticeships are not registered, but that doesn't necessarily mean that the program isn't valid.

To determine if a certain apprenticeship is legitimate, contact your state's apprenticeship agency or a regional office of the OA. You'll find addresses and phone numbers for these regional offices on the following page. You can also visit the OA's Web site at www.doleta.gov/oa/.

OFFICE OF APPRENTICESHIP OFFICES
NATIONAL OFFICE
Office of Apprenticeship
Employment and Training Administration
U.S. Department of Labor
Frances Perkins Building
200 Constitution Avenue, NW
Washington, DC 20210
Phone: 877-US-2JOBS (toll-free)

REGION I: Boston		REGION IV: Dallas	
Ms. Jill Houser Regional Director USDOL/ETA/OA JFK Federal Building Room E-370 Boston, MA 02203 Phone: 617-788-0177 Fax: 617-788-0304 E-mail: houser.jill@dol.gov	Connecticut Maine Massachusetts New Hampshire New Jersey New York Puerto Rico Rhode Island Vermont Virgin Islands	Mr. Steve Opitz Regional Director USDOL/ETA/OA Federal Building 525 S. Griffin Street Room 303 Dallas, TX 75202 Phone: 972-850-4681 Fax: 972-850-4688 E-mail: Opitz.Steve@dol.gov	Arkansas Colorado Louisiana Montana New Mexico North Dakota Oklahoma South Dakota Texas Utah Wyoming
REGION II: Philadelphia		**REGION V: Chicago**	
Mr. Joseph T. Hersh Regional Director USDOL/ETA/OA 170 S. Independence Mall West Suite 820-East Philadelphia, PA 19106-3315 Phone: 215-861-4830 Fax: 215-861-4833 E-mail: Hersh.Joseph@dol.gov	Delaware District of Columbia Maryland Pennsylvania Virginia West Virginia	Mr. Dean Guido Regional Director USDOL/ETA/OA 230 South Dearborn Street Room 656 Chicago, IL 60604 Phone: 312-596-5500 Fax: 312-596-5501 E-mail: guido.dean@dol.gov	Illinois Indiana Iowa Kansas Michigan Minnesota Missouri Nebraska Ohio Wisconsin
REGION III: Atlanta		**REGION VI: San Francisco**	
Mr. Garfield G. Garner Jr. Regional Director USDOL/ETA/OA 61 Forsyth Street SW Room 6T71 Atlanta, GA 30303 Phone: 404-302-5478 Fax: 404-302-5479 E-mail: Garner.Garfield@dol.gov	Alabama Florida Georgia Kentucky Mississippi North Carolina South Carolina Tennessee	Mr. Michael W. Longeuay Regional Director USDOL/ETA/OA 90 7th Street, Suite 17-100 San Francisco, CA 94103 Phone: 415-625-2230 Fax: 415-625-2235 E-mail: Longeuay.Michael@dol.gov	Alaska Arizona California Hawaii Idaho Nevada Oregon Washington

CHAPTER 11

THE MILITARY OPTION

Bet you didn't know that the United States military is the largest employer in the country. There's got to be a good reason that so many people get their paychecks from Uncle Sam!

Find out in this chapter if the military is right for you. And if it is, begin to determine which branch is the best match for you.

SHOULD I WORK FOR THE LARGEST EMPLOYER IN THE UNITED STATES?

Every year, thousands of young people pursue a military career and enjoy the benefits it offers. Yet thousands more consider joining the military and decide against it. Their reasons vary, but many choose not to enlist because they lack knowledge of what a career in the military can offer. Others simply mistrust recruiters based on horror stories they've heard. Sadly, many make the decision against joining the military without ever setting foot in the recruiting office.

But if you are an informed "shopper," you'll be able to make an informed choice about whether the military is right for you.

People rarely buy anything based on their needs—instead, they buy based on their emotions. We see it on a daily basis in advertising, from automobiles to energy drinks. We rarely see an automobile commercial that gives statistics about how the car is engineered, how long it will last, the gas mileage, and other technical specifications. Instead, we see people driving around and having a good time.

The reason for this is that advertising agencies know that you'll probably buy something based on how you feel rather than what you think. Because of this tendency to buy with emotion rather than reason, it is important to separate the feelings from the facts. That way, you can base your decision about whether to join the military primarily on the facts.

You must answer two big questions before you can come to any conclusions.

1. Is the military right for me?
2. If the answer to the first question is yes, which branch is right for me?

Suppose that you have to decide whether to buy a new car or repair your current car. The first choice you make will determine your next course of action. You'll have to weigh the facts to determine if you'll purchase a new car or not. Once you've decided to buy a car rather than repair your old one, you must then decide exactly what make and model will best suit your needs.

> *"Normally the first question we get from people interested in the Air Force is 'What does the Air Force have to offer me?' But I back off and ask them about their qualifications. After all of my questions, some people think it might be easier to apply to an Ivy League school than to join the Air Force because of our stringent requirements."*
>
> Master Sergeant Timothy Little
> United States Air Force

You should make a list of the reasons why you want to join the military before you ever set foot in the recruiter's office. Whether your list is long—with such items as money for college, job security, opportunity to travel, technical training, and good pay—or it contains only one item, such as having full-time employment, the number of items on your list is not what's important. What is important is that you are able to satisfy those reasons, or primary motivators.

Whatever your list contains, the first course of action is to collect your reasons to join the military and put them in order of importance to you. This process, known as rank-ordering, will help you determine if you should proceed with the enlistment process.

Rank-ordering your list is a simple process of deciding which motivators are most important to you and then listing them in rank order.

If we apply the car-buying scenario here, your primary motivators may be finding a car that costs under $20,000, gets at least 30 miles to the gallon, has leather interior, is available in blue, and has a sunroof. If you put those motivators in rank order, your list might look something like this:

1. Costs under $20,000
2. Gets at least 30 mpg
3. Has a sunroof
4. Has leather interior
5. Available in blue

You'll notice that the number one, or most important, motivator in this case is cost, while the last, or least important, motivator is color. The more important the motivator, the less likely you'll be willing to settle for something different or to live without it altogether.

> *"Take 2 people with the same qualifications who are looking for jobs. The person with the Army background will be that much more competitive. That's due to the fact that he or she is disciplined and knows how to act without being told what to do."*
>
> Staff Sergeant Max Burda
> United States Army

After you've rank-ordered your motivators, go down your list and determine whether those motivators can be met by enlisting in the military. If you find that all your motivators can be met by enlisting, that's great; but even if only some of your motivators can be met, you may still want to consider enlisting. Seldom does a product meet all our needs and wants.

CHOOSING WHICH BRANCH TO JOIN

> *"If you like to travel, we offer more than anyone else. The longest you're under way is generally two to three weeks, with three to four days off in every port and one day on the ship. Prior to pulling in, you can even set up tours."*
>
> Chief Petty Officer Keith Horst
> United States Navy

If you are seriously considering joining the military, you probably have checked out at least two of the branches. Check them all out, even if it means just requesting literature and reviewing it. A word of caution: Brochures do not tell the complete story, and it's very difficult to base your decision either for or against a military branch on the contents of a brochure alone. Would you buy a car based solely on the information contained in a brochure? Probably not!

The process of choosing the right branch of the military for you is basically the same process that you used to determine if joining the military was right for you. You should start with your list of primary motivators and use the "yes/no" method to determine whether each branch can meet all or some of those motivators. Once you've determined which branch or branches can best meet your motivators, it's time to compare those branches. Remember to look for the negative aspects as well as the motivators of each of the branches as you compare.

After making your comparisons, you may still find yourself with more than one choice. What do you do then? You could flip a coin, but that's not the wisest idea! Instead, look at some of the following factors.

> *"I tell people that you get paid the same in all the services, and the benefits are the same. What's different about each branch is the environment."*
>
> Infantry Sergeant Ian Bonnell
> United States Marines

Length of enlistment: Some branches may require a longer term for offering the same benefits that you could receive from another branch with a shorter term of enlistment.

Advanced pay grade: You may be entitled to an advanced rank in some branches based on certain enlistment options.

Length and type of training: How long will your training take? Usually the longer the training, the more in-depth and useful it is. You'll also want to consider how useful the training will be once you've left the military.

Enlistment bonuses: Be careful when using an enlistment bonus as the only factor in deciding which branch to choose. However, if it comes down to a tie between two branches and only one offers a bonus, it's not a bad reason to choose that branch.

Additional pay and allowances: You may be entitled to additional pay that only one particular branch can offer. For instance, if you join the Navy, you may be entitled to Sea Pay and Submarine Pay, something obviously not available if you join the Air Force.

Ability to pursue higher education: While all the military branches offer educational benefits, you must consider when you'll be able to take advantage of these benefits. If your job requires 12-hour shifts and has you out in the field a lot, when will you be able to attend classes?

Once you have considered these factors, and perhaps some of your own, you should be able to decide which branch is right for you. If you still haven't been able to select one branch over another, though, consider the following:

- Ask your recruiter if you can speak to someone who has recently joined.
- If you live near a base, you may be able to get a tour of its facilities.
- If you are well versed in Internet chat rooms, you may want to look for those that cater to military members—then ask a lot of questions.
- Talk to friends and family members who are currently serving in the military. Be careful, however, not to talk to people who have been out of the military for a while, as they probably aren't familiar with today's military. Also, avoid people who left the military under less-than-desirable conditions (for example, someone who was discharged from Basic Training for no compatibility).

If you choose to continue with processing for enlistment, your next step will probably be to take the Armed Services Vocational Aptitude Battery (ASVAB).

> *"In the Army, you can get training in everything from culinary arts to truck driving and all the way to aviation mechanics, military intelligence, and computer networking."*
>
> Staff Sergeant Max Burda
> United States Army

THE ASVAB

The ASVAB, a multiple-aptitude battery of tests designed for use with students in their junior or senior year in high school or in a postsecondary school, as well as those seeking military enlistment, was developed to yield results useful to both students and the military. The military uses the results to determine the qualifications of candidates for enlistment and to help place them in military occupational programs. Schools use ASVAB test results to assist their students in developing future educational and career plans.

Frequently Asked Questions about the ASVAB

What is the Armed Services Vocational Aptitude Battery (ASVAB)?

The ASVAB, sponsored by the Department of Defense, is a multi-aptitude test battery consisting of nine short individual tests covering Word Knowledge, Paragraph Comprehension, Arithmetic Reasoning, Mathematics Knowledge, General Science, Auto and Shop Information, Mechanical Comprehension, Electronics Information, and Assembling Objects. Your ASVAB results provide scores for each individual test, as well as three academic composite scores—Verbal, Math, and Academic Ability—and two career-exploration composite scores.

Why should I take the ASVAB?

As a high school student nearing graduation, you are faced with important career choices. Should you go on to college, technical, or vocational school? Would it be better to enter the job market? Should you consider a military career? Your ASVAB scores are measures of aptitude. Your composite scores measure your aptitude for higher academic learning and give you ideas for career exploration.

When and where is the ASVAB given?

ASVAB is administered annually or semiannually at more than 14,000 high schools and postsecondary schools in the United States.

> *"Everyone in the Navy learns how to fight a fire. You get qualified in First Aid and CPR. That's mandatory for every sailor. The only jobs we don't have in the Navy are veterinarians, forest rangers, and rodeo stars."*
>
> Chief Petty Officer Keith Horst
> United States Navy

I'M JOINING THE AIR FORCE

It didn't take Brian Filipek long to decide he wanted to join the Air Force. But that's if you don't count the times he talked to people who had served in the Air Force or the research he did on the Internet to gather information—and that was before he even set foot inside the recruiter's office. By the time an Air Force recruiter responded to a card Brian had sent in, he was pretty sure he liked what he'd seen so far. "The recruiter didn't have to do any work to convince me," says Brian. After that, it was a matter of going through the pre-qualifying process—whether he met the height and weight qualifications—and the security forms he had to fill out.

After he enlisted, Brian didn't stop gathering information. Long before he was sent to Basic Training, he found out about Warrior Week, which is held on one of the last weeks in Basic Training. He was already looking forward to it. "I'm an outdoors kind of person," he says. "I want to do the obstacle course and ropes course."

Though the idea of testing his endurance and strength appeals to him, being away from family will be hard. "Granted, your food is cooked for you, but you're still on your own," he says. However, he knows that it's worth it to achieve his goal of education and free job training. Brian acknowledges that the military is not for everyone, but as far as he's concerned, he's sure he's made the right choice.

Brian Filipek, Enlistee
United States Air Force

Is there a charge or fee to take the ASVAB?

ASVAB is administered at no cost to the school or to the student.

How long does it take to complete the ASVAB?

ASVAB testing takes approximately 3 hours. If you miss class, it will be with your school's approval.

If I wish to take the ASVAB but my school doesn't offer it (or I missed it), what should I do?

See your school counselor. In some cases, arrangements may be made for you to take it at another high school. Your counselor should call 800-323-0513 (toll-free) for additional information.

How do I find out what my scores mean and how to use them?

Your scores will be provided to you on a report called the ASVAB Student Results Sheet. Along with your scores, you should receive a copy of *Exploring Careers: The ASVAB Workbook*, which contains information that will help you understand your ASVAB results and shows you how to use them for career exploration. Test results are returned to participating schools within thirty days.

What is a passing score on the ASVAB?

No one "passes" or "fails" the ASVAB. The ASVAB enables you to compare your scores to those of other students at your grade level.

If I take the ASVAB, am I obligated to join the military?

No. Taking the ASVAB does not obligate you to the military in any way. You are free to use your test results in whatever manner you wish. You may use the ASVAB results for up to two years for military enlistment if you are a junior, senior, or postsecondary school student. The military services encourage all young people to finish high school before joining the armed forces.

If I am planning to go to college, should I take the ASVAB?

Yes. ASVAB results provide you with information that can help you determine your capacity for advanced academic education. You can also use your ASVAB results, along with other personal information, to identify areas for career exploration.

Should I take the ASVAB if I plan to become a commissioned officer?

Yes. Taking the ASVAB is a valuable experience for any student who aspires to become a military officer. The aptitude information you receive could assist you in career planning.

Should I take the ASVAB if I am considering entering the Reserve or National Guard?

Yes. These military organizations also use the ASVAB for enlistment purposes.

What should I do if a service recruiter contacts me?

You may be contacted by a service recruiter before you graduate. If you want to learn about the many opportunities available through military service, arrange for a follow-up meeting. However, you are under no obligation to the military as a result of taking the ASVAB.

Is the ASVAB administered other than in the school testing program?

Yes. ASVAB is also used in the regular military enlistment program. It is administered at approximately sixty-five Military Entrance Processing Stations located throughout the United States. Each year, hundreds of thousands of young men and women who are interested in enlisting in the uniformed services (Army, Navy, Air Force, Marines, and Coast Guard) but who did not take the ASVAB while in school are examined and processed at these military stations.

Is any special preparation necessary before taking the ASVAB?

Yes. A certain amount of preparation is required for taking any examination. Whether it is an athletic competition or a written test, preparation is a *must* to achieve the best results. Your test scores reflect not only your ability but also the time and effort in preparing for the test. The uniformed services use the ASVAB to help determine a person's qualification for enlistment and to help indicate the vocational areas for which the person is best suited. Achieving your maximum score will increase your vocational opportunities. So take practice tests to prepare.

> *"A lot of kids are worried about Marine boot camp. They've seen movies or heard stories. Boot camp is not set up to make you fail. It's challenging, but that's the purpose of it. You're learning that no matter what life throws at you, you will be able to improvise, adapt, and overcome."*
>
> Infantry Sergeant Ian Bonnell
> United States Marines

I SURVIVED BASIC TRAINING

Although Michael Hipszky was eager to join the Navy, it didn't take long for doubts about his decision to hit him. While he was riding the bus to the Navy's Basic Training facility, he asked himself THE QUESTION—"Why am I putting myself through this mess?" Recalls Michael, "It crosses everyone's mind. As far as I know, in my division, everyone had the same thought. 'I want to go home.' Those first few days are intense."

He figures it's because you lose control the minute you walk through the door on the first day of Basic Training. Someone's telling you (in a very loud voice) how to stand at attention, how to stand in line, how to do just about everything. "So many things go through your head," says Michael. He soon found that if he followed three rules, life got a whole lot easier:

1. Keep your mouth shut. "Your mouth is your biggest problem," he warns, "talking when you aren't supposed to and saying dumb things."
2. Pay attention to detail. "They'll say things like, 'Grab the door knob, turn it half to the right, and go through.' A lot of people will just pull it open and get yelled at. They teach you how to fold your clothes and clean the head (toilet). Everything is paying attention to detail," Michael advises.
3. Don't think for yourself. "Wait to be told what to do," Michael says, recalling the time his group was handed a form and told to wait until ordered to fill it out. Many saw that the form was asking for information like name, date, and division and began filling it out, only to get in trouble because they didn't wait.

Having been through Basic Training, Michael now knows that every little thing—from folding T-shirts the exact way he'd been told to do (arms folded in), to sweeping the floor, to marching—is all part of the training process. "You don't realize it until you're done," he says.

Despite all the yelling and push-ups, Michael values the training he got in the classes. He learned how to put out different kinds of fires, how to manage his money, how to identify aircraft—even etiquette. And that's just for starters.

His lowest point was about halfway through Basic, which, he found out, usually happens for everyone at the same time. "The first half of Basic, everything is so surreal. Then you get halfway through, and finishing up Basic seems so far away. You're always busy, whether you're stenciling your clothes or marching. You march a lot," he says. But then he reached his highest point, which was pass in review at the end of the training and winning awards. He knew he'd done well. Looking into his future with the Navy, Michael says, "I want to see the world and have the experiences that the Navy can give you." Having finished Basic Training, he's well on his way.

Airman Michael Hipszky
United States Navy

BASIC TRAINING: WHAT HAVE I GOTTEN MYSELF INTO?

The main objective of Basic Training is to transform civilians into well-disciplined military personnel in a matter of weeks. Performing such a monumental task takes a lot of hard work, both mentally and physically. For most people, Basic Training ends with a parade on graduation day. For others, though, it ends somewhere short of graduation. It is those "horror stories" that make Basic Training one of the biggest fears, or anxiety inducers, for those considering military enlistment.

Unlike the boot camp you may have heard about from your Uncle Louie or have seen on TV, today's Basic Training doesn't include the verbal and physical abuse of yesterday. All of the military branches are ensuring that new enlistees are treated fairly and with dignity. It's not that enlistees aren't yelled at (because they are); however, the vulgarity and demeaning verbal attacks are a thing of the past. From time to time, incidents involving instructors who contradict the military's policies do arise. These violations, however, receive a lot of attention, are thoroughly investigated, and usually end up with disciplinary action taken against those involved in the abuse.

If you are still uncertain of which branch you'd like to join, don't allow the type of Basic Training you'll receive to be your only deciding factor. If, for example, the Marine Corps meets all your needs and is clearly your first choice, don't select the Air Force because its Basic Training seems easier. Conversely, if the Air Force is clearly your first choice, do not select the Marine Corps because it has the "toughest" Basic Training, and you want to prove that you're up to the challenge. Basic Training is a means of transformation from civilian life to military life. It happens in a relatively short period of time compared with the entire length of your enlistment.

Getting Through Basic Training

No matter what you may have heard or read elsewhere, there are no secrets to getting through Basic Training; only common sense and preparation will get you through. The following are some dos and don'ts that should help you survive Basic Training for any of the services. Although following these guidelines will not ensure your success at Basic Training, your chances for success will be greatly improved by following them.

Before Arriving at Basic Training

DO:

- Start an exercise program.
- Maintain a sensible diet.
- Stay out of trouble. (For example, pay any traffic fines promptly before leaving for Basic Training.)
- Ensure that all of your financial obligations are in order.
- Bring all required items.
- Give up smoking.

DON'T:

- Skip preparing yourself physically because you think that Basic Training will whip you into shape.
- Abuse drugs and/or alcohol.
- Have a big send-off party and get drunk the night before you leave for Basic Training.
- Leave home with open tickets, summonses, or warrants.
- Get yourself into heavy debt (such as buying a new car).
- Bring any prohibited items.
- Have your hair cut in a radical manner. (This includes having your head shaved. Men will receive a "very close" haircut shortly after arriving at Basic Training.)
- Have any part of your body pierced, tattooed, or otherwise altered.

PAYING FOR COLLEGE THROUGH THE ARMED SERVICES

You can take any of the following three paths into the armed services—all of which provide opportunities for financial assistance for college.

Enlisted Personnel

All five branches of the armed services offer college-credit courses on base. Enlisted personnel can also take college courses at civilian colleges while on active duty.

ROTC

Thousands of college students participate in Reserve Officers' Training Corps (ROTC). Two-, three-, and four-year ROTC scholarships are available to outstanding students. You can try ROTC at no obligation for two years, or, if you have a four-year scholarship, for one year. Normally, all ROTC classes, uniforms, and books are free. ROTC graduates are required to serve in the military for a set period of time, either full-time on active duty or part-time in the Reserve or National Guard. Qualifying graduates can delay their service to go to graduate or professional school first.

> *"In the Air Force, you're not only getting an education but also experience. You could go to school for a degree in avionics technology, but in the Air Force, you get the teaching and the experience—real-world, hands-on experience—that makes your education marketable."*
>
> Master Sergeant Timothy Little
> United States Air Force

U.S. Service Academies

The United States has five service academies. Openings at the U.S. service academies are few, so it pays to get information as early as your freshman or sophomore year of high school. Every student is on a full scholarship, but free does not mean easy—these intense programs train graduates to meet the demands of leadership and success.

West Point

The U.S. Military Academy (Army) is located in West Point, New York, and offers a broad-based academic program with forty-two majors in various fields of study. The admission process for West Point is almost as rigorous as its academic program. Applicants are evaluated on their academic performance in high school, SAT or ACT scores, demonstrated leadership potential, physical aptitude, and medical qualifications. In addition, as part of the application process, those seeking admission to the U.S. Military Academy must receive a congressional nomination for entry or a service-connected nomination. Service-connected nominations can come from military personnel who have served continuously on active duty for at least eight years. After graduating from the academy, officers must serve five years of active duty and three years in a Reserve Component, for a total of eight years of service. At the U.S. Military Academy, extensive training and leadership experience go hand in hand with academics. *www.usma.edu*

Annapolis

The U.S. Naval Academy (Navy and Marines) is a unique blend of tradition and state-of-the-art technology. Located in Annapolis, Maryland, the Naval Academy emphasizes math, science, and engineering but offers a full academic curriculum of study. Classroom work is supported by practical experience in leadership and professional operations. Annapolis has special learning facilities to support its programs; among these are a learning resource center, a planetarium, wind tunnels, a radio station, a propulsion lab, a nuclear reactor, an oceanographic research vessel, towing tanks, and a flight simulator. Annapolis follows the same rigorous admission process that West Point follows and, in addition to completing a preliminary application, all applicants must include a congressional or service-connected nomination, complete a physical fitness assessment, and undergo a medical examination. If admitted, you'll become a "midshipman" at the Naval Academy. *www.usna.edu*

Air Force Academy

The U.S. Air Force Academy, located north of Colorado Springs, Colorado, prepares and motivates cadets for careers as Air Force officers. All cadets complete a core academic curriculum, which includes classes in the humanities, social sciences, engineering, basic sciences, and physical education. Cadets then specialize in one of thirty-one majors offered by the Academy. Admission into the Air Force Academy mirrors the requirements of other U.S. service academies and should be started as early as your junior year in high school. *www.usafa.af.mil*

Coast Guard Academy

The U.S. Coast Guard Academy is located in New London, Connecticut, and is the smallest of the five U.S. service academies. The Coast Guard Academy offers a four-year bachelor of science degree program and offers thirteen programs of study. This broad-based education includes a thorough grounding in the professional skills necessary for the Coast Guard's work. Admission into the Coast Guard Academy is similar to that of other U.S. service academies, but a congressional nomination is not required. Admittance is based solely on personal merit. *www.cga.edu*

Merchant Marine Academy

The U.S. Merchant Marine Academy is located in Kings Point, New York, and offers classes in marine transportation, marine engineering, maritime operations and technology, and logistics and intermodal transportation, to name just a few. The academic year runs eleven months, from July to June, and is divided into trimesters, or three academic terms of thirteen weeks each. The admission process for the U.S. Merchant Marine Academy is similar to that of the other service academies; you will need to submit an application, an essay, high school transcripts, SAT or ACT scores, three letters of recommendation, and a congressional letter of nomination. A medical exam and candidate fitness assessment are also required. In addition, during the application process, a candidate must list a tentative major, which does not have to be affirmed until the second trimester. *www.usmma.edu*

WHAT'S MY JOB?—OH, I JUST DRIVE AN ARMORED CARRIER AROUND

Justin Platt thought maybe he would join the Army, but first he had a few doubts to overcome. A big one was his reluctance to be away from friends and family. Another one was the overseas duty—something he definitely didn't want. But his desire to get his foot in the door of medical training won out. When he found out that he could get an education in the Army to become a nurse, his fears flew out the window, and Justin joined the Army. He's glad he did.

Stationed at Fort Carson in Colorado, Justin's been through Basic Training and is on his first stint of active duty working in—you guessed it—the medical field. "I work in an aid station, which is like a mini hospital," he says. He's the one who does the screening for anyone in his battalion who comes into sick call. Okay, it's from 5 a.m. to 7 p.m., but Justin doesn't mind.

Justin's job on active duty doesn't just consist of handing out Band-Aids and cough drops. He's also learning how to drive an armored carrier—not your usual medical training. But in the field, Army medics have to be able to pick up the wounded, which means knowing how to drive what he describes as a souped-up SUV—only instead of tires, it has tracks.

Justin plans to get enough rank to go from green to gold—enlisted to officer. "I'll have to take additional college courses to get a four-year degree," he says. It'll take him about seven years, including his Army duty. Not bad for someone who once had doubts about joining the military.

Financing Higher Education During and After Service in the Armed Forces

The U.S. military provides a number of options to help students get financial aid for postsecondary education.

The Active Duty Montgomery GI Bill

The Active Duty Montgomery GI Bill, called ADMGIB for short, provides up to thirty-six months of education benefits to eligible veterans for college, business, technical or vocational courses, correspondence courses, apprenticeship/job training, and flight training. You may be an eligible veteran if you get an Honorable Discharge; you have a high school diploma or GED, or, in some cases, 12 hours of college credit; AND you meet the necessary requirements related to military service. You MUST have elected to participate in the ADMGIB, which involves giving up $100 of your pay per month for the first twelve months of military service. The monthly benefit paid to you is based on the type of training you take, length of your service, your category, and if the Department of Defense put extra money in your College Fund (called "kicker"). You usually have ten years to use your MGIB benefits, but the time limit can vary.

The Selected Reserve Montgomery GI Bill

The Selected Reserve Montgomery GI Bill (SRMGIB) may be available to you if you are a member of the Selected Reserve. The Selected Reserve includes the Army Reserve, Navy Reserve, Air Force Reserve, Marine Corps Reserve, and Coast Guard Reserve, and the Army National Guard and the Air National Guard. You may use this education assistance program for degree programs, certificate or correspondence courses, cooperative training, independent study programs, apprenticeship/on-the-job training, and vocational flight training programs. Remedial, refresher, and deficiency training are available under certain circumstances. Eligibility for this program is determined by the Selected Reserve components. The U.S. Department of

Veterans Affairs (VA) makes the payments for this program. You may be entitled to receive up to thirty-six months of education benefits. Your eligibility typically ends on the day you leave the Selected Reserve.

Call 888-GI-BILL-1 (toll-free) for more information, or visit the Web site at http://www.gibill.va.gov/post-911/montgomery-gi-bill/selected-reserve.html.

Tuition Assistance

All branches of the military pay up to 75 percent of tuition for full-time, active-duty enlistees who take courses at community colleges or by distance learning during their tours of duty. Details vary by service.

The Community College of the Air Force

Enlisted Air Force personnel can convert their technical training and military experience into academic credit, earning an associate degree, an occupational instructor's certificate, or a trade school certificate. Participants receive an official transcript from this fully accredited program. You can visit the Community College of the Air Force online at www.au.af.mil/au/ccaf.

Educational Loan-Repayment Program

The Armed Services can help repay government-insured and other approved loans. Each of the services is free to offer such programs, but individual policies differ.

Other Forms of Tuition Assistance

Each branch of the military offers its own education incentives. To find out more, check with a local recruiting office.

SAMPLE CONGRESSIONAL NOMINATION REQUEST LETTER

Name
Street Address
City, State, ZIP Code
Date

The Honorable __________ OR The Honorable __________
United States Senate House of Representatives
Washington, DC 20510-0001 Washington, DC 20515-0001
Dear Senator __________: Dear Representative __________:

OR

Vice President __________
The Old Executive Office Building, Room 490
Washington, DC 20501
Dear Vice President __________:

I desire to attend the (name of military academy) and to be commissioned in the (name of military branch). I respectfully request that I be considered as one of your nominees for the class entering (name of military academy) in (month, year).

The following data are furnished for your information:

Full Name of Applicant: ______________________________
Names of Parents: ______________________________
Permanent Address: ______________________________
Telephone Number: ______________________________
Temporary Address and Telephone Number (if different from preceding): ______________________________
____
Date of Birth: ______________________________
Place of Birth: ______________________________
Social Security Number: ______________________________
Sex: __________
High School (name and location): ______________________________
Date of Graduation: ______________
Class Standing: __________ in a class of __________ students

I have/have not requested a pre-candidate file from the (name of military academy).

I have requested that my high school transcript of work completed to date be sent to your office as soon as possible.

On the next page, please find my ACT/SAT scores and information about my involvement in extracurricular activities.

I would greatly appreciate your consideration of my request for one of your nominations.

Sincerely,

(Your signature)

(Type your name below signature)

PART 4
YOU AND THE WORKPLACE

Some of you will go to college first and then look for jobs. Some of you might work for a few years and then go to college. And many of you will go immediately into the workforce and bypass college altogether. Whenever you become an employee, you'll want to know what you can do to succeed on the job and move to both higher levels of responsibility and more pay.

CHAPTER 12

JUMP INTO WORK

Almost everyone ends up in the workforce at some point. No matter when you plan to receive that first full-time paycheck, you'll need to do a few things to prepare yourself for the world of work.

At each grade level, you should take specific steps regardless of whether you plan to attend college immediately following high school. In fact, college and career time lines should coincide, according to guidance counselors and career specialists, and students should take college-preparatory courses, even if they aren't planning on attending college.

THE CAREER/COLLEGE TIME LINE

The following time line will help you meet college requirements and prepare you for work. In an effort to make sure that you are adequately preparing for both school and work, incorporate these five steps into your career/college time line:

1. **Take an aptitude test.** You can do this as early as the sixth grade, but even if you don't do this until high school, it's not too late. By doing so, you'll begin to get a feel for what areas you might be good at and enjoy. Your guidance counselor should have a test in his or her office for you to take, or you can try the Armed Services Vocational Aptitude Battery (ASVAB) (see Chapter 11). Thousands of high school students take this test every year to discover possible career paths—and taking the ASVAB doesn't require you to join the military.

2. **Beginning in middle school, you should start considering what your options are after high school.** However, if you're only starting to think about this in high school, that's okay, too. Keep a notebook of information gathered from field trips, job-shadowing experiences, mentoring programs, and career fairs to help you make sense of the possibilities open to you. This process should continue through high school. Many schools offer job shadowing and internship programs for students to explore different vocational avenues. Take advantage of these opportunities if you can. Too often, students don't explore the workplace until after they've taken the courses necessary to enter a particular profession, only to discover it wasn't the career they dreamed of after all.

3. **No later than the tenth grade, visit a vocational center to look at the training programs offered.** Some public school systems send students to vocational and career program centers for career exploration.

4. **During your junior and senior years, be sure to create a portfolio of practice resumes, writing samples, and a list of work skills.** This portfolio should also include your high school transcript and letters of recommendation. It will serve as a valuable reference tool when it comes time to apply for jobs.

5. **By tenth or eleventh grade, you should begin focusing on a specific career path.** More employers today are looking for employees who have both the education and work experience that relates to the career field for which they're interviewing. If you are looking for part-time employment, you should consider jobs that pertain to your field of study. Until you start interacting with people in the field, you won't have a realistic feel of what's involved in that profession. If you're planning on heading into the workplace right after high school, take a look at the following pages for a list of careers that don't require a four-year degree.

TAKING A BREAK BETWEEN HIGH SCHOOL AND COLLEGE

Because of the soaring costs of college tuition today, college is no longer a place to "find yourself." It is a costly investment in your future. The career you choose to pursue may or may not require additional education; your research will determine whether or not it's required or preferred. If you decide not to attend college immediately after high school, however, don't consider it to be a closed door. Taking some time off between high school and college is considered perfectly acceptable by employers. Many students simply need a break after thirteen years of schooling. Many experts agree that it's better to be ready and prepared for college; many adults get more out of their classes after they've had a few years to mature.

Source: Street Smart Career Guide: A Step-by-Step Program for Your Career Development

WRITING YOUR RESUME

Resumes are a critical part of getting a job. A resume is an introduction of your skills to a potential employer. For that reason, your resume must stand out in a crowd because some employers receive dozens of resumes each week. A resume that is too long, cluttered, or disorganized may find its way to the "circular file," also known as the trash can. You can avoid this hazard by creating a resume that is short, presentable, and easy to read.

Remember that a resume is a summary of who you are, with an outline of your experiences, skills, and goals. While writing it, you may discover some talents that you weren't aware you had, and that will help boost your confidence for the job search.

Begin by collecting facts about yourself, including where you went to high school, your past and present jobs, activities, interests, and leadership roles. Next to the individual activities, write down what responsibilities you had. For example, something as simple as babysitting requires the ability to settle disagreements and supervise others.

Next, decide on how you would like to format your resume. Most hiring managers expect to see one of two types of resumes: chronological or functional. The chronological resume is the most traditional, supplying the reader with a sequential listing (from present to past) of your accomplishments. Because the emphasis here is on past employment experience, high school and college students with little or no employment history might want to avoid this resume type. A functional resume, on the other hand, highlights a person's abilities rather than his or her work history. Entry-level candidates who want to focus on skills rather than credentials should consider using a functional resume.

Parts of a Resume

At the very least, your resume should include the following components:

Heading—Centered at the top of the page should be your name, address, home phone number, cell number, and e-mail address.

Objective—In one sentence, tell the employer the type of work for which you are looking.

Education—Beginning with your most recent school or program, include the date (or expected date) of completion, the degree or certificate earned, and the address of the institution. Don't overlook any workshops or seminars, self-study, or on-the-job training in which you have been involved. If any courses particularly lend themselves to the type of work for which you are applying, include them. Mention grade point averages and class rank when they are especially impressive.

SAMPLE FUNCTIONAL RESUME

Jane A. Smith
1234 Main Street
Atlanta, Georgie 30308
404-555-6789
E-mail: jane.a.smith_123@email.com

OBJECTIVE:
Seeking a sales position in the wireless phone industry

EDUCATION:
High School Diploma, June 2011
John F. Kennedy High School, Atlanta, Georgia

SKILLS:
Computer literate on both PC and MAC; MS Word, Excel, PowerPoint

ACTIVITIES:
Varsity Swim Club (Captain; MVP Junior, Senior; Sportsmanship Award)
Outstanding Community Service Award, 2010

EXPERIENCE:
Sales Clerk, The Limited, Atlanta, Georgia; part-time, October 2009 to present
Cashier, Winn-Dixie Supermarkets, Atlanta, Georgia, Summers 2008 and 2009

INTERESTS:
Swimming, reading, computers

REFERENCES:
Available upon request

Skills and abilities—Until you've actually listed these on paper, you can easily overlook many of them. They may be as varied as the ability to work with computers or being captain of the girls' basketball team.

Work experience—If you don't have any, skip this section. If you do, begin with your most recent employer and include the date you left the job, your job title, the company name, and the company address. If you are still employed there, simply enter your start date and "to present" for the date. Include notable accomplishments for each job. High school and college students with little work experience shouldn't be shy about including summer, part-time, and volunteer jobs, such as lifeguarding, babysitting, delivering pizzas, or volunteering at local parks.

Personal—This section is your opportunity to include special talents and interests as well as notable accomplishments or experiences.

References—Most experts agree that it's best to simply state that references are available upon request. If you do decide to list names, addresses, and phone numbers, however, limit yourself to no more than three. Make sure you inform any people whom you have listed that they may be contacted.

Resume-Writing Tips

These tips will help as you begin constructing your resume:

- Keep the resume short and simple. Although senior executives may use as many as two or three pages, recent graduates should limit themselves to one page.
- Capitalize headings.
- Keep sentences short; avoid writing in paragraphs.
- Use language that is simple, not flowery or complex.
- Be specific, and offer examples when appropriate.
- Emphasize achievements.
- Be honest.
- Don't include information about salary or wages unless specifically requested.
- For snail mail, use high-quality, white, beige, or gray, 8 ½″ × 11″ paper.
- Make good use of white space by leaving adequate side and top margins on the paper.

- Make what you write presentable and use good business style.
- Because your resume should be a reflection of your personality, write it yourself.
- Avoid gimmicks such as colored paper, photos, or clip art.
- Make good use of bullets or asterisks, underlining, and bold print.
- Proofread your work, and have someone you trust proofread it also.
- Be neat and accurate.
- Never send a resume without a cover letter.

The Cover Letter

Every resume should be accompanied by a cover letter. This is often the most crucial part of your job search because the letter will be the first thing that a potential employer reads. When you include a cover letter, you're showing the employer that you care enough to take the time to address him or her personally and that you are genuinely interested in the job.

Always call the company and verify the name and title of the person to whom you are addressing the letter. Although you'll want to keep your letter brief, introduce yourself and begin with a statement that will catch the reader's attention. Indicate the position you are

SAMPLE COVER LETTER

Take a look at how this student's cover letter applied the facts outlined in her resume to the job to which she's applying. You can use this letter to help you get started on your own cover letters. Text that appears in all caps below indicates the kind of information you need to include in that section. Before you send your letter, proofread it for mistakes, and ask a parent or friend you trust to look it over as well.

(DATE)
June 29, 2011

(YOUR ADDRESS)
1234 Main Street
Atlanta, Georgia 30308
Phone: 404-555-6789
E-mail: jane.a.smith@email.com

(PERSON—BY NAME—TO WHOM YOU'RE SENDING THE LETTER)
Mr. Charles E. Jones
Manager, Human Resources
Cell Wireless, Inc.
20201 East Sixth Street
Atlanta, Georgia 30372

Dear Mr. Jones:

(HOW YOU HEARD OF THE POSITION)
Your job announcement in the *Atlanta Gazette* for an entry-level sales position asked for someone who has both computer and sales skills. (SOMETHING EXTRA THAT WILL INTEREST THE READER) My training and past job experience fit both of those categories. I also bring an enthusiasm and desire to begin my career in a communications firm such as Cell Wireless, Inc.

(WHAT PRACTICAL SKILLS YOU CAN BRING TO THE POSITION)
I recently graduated from John F. Kennedy High School here in Atlanta. While in school, I concentrated on gaining computer skills on both IBM and Macintosh machines and participated in organizations such as the Key Club, in which I was vice president, and the Future Business Leaders of America.

(RELATE PAST EXPERIENCE TO DESIRED JOB)
As you will see from my resume, I worked as a cashier at Winn-Dixie Supermarket for two summers and am currently employed as a sales clerk at The Limited. From these two positions, I have gained valuable customer service skills and an attention to detail, qualities which I am sure are of utmost importance to you as you make your hiring decision.

I would very much like to interview for the position and am available at your convenience. I look forward to hearing from you soon.

Sincerely,

Jane A. Smith

applying for and mention if someone referred you or if you are simply responding to an ad. Draw attention to yourself by including something that will arouse the employer's curiosity about your experience and accomplishments. A cover letter should request something, most commonly an interview. Follow up with a phone call a few days after you're sure the letter has been received. Persistence pays!

JOB HUNTING 101

High school is a time for taking classes and learning, developing relationships with others, becoming involved in extracurricular activities that teach valuable life skills, and generally preparing for college or a job. Regardless of where you're headed after high school, you need to learn how to create a favorable impression. That can mean setting some clear, attainable goals for yourself, putting them down on paper in the form of a resume and cover letter, and convincing interviewers that you are, indeed, the person for whom they are looking. In short, learn how to sell yourself. A brief course in Job Hunting 101 will help you do just that.

Marketing Yourself

You can use several approaches to market yourself successfully. Networking, the continuous process of contacting friends and relatives, is a great way to get information about job openings. Seventy-five percent of the job openings in this country are not advertised but are filled by friends, relatives, and acquaintances of current employees. From the employer's perspective, hiring someone recommended by an employee is less risky than hiring someone unknown. Networking is powerful. Everyone has a primary network of people they know and talk to frequently. Those acquaintances know and talk to networks of their own, thereby creating a secondary network for you and multiplying the number of individuals who know what you're looking for in a job.

Broadcasting is another marketing method in which you gather a list of companies that interest you and then mail them letters asking for job interviews. Although the rate of return on your mailings is small, two thirds of all job hunters use this approach, and half of those who use it find a job. You'll increase your response rate by addressing your letter to a particular person—the one who has the power to hire you—and by following up with a phone call a few days after the letter has been received. To obtain the manager's name, simply call the company and ask the receptionist for the person's name, job title, and correct spelling. Good resources for finding potential employers include referrals, community agencies, job fairs, newspaper ads, trade directories, trade journals, state indexes, the local chamber of commerce, the Yellow Pages, and the Internet. The following tips can help as you begin hunting for the perfect job:

- Job hunting is time-intensive. Do your homework and take it seriously by using every opportunity available to you.
- Prepare yourself for the fact that you'll likely receive far more rejections than acceptances.
- Consider taking a temporary job while you continue the job hunt. It will help pay the bills and give you new skills to boost your resume at the same time.
- Research the activities of potential employers and show that you have studied them when you're being interviewed.
- Keep careful records of all contacts and follow-up activities.
- Don't ignore any job leads—act on every tip you get.
- Stay positive.

With all these thoughts in mind, you should be ready to begin the process of making people believe in you, and that's a major part of being successful in your job hunt.

THE JOB INTERVIEW

You can prevent some of the pre-interview jitters by adequately preparing. Remember that you have nothing to lose and that you, too, are doing the choosing. Just as you are waiting and hoping to be offered a job, you have the option of choosing whether to accept an offer. It's all right to feel somewhat anxious, but keep everything in perspective. This is an adventure, and you are in control. Most important, remember to be yourself. With all of this in mind, consider some of the following points of the interview process:

- Speak up during the interview, and furnish the interviewer with the information he or she needs to make an informed decision. It is especially impressive if you can remember the names of people to whom you've been introduced. People like to be called by name, and it shows that you took the initiative to remember them.
- Always arrive a few minutes early for the interview, and look your best. The way you act and dress tells the interviewer plenty about your attitude and personality. Sloppy dress, chewing gum, and cigarettes have no place at an interview. Instead, dress professionally and appropriately for the job. Avoid heavy makeup, short skirts, jeans, and untidy or flashy clothing of any kind.

The best way to prepare for the interview is to practice. Have a friend or relative play the role of the interviewer, and go over some of the most commonly asked questions. Learn as much as you can about the company you're interviewing with—it pays to do your homework. When you show a potential employer that you've taken the time and initiative to learn about his or her company, you're showing that you'll be a motivated and hardworking employee. Employers fear laziness and minimal effort, looking instead for workers who don't always have to be told what to do and when to do it.

The following is a list of interview questions you can expect to have to answer:

- **Tell me a little bit about yourself.** This is your chance to pitch your qualifications for the job in 2 minutes. Provide a few details about your education, previous jobs you've held, and extracurricular activities that relate to the position for which you're interviewing.
- **Are you at your best when working alone or in a group?** The safest answer is "Both." Most companies today cluster their employees into work groups, so you'll need strong interpersonal skills. On occasion, however, you may be required to work on projects alone.
- **What did you like the most about your last job? What did you dislike the most about it?** You should always accentuate the positives in an interview, so focus primarily on what you liked. Also be honest about what you disliked, but then explain how facing the negatives helped you grow as an employee.
- **What are your career goals?** Be sure you've done some research on the company and industry before your interview. When this question comes up, talk realistically about how far you believe your skills and talents will take you and what actions you plan to take to ensure this happens, such as pursuing more education.

Take the time to prepare some answers to these commonly asked questions. For instance, if you haven't set at least one career goal for yourself, do it now. Be ready to describe it to the interviewer. Likewise, you should be able to talk about your last job, including what you liked the most and the least. Adapt your answers so they apply to the job for which you are now interviewing. Other questions that might be asked include the following:

- What qualifications do you have?
- Why do you want to work for us?

- Do you enjoy school? Why or why not?
- Do you plan to continue your education?
- What do you plan to be doing five years from now?
- What motivates you to do a good job?

If you are seeking a job as a manager, you might respond by saying you liked the varied responsibilities of your past job. Recall that you enjoyed the unexpected challenges and flexible schedule. And when describing what you liked least, make sure you respond with some function or area of responsibility that has nothing to do with the responsibilities of the job you hope to get.

More than likely, you'll be asked to tell the interviewer something about yourself. This is your chance to "toot your horn," but don't ramble. You might ask the interviewer specifically what he or she would like to hear about: your educational background or recent experiences and responsibilities in your present or last job. After he or she chooses, stick to the basics; the next move belongs to the interviewer.

When asked about personal strengths and weaknesses, given that the question is two parts, begin with a weakness so you can end on a strong note with your strengths. Again, try to connect your description of a strength or weakness with the requirements for the job. Naturally, it wouldn't be wise to reveal a serious weakness about yourself, but you can mention how you have changed your shortcomings. You might say, "I like to get my work done fast, but I consciously try to slow down a little to make sure I'm careful and accurate." When it comes to strengths, don't exaggerate, but don't sell yourself short either.

FINDING JOBS ON THE WEB

As mentioned, you can find jobs through your network of friends, family, and acquaintances; through classified ads in the newspaper; and through career Web pages. The following are some popular Web sites that not only offer job search technology but also information on resume writing, interviewing, and other important career advice.

www.monster.com
www.careerbuilder.com
www.simplyhired.com
www.vault.com
www.idealist.org
www.indeed.com

Asking Questions

You can ask questions, too. In fact, the interviewer expects you to ask questions to determine if the job is right for you, just as he or she will be trying to find out if you'll be successful working for his or her company. When you ask questions, it shows that you're interested and want to learn more. When the type of question you ask indicates that you've done your homework regarding the job and the company, your interviewer will be impressed. Avoid asking questions about salary or fringe benefits, anything adversarial, or questions that show you have a negative opinion of the company. It's all right to list your questions on a piece of paper; it's the quality of the question that's important, not whether you can remember it. The following are a few sample questions that you should consider asking if the topics don't come up in your interview:

- What kind of responsibilities come with this job?
- How is the department organized?
- What will be the first project for the new hire to tackle?
- What is a typical career advancement path for a person in this position?
- Who will be the supervisor for this position, and can I meet him or her?

- What is the office environment like? Is it casual or corporate?
- When do you expect to reach a hiring decision?

Following Up

After the interview, follow up with a thank-you note to the interviewer. Not only is it a thoughtful gesture, it triggers the interviewer's memory about you and shows that you have a genuine interest in the job. Your thank-you note should be written in a business-letter format and should highlight the key points in your interview. During the interview process, remember that you won't appeal to everyone who interviews you. If your first experience doesn't work out, don't get discouraged. Keep trying.

WHAT EMPLOYERS EXPECT FROM EMPLOYEES

As part of the National City Bank personnel team in Columbus, Ohio, Rose Graham works with Cooperative Business Education (CBE) coordinators in the area who are trying to place high school students in the workplace. When asked what skills she looks for in potential employees, she quickly replies that basic communication skills are at the top of her list. She stresses, "The ability to construct a sentence and put together words cannot be overemphasized." She cites knowledge of the personal computer, with good keyboarding skills, as essential.

In an article published in the *Nashville Business Journal*, Donna Cobble of Staffing Solutions outlined these basic skills for everyday life in the workplace:

Communication—Being a good communicator means not only having the ability to express oneself properly in the English language, but also being a good listener. If you feel inferior in any of these areas, it's a good idea to sign up for a public speaking class, read books on the subject, and borrow techniques from professional speakers.

Organization—Organization is the key to success in any occupation or facet of life. The ability to plan, prioritize, and complete a task in a timely fashion is a valuable skill. Check out Chapter 13 for tips on improving your time-management skills.

Problem solving—Companies are looking for creative problem solvers—people who aren't afraid to act on a situation and follow through with their decision. Experience and practice play a major role in your ability to determine the best solution. You can learn these techniques by talking with others about how they solve problems as well as observing others in the problem-solving process.

Sensitivity—In addition to being kind and courteous to their fellow workers, employees need to be sensitive to a coworker's perspective. That might mean putting yourself in the other person's shoes to gain a better understanding of that person's feelings. Employers look for individuals who are able to work on a team instead of those concerned only with their own personal gain.

Good judgment—Although closely related to problem solving, good judgment shows up on many different levels in the workplace. It is the ability to assess a situation, weigh the options, consider the risks, and make the necessary decision. Good judgment is built on experience and self-confidence.

Concentration—Concentration is the ability to focus on one thing at a time. Learning to tune out distractions and relate solely to the task at hand is a valuable asset for anyone.

Cooperation—Remember that you're being paid to do a job, so cooperate.

Honesty—Dishonesty shows up in many different ways, ranging from stealing time or property to divulging company secrets. Stay honest.

Initiative—Don't wait to be told exactly what to do. Show some initiative and look around to see what needs to be done next.

SAMPLE THANK-YOU LETTER

After you've interviewed for a job, it's important to reiterate your interest in the position by sending a thank-you letter to those who interviewed you. Take a look at Michele's letter to the manager she interviewed with at NexAir. You can use this letter as a model when the time comes for you to write some thank-you letters.

July 17, 2011

Jane A. Smith
1234 Main Street
Atlanta, Georgia 30308
Phone: 404-555-6789
E-mail: jane.a.smith@email.com

Mr. Charles E. Jones
Manager, Human Resources
Cell Wireless, Inc.
20201 East Sixth Street
Atlanta, Georgia 30372

Dear Mr. Jones:

It was a pleasure meeting with you Monday to discuss the sales opportunity at the downtown location of Cell Wireless, Inc. After learning more about the position, it is clear to me that with my background and enthusiasm, I would be an asset to your organization.

As we discussed, my experiences as a cashier at Winn-Dixie Supermarket and as a sales clerk at The Limited have provided me with the basic skills necessary to perform the responsibilities required of a sales representative at Cell Wireless, Inc. I believe that with my ability to learn quickly and communicate effectively, I can help Cell Wireless increase sales of its wireless products.

Thank you for the opportunity to interview with your organization. If there is any additional information I can provide about myself, please do not hesitate to call me. I look forward to hearing your decision soon.

Sincerely,

Jane A. Smith

Willingness to learn—Be willing to learn how things are done at the company instead of doing things the way you want to do them.

Dependability—Arrive at work on time every day and meet your deadlines.

Enthusiasm—Although not every task you're assigned will be stimulating, show enthusiasm for your work at all times.

Acceptance of criticism—Constructive criticism is necessary for any employee to learn how things should be done. Employees who view criticism as a way to improve themselves will benefit from it.

Loyalty—The workplace has no room for negativity. You simply won't be happy working for an employer to whom you're not loyal.

Never fail to show pride in your work, the place where you work, and your appearance. By making these traits a part of your personality and daily performance, you'll demonstrate that you are a cut above other employees with equal or better qualifications.

JUMPING ON THE SALARY FAST TRACK

So the job offer comes, and it's time to talk about money. Unless you are an undiscovered genius, you most likely will start near the bottom of the salary scale if you're heading straight to the workplace after graduating from high school. There's not much room to negotiate a salary since you probably won't be able to say, "Well, I've done this, this, and this. I know what my experience is worth." You'll find that most people hiring first-time employees will have a "take-it-or-leave-it" attitude about salary offers. However, according to Amryl Ward, a human resources consultant who has been hiring employees for more than twenty-five years in various human resource positions, entry-level employees can do a few things to make themselves more easily hired and, once hired, to get themselves on the fast track toward higher pay:

- As you interview for the job, be prepared to tell a potential employer why you're worth hiring. "Bring your skills to the table," says Ward. For instance, you might not think that the job you had during the summer at that big office supply store did anything more than earn you spending money. On the contrary, you learned valuable skills, such as how to be part of a team and how to deal with customers. What about that after-school office job you had? You learned how to answer the phones and how to work with certain software. Think carefully about the jobs you had in high school and what you learned from them. Those are called transferable skills.
- Once you're hired, be willing to do more than just what the job requires. Sure, you may be frying fries at the start. But if you come in early and stay late, if you pitch in to help another employee with his or her job, or if you voluntarily clean up the counters and sweep the floor, that says to management, "This employee is a winner. Let's keep him or her in mind the next time a promotion comes up." Soon, you might be managing a crew and then the store.

ON THE JOB

Once you snag that perfect job, you'll have no time to rest easy. You need to keep your manager happy and instill trust in your coworkers. And at the same time you're doing this, you'll want to watch out for yourself, keep yourself happy, and stay ahead of the learning curve. The following are some ways for you to do just that.

Minding Your Office Etiquette

Okay, so maybe you didn't know which fork to use to eat the salad at your cousin's wedding reception. Most likely, though, you can name a few basic rules of etiquette, like not chewing with your mouth open at the dinner table. Now, what about the manners you're supposed to have in the workplace? That usually draws a blank if you've never worked in an office setting. How would you know what's the right way to answer the phone or talk to your boss or customers?

Those who succeed in the workplace do so because they know how to present themselves in a professional situation. Those who don't succeed have no clue how to act in a professional environment. They don't realize that when they're working in an office with a group of people, they have to go out of their way to get along and follow the unwritten rules of that workplace. When you first enter a new work environment, you'll have to size up how others dress and try to match the tone of the office. For instance, if you work in a business office, most likely you'd wear slacks and a button-down shirt or a nice skirt and top. If you work in a golf pro shop, you'd wear a golf shirt and shorts. It's fine to want to be an individual, but you have to fit in when you're in a business setting.

A lot of young people don't grasp how important office etiquette is and blow it off as just some silly rules imposed by adults. Refusing to follow the norms of office etiquette, however, can make or break a job. You can have all the technical talent and know all the latest software applications, but if you're not up on how to properly dress, talk, and conduct business, your job probably won't last very long. When it comes to getting a job, first impressions are important, and engaging in bad office etiquette can ruin the impression you make. The best advice that we can offer is that if you're not sure what the policy is about answering phones, using e-mail or the Internet on the job, or dressing appropriately, ask your boss. He or she won't steer you wrong and will be pleased that you were concerned enough to ask.

Finding a Friendly Face at Work

There you are on the first day of a new job. Everyone looks like they know what they're doing while you stand there feeling really dumb. Even for the most seasoned employee, those first few weeks on the job are tough. Of course, everyone else looks like they know what they're doing because they've been doing it for quite some time. Wouldn't it be nice, though, if you had someone to help you adjust? Someone who would give you those inside tips that everyone else learns with experience. Someone to caution you about things that could go wrong or give you a heads-up when you're doing something that could lead to a reprimand. If you look around the office, you'll find such a person, says Robert Fait, Career Counselor and Curriculum Specialist, who is associated with Career and Technical Education in the Katy Independent School District in Katy, Texas. You might not realize that such a person is a mentor, but in the strict definition of the word, that's what he or she is. Or, as Fait puts it, "Mentors are role models who are willing to assist others with personal education and career goal setting and planning. This caring person shares a listening ear, a comforting shoulder, and an understanding heart." In other words, a mentor is someone who will make you feel comfortable in a new working environment, show you the procedures, and, in the end, help you become more productive.

Unless the company you're working for has a formal mentoring program, mentors don't come with huge signs around their necks that read "Look here. I'm a mentor. Ask me anything." You have to look for them. Fait advises new employees to look closely at their coworkers and take notice of who demonstrates positive behavior, has strong work habits, and seems trustworthy. Those are the people to approach. "Such workers are usually willing to share their knowledge and insights with others," says Fait.

Who knows? You could become a mentor yourself after you've been on the job for a while. Maybe you'll be able to help some new employee who looks kind of bewildered and in need of a friendly hand because you'll remember what it was like to be that new person.

CAREERS WITHOUT A FOUR-YEAR DEGREE

Some students spend a few years in the workplace before going to college. Others begin their career with a high school diploma, a vocational certificate, or up to two years of education or training after high school.

With that in mind, sometimes it's easier to know what you don't want rather than what you do want. Take a look at the list below, and check off the careers that interest you. Perhaps you've thought of something you'd like to do that isn't on this list. Well, don't dump your hopes. There are many different levels of training and education that can lead you to the career of your dreams. Since this list is not all-inclusive, you should check with your high school counselor or go online to research the training you'll need for the job or career you want—without a four-year degree. Then talk to your guidance counselor, teacher, librarian, or career counselor for more information about the careers on the following list or those you've researched on your own.

AGRICULTURE AND NATURAL RESOURCES

High school/vocational diploma

- ❑ Fisher
- ❑ Groundskeeper
- ❑ Logger
- ❑ Pest Controller

Up to two years beyond high school

- ❑ Fish and Game Warden
- ❑ Tree Surgeon

APPLIED ARTS (VISUAL)

High school/vocational diploma

- ❑ Floral Arranger
- ❑ Merchandise Displayer
- ❑ Painter (artist)

Up to two years beyond high school

- ❑ Cartoonist
- ❑ Commercial Artist
- ❑ Fashion Designer
- ❑ Interior Decorator
- ❑ Photographer

APPLIED ARTS (WRITTEN AND SPOKEN)

High school/vocational diploma

- ❑ Proofreader

Up to two years beyond high school

- ❑ Advertising copywriter
- ❑ Legal Assistant

BUSINESS MACHINE/COMPUTER OPERATION

High school/vocational diploma

- ❑ Data Entry
- ❑ Statistical Clerk
- ❑ Telephone Operator

Up to two years beyond high school

- ❑ Computer Operator
- ❑ Motion Picture Projectionist

CONSTRUCTION AND MAINTENANCE

High school/vocational diploma

- ❑ Bricklayer
- ❑ Construction Laborer
- ❑ Elevator Mechanic
- ❑ Floor Covering Installer
- ❑ Heavy Equipment Operator
- ❑ Janitor
- ❑ Maintenance Mechanic

Up to two years beyond high school

- ❑ Building Inspector
- ❑ Carpenter
- ❑ Electrician
- ❑ Insulation Worker
- ❑ Lather
- ❑ Painter (construction)
- ❑ Pipefitter
- ❑ Plumber
- ❑ Roofer
- ❑ Sheet Metal Worker
- ❑ Structural Steel Worker
- ❑ Tile Setter

CRAFTS AND RELATED SERVICES

High school/vocational diploma

- ❑ Baker/Cook/Chef
- ❑ Butcher
- ❑ Furniture Upholsterer
- ❑ Housekeeper (hotel)
- ❑ Tailor/Dressmaker

Up to two years beyond high school

- ❑ Dry Cleaner
- ❑ Jeweler
- ❑ Locksmith
- ❑ Musical Instrument Repairer

CREATIVE/PERFORMING ARTS

High school/vocational diploma

- ❑ Singer
- ❑ Stunt Performer

Up to two years beyond high school

- ❑ Actor/Actress
- ❑ Dancer/Choreographer
- ❑ Musician
- ❑ Writer/Author

EDUCATION AND RELATED SERVICES

High school/vocational diploma

- ❑ Nursery School Attendant
- ❑ Teacher's Aide

ENGINEERING AND RELATED TECHNOLOGIES

High school/vocational diploma

- ❑ Biomedical Equipment Technician
- ❑ Laser Technician

Up to two years beyond high school

- ❑ Aerospace Engineer Technician
- ❑ Broadcast Technician
- ❑ Chemical Laboratory Technician
- ❑ Civil Engineering Technician
- ❑ Computer Programmer
- ❑ Computer Service Technician
- ❑ Electronic Technician
- ❑ Energy Conservation Technician
- ❑ Industrial Engineering Technician
- ❑ Laboratory Tester
- ❑ Mechanical Engineering Technician
- ❑ Metallurgical Technician
- ❑ Pollution Control Technician
- ❑ Quality Control Technician
- ❑ Robot Technician
- ❑ Surveyor (land)
- ❑ Technical Illustrator
- ❑ Tool Designer
- ❑ Weather Observer

FINANCIAL TRANSACTIONS

High school/vocational diploma

- ❑ Accounting Clerk
- ❑ Bank Teller
- ❑ Cashier
- ❑ Payroll Clerk
- ❑ Travel Agent

Up to two years beyond high school

- ❑ Bookkeeper
- ❑ Loan Officer

HEALTH CARE (GENERAL)

High school/vocational diploma

- ❑ Dental Assistant
- ❑ Medical Assistant
- ❑ Nursing/Psychiatric Aide

Up to two years beyond high school

- ❑ Dietetic Technician
- ❑ Nurse (practical)
- ❑ Nurse (registered)
- ❑ Optometric Assistant
- ❑ Physical Therapist's Assistant
- ❑ Physician's Assistant
- ❑ Recreation Therapist

HEALTH-CARE SPECIALTIES AND TECHNOLOGIES

High school/vocational diploma

- ❑ Dialysis Technician

Up to two years beyond high school

- ❑ Dental Hygienist
- ❑ Dental Laboratory Technician
- ❑ EEG Technologist
- ❑ EKG Technician
- ❑ Emergency Medical Technician
- ❑ Medical Laboratory Technician
- ❑ Medical Technologist
- ❑ Nuclear Medicine Technologist
- ❑ Operating Room Technician
- ❑ Optician
- ❑ Radiation Therapy Technologist
- ❑ Radiologic Technologist
- ❑ Respiratory Therapist
- ❑ Sonographer

HOME/BUSINESS EQUIPMENT REPAIR

High school/vocational diploma

- ❑ Air-Conditioning/Refrigeration/ Heating Mechanic
- ❑ Appliance Servicer
- ❑ Coin Machine Mechanic

Up to two years beyond high school

- ❑ Communications Equipment Mechanic
- ❑ Line Installer/Splicer
- ❑ Office Machine Servicer
- ❑ Radio/TV Repairer
- ❑ Telephone Installer

INDUSTRIAL EQUIPMENT OPERATIONS AND REPAIR

High school/vocational diploma

- ❑ Assembler
- ❑ Blaster
- ❑ Boilermaker
- ❑ Coal Equipment Operator
- ❑ Compressor House Operator
- ❑ Crater
- ❑ Dock Worker
- ❑ Forging Press Operator
- ❑ Furnace Operator
- ❑ Heat Treater
- ❑ Machine Tool Operator
- ❑ Material Handler
- ❑ Miner
- ❑ Sailor
- ❑ Sewing Machine Operator

Up to two years beyond high school

- ❑ Bookbinder
- ❑ Compositor/Typesetter
- ❑ Electronic Equipment Repairer
- ❑ Electroplater
- ❑ Firefighter
- ❑ Instrument Mechanic
- ❑ Lithographer
- ❑ Machine Repairer
- ❑ Machinist
- ❑ Millwright
- ❑ Molder
- ❑ Nuclear Reactor Operator
- ❑ Patternmaker
- ❑ Photoengraver
- ❑ Power House Mechanic
- ❑ Power Plant Operator
- ❑ Printing Press Operator
- ❑ Stationery Engineer
- ❑ Tool and Die Maker
- ❑ Water Plant Operator
- ❑ Welder
- ❑ Wire Drawer

MANAGEMENT AND PLANNING

High school/vocational diploma

- ❑ Administrative Assistant
- ❑ Food Service Supervisor
- ❑ Postmaster
- ❑ Service Station Manager

Up to two years beyond high school

- ❑ Benefits Manager
- ❑ Building Manager
- ❑ Caterer
- ❑ Contractor
- ❑ Credit Manager
- ❑ Customer Service Coordinator
- ❑ Employment Interviewer
- ❑ Executive Housekeeper
- ❑ Funeral Director
- ❑ Hotel/Motel Manager
- ❑ Importer/Exporter
- ❑ Insurance Manager
- ❑ Manager (small business)
- ❑ Office Manager
- ❑ Personnel Manager
- ❑ Restaurant/Bar Manager
- ❑ Store Manager
- ❑ Supermarket Manager

MARKETING AND SALES

High school/vocational diploma

- ❑ Auctioneer
- ❑ Bill Collector
- ❑ Driver (route)
- ❑ Fashion Model
- ❑ Product Demonstrator
- ❑ Salesperson (general)
- ❑ Sample Distributor

Up to two years beyond high school

- ❑ Claims Adjuster
- ❑ Insurance Worker
- ❑ Manufacturer's Representative
- ❑ Real Estate Agent
- ❑ Sales Manager
- ❑ Travel Agent
- ❑ Travel Guide

PERSONAL AND CUSTOMER SERVICE

High school/vocational diploma

- ❑ Barber
- ❑ Bartender
- ❑ Beautician
- ❑ Child-Care Worker
- ❑ Counter Attendant
- ❑ Dining Room Attendant
- ❑ Electrologist
- ❑ Flight Attendant
- ❑ Host/Hostess
- ❑ Houseparent
- ❑ Manicurist
- ❑ Parking Lot Attendant
- ❑ Porter
- ❑ Private Household Worker
- ❑ Waiter/Waitress

RECORDS AND COMMUNICATIONS

High school/vocational diploma

- ❑ Billing Clerk
- ❑ Clerk (general)
- ❑ File Clerk
- ❑ Foreign Trade Clerk
- ❑ Hotel Clerk
- ❑ Meter Reader
- ❑ Postal Clerk
- ❑ Receptionist
- ❑ Stenographer

Up to two years beyond high school

- ❑ Court Reporter
- ❑ Legal Secretary
- ❑ Library Assistant
- ❑ Library Technician
- ❑ Medical Records Technician
- ❑ Medical Secretary
- ❑ Personnel Assistant
- ❑ Secretary
- ❑ Travel Clerk

SOCIAL AND GOVERNMENT

High school/vocational diploma

- ❑ Corrections Officer
- ❑ Police Officer
- ❑ Security Guard
- ❑ Store Detective

Up to two years beyond high school

- ❑ Detective (police)
- ❑ Hazardous Waste Technician
- ❑ Recreation Leader
- ❑ Personal/Customer Services

STORAGE AND DISPATCHING

High school/vocational diploma

- ❑ Dispatcher
- ❑ Mail Carrier
- ❑ Railroad Conductor
- ❑ Shipping/Receiving Clerk
- ❑ Stock Clerk
- ❑ Tool Crib Attendant
- ❑ Warehouse Worker

Up to two years beyond high school

- ❑ Warehouse Supervisor

VEHICLE OPERATION AND REPAIR

High school/vocational diploma

- ❑ Automotive Painter
- ❑ Bus Driver
- ❑ Chauffeur
- ❑ Diesel Mechanic
- ❑ Farm Equipment Mechanic
- ❑ Forklift Operator
- ❑ Heavy Equipment Mechanic
- ❑ Locomotive Engineer
- ❑ Railroad Braker
- ❑ Refuse Collector
- ❑ Service Station Attendant
- ❑ Taxicab Driver
- ❑ Truck Driver

Up to two years beyond high school

- ❑ Aircraft Mechanic
- ❑ Airplane Pilot
- ❑ Auto Body Repairer
- ❑ Automotive Mechanic
- ❑ Garage Supervisor
- ❑ Motorcycle Mechanic

CHAPTER 13

SURVIVAL SKILLS

Whether you're headed to college or work, you're going to come face-to-face with some intimidating stuff after graduation.

Your level of stress will most likely increase due to the demands of your classes or job and your exposure to alcohol or drugs. Various forms of conflict will arise, and you're going to have to keep up with your own health and nutrition. Seem daunting? It's really not if you keep a level head about you and stick to your core values. This chapter will help you work through the muddier side of life after high school.

HOW TO SAY "NO THANKS" TO STRESS

Jump out of bed and into the shower. What to wear? Throw that on. Yuck—what's that stain? "Mom, where are my clean socks?" Tick, tock. No time to grab a bite if you want to make the homeroom bell. Skid around the corner and race for the classroom just as the final bell rings. Whoops, forgot your bio book. Sports, clubs, job, homework, friends on the Internet, and finally (sigh) sleep.

Sound like your life? If you're like most high school students, that description probably hits pretty close to home. So now we'll take your already-hectic schedule and throw in the fact that you'll soon be graduating and have to figure out what to do with your life. Can you say "stress"?

Some people say that stress actually motivates them to perform better, but we won't talk about those perfect people. For most of you, stress means that you may snap at the dog, slam a few doors, get mad at your dad, and feel down. Maybe you'll even have physical symptoms—upset stomach, rapid heartbeat, sweaty palms, dizziness. The list goes on. Not a good place to be when you're dealing with a huge list of things to do, plus graduation staring you in the face.

How to handle stress has been written about countless times, but, of all the advice that's out there, a few simple pointers can really help you prevent the sweaty palms and nauseated feeling in the pit of your stomach.

- Greasy food out, healthy food in. Eat at least one hot, balanced, healthy meal a day. *Healthy*, as in veggies, fruits, meats, cheese, grains. Read further along in this chapter for more information about nutrition and health.
- Sleep. 7, 8, 10 hours a day. Easier said than done but well worth it. Sleep will not only get you through high school but also your college and career lives, and it will help you stop feeling like such a frazzled bunch of nerve endings.
- Hug your dog, cat, rabbit, friend, or mom. Loneliness breeds stress because then all you've got is yourself and those stressed-out thoughts zooming around in your head.
- Hang out with friends. That takes time, but being with people you like and doing fun things eases stress—as long as you don't overdo it.
- Exercise. This does not include running down the hall to make the bell. We're talking 20 minutes of heart-pounding perspiration at least three times a week. It's amazing what a little sweat can do to relax you. Believe it or not, good posture helps too.
- Don't smoke, drink, or use excessive amounts of caffeine. Whoever told you that partying is the way to relieve stress got it all wrong. Nicotine and alcohol actually take away the things your body needs to fight stress.
- Simplify your expenses. Money can be a big stress factor. Think of ways to spend less so that the money you have doesn't have to be stretched so far. Be creative. Share resources. Sell items you no longer use. Maybe put off buying something you've been wanting.
- Let your feelings out of your head. It takes time and energy to keep them bottled up inside. Have regular conversations with your parents and siblings so that minor annoyances can be solved when they're still minor.
- Organize your time. As in prioritizing and dealing with one small part of your life instead of trying to solve everything in one shot. Read on for more information about time management.
- Lighten up. When you've graduated and are into whatever it is you end up doing, you'll

look back and realize that this was a teensy little part of your life. So look on the bright side. The decisions you'll be making about your future are heavy, but they won't be cut in stone. You can change them if they don't work out.

Stress Busters

Most people get stressed when things are out of control—too many things to do, too many decisions to make, or too much information to digest. If you add not having enough time, enough money, or enough energy to get it all done, you have the perfect recipe for stress. In the space below, identify what's causing your stress:

____

____

____

____

____

____

Then, choose from these three stress-busting options:

1. **Alter the situation.** Some things you can't control, and some things you can. Change the ones you can. If you have too much on your plate and can't possibly do it all, push a few things aside. You have to be able to get rid of something on the list. (And no, homework is not a choice.) Maybe you need to be able to say no to extra demands. Concentrate on what is important. Make a list of your priorities from the most important to the least, and work your way down.

2. **Avoid the situation—for now.** Step back and ask, "Is this really a problem? Do I really need to solve it now?" This doesn't mean you should procrastinate on things that need to get done. Think of this stress buster as buying some time, taking a break, catching your breath, getting advice, and airing out the situation so that you can deal with it when you're better prepared to handle it.

3. **Accept the situation.** How you perceive your circumstances has a lot to do with how you make decisions about them. Put whatever is stressing you in the perspective of the big picture. How will this really affect me next year or even ten years from now? Look at your circumstances through the lens of your personal values. Think about what feels right to you, not someone else.

Quick Fixes

If you're still feeling like you're being pulled in a million directions, use these quick fixes to help you calm down.

- Make the world slow down for a bit. Take a walk. Take a shower. Listen to some soothing music.
- Breathe deeply. Get in tune with the rhythm of your own breathing. Lie or sit down for 15 minutes, and just concentrate on relaxing.
- Relax those little knots of tension. Start at your head and work down to your toes.
- Close your eyes and clear your mind. Get rid of the clutter. Imagine yourself in your favorite place: the beach, under a tree, whatever works best for you.
- Close the door to your bedroom, and let out a blood-curdling scream. Walt Whitman knew what he was talking about when he said, "I sound my barbaric yawp over the roofs of the world." Just let your family know what you're doing so they don't come running to your room in fear. You'll be amazed at how much better you feel.
- When all else fails, watch a funny movie. Read the comics. Get in a giggly frame of mind. Those big challenges will quickly be brought down to size.

WINNING THE TIME-MANAGEMENT GAME

What is the value of time? Ten dollars an hour? The price of a scholarship because your application was a day late? Time can be a very expensive resource or something you can use to your advantage. Even if you recognize the value of time, managing it is a challenge.

When you live with enough time, life is relaxed and balanced. To find that balance, you have to prioritize and plan. Decide what you want and what is important to you. Organize logically and schedule realistically. Overcome obstacles. Change bad habits. Simplify and streamline. Save time when you can. Sound impossible? It's not easy, but you can do it. The secret is held in a Chinese proverb: The wisdom of life is the elimination of nonessentials.

It's All About Control

The good thing about time is that much of it is yours to do with as you wish. You may feel out of control and as if you must run to keep up with the conflicting demands and expectations of your life. But we all have the same number of hours in each day. The key is in how we spend them. The following tips are designed to help you spend your time wisely and to keep you in control of your life.

Prepare a list of your goals and the tasks necessary to accomplish them. This could be by day, week, month, semester, or even year. You may also want to break the list into sections, such as friends and family, school, work, sports, health and fitness, home, personal development, and college preparation.

Prioritize based on time-sensitive deadlines. Use a grading system to code how important each task is. A is "Do It Now," B is "Do It Soon," C is "Do It Later." Understand the difference between "important" and "urgent."

Be realistic about how much you can really do. Analyze how you spend your time now. What can you cut? How much time do you truly need for each task?

Think ahead. How many times have you underestimated how long it will take to do something? Plan for roadblocks, and give yourself some breathing space.

Accept responsibility. Once you decide to do something, commit yourself to it. That doesn't mean that a task that was on the "A" list can't be moved to the "C" list. But be consistent and specific about what you want to accomplish.

Divide and conquer. You may need to form a committee, delegate tasks to your parents, or ask for help from a friend. That is why it is called time management.

Take advantage of your personal prime time. Don't schedule yourself to get up and do homework at 6 a.m. if you are a night owl. It won't work. Instead, plan to accomplish complex tasks when you are most efficient.

Avoid procrastination. There are a million ways to procrastinate. And not one of them is good if you really want to get something done. Have you ever noticed that you always find time to do the things you enjoy?

Do the most unpleasant task first. Get it over with. Then it will be all downhill from there.

Don't over-prepare. That is just another way to procrastinate.

Learn to say no to the demands on your time that you cannot afford.

Be enthusiastic, and share your goals with others.

If you work on too many goals at once, you'll overwhelm yourself from the start. Remember, what is important is the quality of the time you spend on a task, not the quantity. It doesn't make any difference if you study for 10 hours if you don't recall a thing you've reviewed. The overall goal is to be productive, efficient, and effective—not just busy. You'll also need to pace yourself. All work and no play makes for an unbalanced person.

Use all the benefits of modern technology to help you manage time. You can save lots of time by using fax, e-mail, or voice mail. If you don't already use a day planner or calendar, you would be wise to invest in one. Write in all the important deadlines, and refer to it often. Block out commitments you know you have so you won't over-schedule yourself. When you do over-schedule yourself or underestimate the time it takes to accomplish a task, learn from your mistakes. But don't get too down on yourself. Give yourself a pep talk every now and then to keep yourself positive and motivated.

MOVING OUT ON YOUR OWN?

As you consider moving away from home either to a college dorm or your own place, some pretty wonderful expectations of what it no doubt will be like will come floating into your head. No more parental rules. Making your own decisions. Hamburgers forever! Coming and going when you want to. But wait, what's this? Looks like you're out of clean clothes to wear. No more cereal bowls—they're all in the sink, and they're dirty. Out of milk and the refrigerator's empty. Yikes! What happened to all those warm, fuzzy thoughts about being on your own?

Sure, it's nice to be able to come and go as you please, but before you get too far into that pleasant—and unrealistic—mind-set, the following are some important things to consider as you make plans to become independent. Ozzie Hashley, a guidance counselor at Clinton Community Schools in Clinton, Michigan, works with high school juniors and seniors. Here is what he says are the realities of independent life.

1. **If you rent your own place, have you thought about the extra charges in addition to the rent?** Says Hashley, "Many students think only of paying the rent. They don't realize that they'll be responsible for utilities in many cases. Or the money it will take to wash and dry their clothes."

2. **Subsisting on hamburgers and fries sounds yummy, but as you watch a fast-food diet eat its way into your paycheck, you'll most likely think about cooking up something yourself.** What will you cook? Who will buy the food? More important, who will do the dishes? Dividing up the responsibilities of preparing food is a big aspect of being on your own, especially when sharing a living space.

3. **Medical insurance may not be on your mind as you prepare to graduate—you're probably on your parents' insurance plans right now.** Thanks to the Patient Protection and Affordable Care Act of 2010, however, you can remain on your parents' insurance plans until you are 26 whether or not you are

   - married;
   - living with your parents;
   - in school;
   - financially dependent on your parents; and/or
   - eligible to enroll on your employer's plan.

   Though health-care laws have changed, you should understand that medical insurance is a big expense; however, if you need health care and don't have medical insurance, the bills will be much, much larger.

4 There's no one to tell you when to come home when you're on your own. There's also no one to tell you that you're really disorganized when it comes to managing your time. Time management might not sound like a big deal now, but when you have to juggle all the facets of being independent—your job, taking care of your living space and car, your social life—then being able to manage time becomes an important part of life.

5 Managing your money moves into a whole other realm when you are on your own. You have to make sure you have enough to pay the rent, your car loan, and insurance, not to mention that movie you want to see, the video game you'd like to buy, or those jeans you saw at the mall last week. If you want to eat at the end of the month, budgeting will become an important part of your new independent vocabulary. Ask your parents or an adult you trust to help you set up your budget. Also learn how to balance your checkbook. It's a lot easier to manage your money when you keep track of how much you have in your bank account and how much you spend!

SMART CREDIT FOR TEENS

With age comes responsibility, and that includes financial responsibility. If you plan to move out and live on your own, it's a good idea to develop sound financial habits from the beginning—especially when it comes to credit cards and credit debt. Parents and teens can work together to establish good credit habits early on.

Prepaid credit cards allow parents to put money on a credit card, almost like a gift card, for teens to spend. Prepaid credit cards are a great way to limit teens' spending, while still giving them the flexibility of a credit card.

Low-limit credit cards are another alternative. Parents co-sign for their teens to obtain these cards, but the limit is usually set at around $200 to $500. By setting such low limits, teens avoid falling into debt and spending more than they can realistically afford.

ARE CREDIT CARDS OKAY FOR TEENS?

Prepaid and low-limit credit cards are excellent ways for teens to learn smart money management and avoid burying themselves in credit card debt when they move out on their own. These cards can also help teens establish good credit early in their lives.

Before getting and using credit cards, however, teens should learn to manage their own checking accounts. Today most checking accounts come with a debit card that can also be used as a credit card. These cards withdraw money directly from the checking account whenever a purchase is made with the card. Such checking accounts allow teens to master the art of balancing a checkbook, tracking expenses, and developing good spending habits. You can learn more about checking accounts and credit and debit cards by visiting a branch of your local bank.

DRUGS AND ALCOHOL: ARE YOU AT RISK?

At risk? Wait a minute. How could you be at risk when the legal drinking age in all fifty states is 21? Chances are, if you're reading this, you're not 21 yet. It's also illegal to smoke or buy any tobacco product before age 18, and possession of any drug for recreational use is illegal, period. So if you drink alcohol before age 21; smoke or buy cigarettes, cigars, or chewing tobacco before age 18; or take any illegal drugs, you could

- be arrested for driving under the influence (DUI);
- be convicted;
- be required to pay steep fines;
- have your driving privileges suspended;
- get kicked out of school (that's any kind of school, college included);
- get fired;
- go to jail; and/or
- end up with a criminal record.

A criminal record . . . so what?

Consider this true story. A 29-year-old man who recently received his graduate degree in business was offered a job with a major Fortune 100 corporation. We're talking big bucks, stock options, reserved parking space—the whole nine yards. When the company did a background check and found that he was arrested for a DUI during his freshman year of college, they rescinded their offer. The past can, and will, come back to haunt you. Let's not even think about what would happen down the line if you decide to run for public office.

Think about why you might want to try drinking or doing drugs. For fun? To forget your troubles? Seriously, are your reasons good enough? Remember the consequences before you make a decision.

How Can I Say No?

"It takes a lot more guts to stay sober, awake, and aware than to just get high, get numb, and learn nothing about life," says one former user. "Laugh at people who suggest you drink or take drugs, and then avoid them like the plague."

Friends worth having will respect your decision to say no. And girls—if a guy pressures you to drink or get high, ditch him pronto. You can vice-versa that for guys, too. According to the National Institute on Drug Abuse (NIDA), alcohol and club drugs like GHB or Rohypnol (roofies) make you an easy target for date rape.

The Nitty Gritty

Along with the temporary pleasure they may give you, all drugs (including club drugs, alcohol, and nicotine) have a downside. Alcohol, for example, is a depressant. Even one drink slows down the part of your brain that controls your reasoning. So your judgment gets dull just when you're wondering, "Should I drive my friends home? Should I talk to this guy? Should I have another drink?"

Your body needs about an hour to burn up the alcohol in one drink (one shot of hard liquor, straight or mixed in a cocktail; one glass of wine; or one 12-ounce beer). Nothing, including coffee, will sober you up any faster.

Alcohol helps smart people make bad decisions. In fact, many drugs make you believe that you're thinking even more clearly than usual. Well, guess what? You aren't. Depending on what drug you take, how much, and what you do while you're on it, you're also risking confusion, nausea, headache, sleep problems, depression, paranoia, rape (especially "date rape"), unwanted pregnancy, sexually transmitted diseases (STDs) ranging from herpes to HIV/AIDS, having a baby with a birth defect, memory impairment, persistent psychosis, lung damage, cancer, injuring or killing someone else, and your own death.

Take a moment now, when your brain is razor-sharp, to decide if those consequences are worth the escape you get for 20 minutes one night. You may be saying, "Oh, come on. Only addicts have problems like that." Getting drunk or high doesn't necessarily mean that you're an alcoholic or an addict—but it always means a loss of control.

"So much of addiction is about denial," says one member of Alcoholics Anonymous. "I just didn't think I looked or acted or thought or smelled or lied or cheated or failed like an alcoholic or addict. It was when the drugs and alcohol use started to cause problems in multiple areas of my life that I began to think the problem might reside with me. Friends leaving—in disgust—was what opened my eyes."

DID YOU KNOW?

- ✓ Nicotine is as addictive as cocaine and heroine, according to the American Cancer Society.
- ✓ Drinking a lot of alcohol fast can kill you on the spot, according to Keystone College.
- ✓ MDMA (Ecstasy, X, Adam, Clarity, Lover's Speed), according to NIDA, may permanently damage your memory.

DO I HAVE A PROBLEM?

Take the quiz below to see if you're in real trouble with drugs or alcohol.

1. **Do you look forward to drinking or using drugs?**
2. **Do most of your friends drink or do drugs?**
3. **Do you keep a secret supply of alcohol or drugs?**
4. **Can you drink a lot without appearing drunk?**
5. **Do you "power-hit" to get high faster, by binge-drinking, funneling, or slamming?**
6. **Do you ever drink or do drugs alone, including in a group where no one else is doing so?**
7. **Do you ever drink or use drugs when you hadn't planned to?**
8. **Do you ever have blackouts where you can't remember things that happened when you were drunk or high?**

If you answered yes to any of these questions, you probably need help. If you have a friend who fits the picture, find a respectful way to bring up your concerns. Don't be surprised if he or she tells you to back off—but don't give up, either. If someone in your family has an alcohol or drug problem, be aware that you may be prone to the same tendency.

Source: Keystone College, La Plume, Pennsylvania

Where Can I Get Help?

If you think you have a problem, or if you think a friend has a problem, try Alcoholics Anonymous or Narcotics Anonymous. If you're not sure, ask yourself the questions in "Do I Have a Problem?".

Talk to any adult you trust: maybe your doctor, a clergy member, a counselor, or your parents. Health clinics and hospitals offer information and treatment. The American Cancer Society can help you quit smoking. These are only a few places to turn—check out the Yellow Pages and the Web for more.

Alcoholics Anonymous
212-870-3400
www.aa.org

American Cancer Society
800-ACS-2345
www.cancer.org

Narcotics Anonymous
818-773-9999
www.na.org

So, that's the straight stuff. You're at a tough but wonderful age, when your life is finally your own and your decisions really matter. Think about what you value most—and then make your choices.

CONFLICT: HOW TO AVOID IT OR DEFUSE IT

You're walking along and you see a group of kids up ahead . . . and suddenly you're afraid. Or you're about to talk to someone you have a disagreement with, and already you're tense. Or your boyfriend's jealousy is freaking you out. What should you do?

All of these situations involve potential conflicts that could get out of hand. Even if you never get into a violent situation, you'll face conflicts with others, as we all do. Learning to spot the warning signs of violence and how to handle conflicts well will bring you lifelong benefits.

What's Your Style?

What do you do when you're faced with a potential conflict? Do you try to get away, no matter what? Do you find yourself bowing to pressure from others? Do you feel like you have to stand and fight, even if you don't want to? Do you wish you had some new ways to handle conflict?

Different situations call for different strategies. First, let's talk about situations where violence is a real possibility. Most of us get a bad feeling before things get violent, but too often, we ignore the feeling. Trust your gut feeling! And whether you're on the street or in school, officials at the Crime Prevention Association of Philadelphia suggest that you keep in mind these tips for avoiding violence:

- Walk like you're in charge and you know where you're going.
- Stick to lighted areas.
- Travel with a trusted friend when possible. On campus, get an escort from security at night. Loners are targets.
- If a person or group up ahead makes you nervous, cross the street immediately—and calmly—as if you'd intended to anyway.
- Call out to an imaginary friend, "Hey, Joe! Wait up!" and then run toward your "friend," away from whoever is scaring you.
- Go right up to the nearest house and ring the bell. Pretend you're expected: "Hey Joe, it's me!" You can explain later.
- If someone threatens you physically, scream.
- If someone assaults you, scream, kick where it hurts, scratch—anything.
- Don't ever get in a car with someone you don't know well or trust, even if you've seen that person around a lot.
- Strike up a conversation with an innocent bystander if you feel threatened by someone else, just to make yourself less vulnerable for a few minutes.
- Wear a whistle around your neck or carry a personal alarm or pepper spray.
- If someone mugs you, hand over your purse, wallet, jewelry—whatever he or she asks for. None of it is worth your life.
- Don't go along with something your gut says is wrong, no matter who says it's okay.

Remember that it's not a sign of weakness to back down if someone's egging you on to fight. According to Bill Tomasco, former principal of Furness High School in Philadelphia, pressure from other kids to fight creates much of the violence in schools. If you're being pushed to fight, show true strength: Know that your opponent has a good side too, speak only to that good side, and don't give in to the pressure of the crowd.

Are You Safe at Home?

Locking doors and windows makes sense—but sometimes the danger lies within. A lot of violence occurs in abusive relationships, says Amy Gottlieb, a marriage and family therapist in West Los Angeles. To find out if you're at risk, ask yourself whether your partner, roommate, or family member does any of the following things:

- Uses jealousy to justify controlling you
- Puts you down, humiliates you, or pulls guilt trips on you
- Threatens to reveal your secrets or tells lies about you
- Makes all the decisions
- Frightens you, especially if it's on purpose
- Threatens you in any way
- Makes light of abusive behavior or says you provoked it

If any of this is going on in your relationship, talk about it to an adult you trust, and ask for help.

Talking It Out

If your instincts tell you to get away from a situation, do it. But you can resolve many actual or potential conflicts face-to-face and gracefully so that everyone walks away feeling good. Read on for some tips on handling conflict from Kare Anderson, a communications expert in Sausalito, California.

Most of us make the mistake of reacting quickly, thinking only of our own needs, and not listening, says Anderson. Try doing the opposite. First and foremost, think about what you really want from the situation, and keep your goal in mind the whole time. But bring up the other person's concerns first. Then, discuss how the situation affects you both. Offer a solution that will benefit you both—and only then talk about how your solution addresses your own needs.

When the other person is talking, really listen—don't just come up with retorts in your head. Always show that you've heard the person before you give your response, especially if you're talking with someone of a different sex, size, or race. Those differences can distract us so much that we actually hear less. If you're female, you may need to s-l-o-w yourself down. Say less than you think you need to. Guys, don't shut down altogether—keep the communication going.

Even if the other person acts like a jerk, be gracious and respectful. Ask questions instead of criticizing. Let someone save face instead of looking like a fool. If you insult or embarrass someone, you may never have that person's full attention again. In short, treat the other person as you'd like to be treated.

What should you do if you're really angry? One teen said, "Thinking about things calms me down." Another said, "Once in a while, we have to cool off for a day and then come back to the discussion." Anger almost always covers up fear. What are you afraid of? Is the reward you want out of this negotiation bigger than your fear? Focus on that reward. Don't forget to breathe—long, slow breaths.

Think about these strategies often, so you'll be more likely to use them when a situation gets sticky, instead of just reacting blindly. Use them to plan for negotiations ahead of time, too. Learning to resolve problems with people takes most of us a lifetime—get a jump on it now!

Cyberbullying

In days past, you could escape a conflict with someone at school or work within the confines of your own home, but that's no longer the case. Technological advancements such as cell phones and computers and social networking sites such as Facebook® and Twitter™ allow you to stay in touch with your friends 24/7. However, they also have helped cyberbullies to break down your front door.

Cyberbullying is willful and repeated harm inflicted through the use of computers, cell phones, and other electronic devices. Constant hurtful text messages and the constant spreading of rumors via phone,

Internet, and social networking sites are forms of cyberbullying. According to the Cyberbullying Research Center (www.cyberbullying.us), in 2010, about 20 percent of more than 4,400 randomly selected teens between the ages of 10 and 18 indicated that they had been victims of cyberbullying at some point in their lives. About the same number admitted to cyberbullying others. Cyberbullies, and even friends, can use video and camera capabilities on their phones to record incriminating moments and text them or post them online. Privacy is a thing of the past.

So, what does this mean for you? First, you must learn to guard your privacy. Second, be very careful about the choices you make and the things you do in public or online.

Stopping a Cyberbully

When something bothers you, it's helpful to talk it out. Try to develop a relationship with an adult whom you trust, such as a parent, a teacher, or a coach, and to whom you can speak openly about online situations that make you feel uncomfortable. If you think you are a victim of cyberbullying, save all the evidence. Save the text messages, and add any Web pages to your "favorites." If you have a Facebook page, take advantage of the privacy settings that are available, and allow only your friends to access your information. If you repeatedly receive hurtful texts from someone, block the number on your cell phone so you'll no longer receive them.

10 FACTS ABOUT CYBERBULLYING

1. Nearly 42 percent of kids have been threatened online, and almost 1 in 4 kids have been threatened more than once.
2. Among these kids, the most common forms of cyberbullying were being ignored and being disrespected.
3. Nine in ten middle school students have had their feelings hurt online.
4. About 75 percent have visited a Web site that bashes another student.
5. Four in ten middle school students have had their password(s) stolen and changed by a bully who locked them out of their own account or sent communications posing as them.
6. About 21 percent of kids have received mean or threatening e-mails.
7. The psychological and emotional outcomes of cyberbullying are similar to real-life bullying outcomes. The exception, however, is that cyberbullying allows no escape from the torment. School ends at 3 p.m., but the Internet is available all the time.
8. The primary cyberbullying location where victimizing occurs is in the chat room.
9. Girls are about twice as likely as boys to be victims *and* perpetrators of cyberbullying.
10. About 58 percent of kids admit that someone has said mean or hurtful things to them online. More than four in ten say it has happened more than once.

Sources: DoSomething.org, Stop Cyberbullying, LovetoKnow, New York State School Counselor Association, National Crime Prevention Council

If someone you know is being cyberbullied or if you have witnessed a cyberbully in action, understand that you can make a difference. A bully will continue to harass someone only as long as he or she has an audience. Don't support the bully, and try to support the victim if you can. Note all incidents that occur, and tell an adult who can step in to stop the situation.

THE LOWDOWN ON SEXUAL HARASSMENT

Has someone ever looked at you, talked to you, or touched you in a way that gave you the creeps, made you self-conscious about your body, or created a sexual mood when it wasn't appropriate? And did you begin to dread seeing this person because he or she just wouldn't quit?

If so, you've encountered sexual harassment. Sexual harassment is inappropriate behavior that is

- happening to you because of your sex
- unwanted (you don't like it)
- objectively offensive (to a hypothetical "reasonable" man or woman)
- either severe, persistent, or pervasive
- interfering with your work or school experience

According to a domestic and sexual violence prevention educator in Portland, Oregon, in most cases—just as with crimes like rape—men harass women. But teenage girls are a bit more likely than older women to sexually harass someone, more girl-on-girl harassment goes on with teens, and guys get harassed, too. In some of the most brutal cases coming to light, gay men (or men perceived to be gay) are the targets.

People who sexually harass others generally fall into three camps. Some just seem to be misguided and insensitive. Others get turned on by harassing someone. And a third group does it to intimidate—for example, to drive someone away from a job or just to make him or her feel bad about himself or herself.

So What Do I Do If Someone's Harassing Me?

Experts in self-defense say the best technique is to name the behavior that's bugging you and request that it stop. You might say, "Your hand is on my knee. Please remove it." If the person doesn't quit, you might try writing a letter spelling out what's bothering you and requesting that the person stop. This way, you've confronted the situation directly, and you also have a record of your complaint.

But here's the good news: You are not expected to handle harassment on your own, especially if the person harassing you is in a position of authority over you, such as a teacher, sergeant, or boss. The authorities at your school or your job should handle it—but they can't do that unless you tell them what's going on.

If you file a complaint, be prepared to describe what happened, when, and where. And make sure you report your concerns to someone who has clear authority to handle sexual harassment complaints, such as the principal or the personnel director.

Often, the person harassing you will stop as soon as he or she gets the clear message that the behavior isn't okay with you, especially if your complaint goes to someone higher up as well. Most harassment cases don't end up involving lawyers and lawsuits. You may choose, in serious cases, to register your complaint with the Office of Civil Rights (if you're being harassed at school) or the Equal Employment Opportunity Commission (if you're being harassed at work). You can also file your complaint on different levels at the same time: for example, with your school and the police.

You have the legal right to a school and workplace free from discrimination based on your race, color, religion, sex, national origin, and—depending on where you live, as state and local laws vary—your sexual orientation. You have the right to protection from retaliation if you file a complaint of harassment. So don't be afraid to report a situation if it truly offends you and interferes with your life.

What If I'm Just Being Hypersensitive?

If someone's words or actions make you uncomfortable, that's all the reason you need to ask that person to stop the behavior, no matter how innocent the behavior may be. Trust your feelings—especially if you find you're trying to convince yourself that nothing is wrong.

What Will Happen to the Person Who Has Been Harassing Me?

If your complaint is successfully handled, the main thing that will happen is that the person will stop harassing you. People aren't "charged" with sexual harassment unless their behavior includes criminal conduct. But your harasser may face disciplinary action, loss of privileges, suspension, expulsion, lawsuits, or criminal action, depending on the severity of his or her behavior.

How Can I Avoid Harassing Someone?

Sometimes the line between harmless flirting, joking, or complimenting and harassment is pretty thin. How can you stay on the right side of that line?

First, pay attention to your own motives. Be honest with yourself. Do you enjoy watching someone get uncomfortable when you say or do certain things? Do you feel angry with the person for some reason? Do you enjoy exercising your authority over this person in some way? Do you find yourself obsessing about the person? If any of these is true, whatever you're saying or doing probably isn't harmless.

Even if your motives seem harmless to you, be extraordinarily careful about whom and how you touch. You may be comfortable touching people casually—perhaps you'll touch someone's hand or shoulder in conversation—but remember that other people's boundaries may differ from yours.

Pay attention to the person's reactions to you. Are you getting clear green signals when you do or say things around this person, or does the person seem to shrink away from you? Does the person shut down or seem upset when you do or say certain things? If someone's told you clearly that she or he doesn't like it when you do or say certain things, apologize and stop at once. And remember, no means no.

So, if you're faced with something that feels like sexual harassment, remember to trust your feelings, convey them clearly, and get help promptly if you need it.

STAYING HEALTHY IN SPITE OF YOURSELF

When someone—like your mom—asks if you're eating right, do you ever want to say, "Hey, have you looked at my life lately? Do you see a lot of time there for eating right?" Well, how about exercise—are you getting enough? "Yeah, right. I bench-press my backpack when I'm not doing wind sprints to my next class," may be how you reply. If you're feeling like you can't escape your stress and fatigue, you might be surprised by how much better you'll feel if you keep active and don't just eat junk. Your workload will seem easier. You'll sleep better. You'll look fantastic. And you can stay healthy—even if time and money are in short supply.

There are two halves to the exercise equation:

1. Cardiovascular Training—walking, running, biking, etc.
2. Strength Training—using resistance bands, lifting weights, etc.

Unfortunately, most people think of exercise as just the cardio half. That's a big mistake! Cardio exercises generally help you burn calories while you are performing the exercise. Strength exercises build lean muscle that burns calories for the other 23 hours in the day, even while you are resting or sitting at your desk studying! The best exercise workout is one that combines both cardiovascular *and* strength training.

> *Physical fitness is not only one of the most important keys to a healthy body, it is the basis of dynamic and creative intellectual activity.*
> *~John F. Kennedy*

TIPS FOR INCREASING PHYSICAL ACTIVITY

Make physical activity a regular part of the day

- Choose activities that you enjoy and can do regularly. Keep it interesting by trying something different on alternate days.
- Every little bit adds up, and doing something is better than doing nothing.
- Make sure to do at least 10 minutes of activity at a time; shorter bursts of activity will not have the same health benefits. For example, walking the dog for 10 minutes before and after school or adding a 10-minute walk at lunchtime, if your school permits you to go outside, can add to your weekly goal.
- Mix it up and have fun! Here are some suggestions:
  - ✓ Walk or run with your dog—don't just watch your dog walk or run around.
  - ✓ Get off the bus or subway one stop early and walk or jog the rest of the way.
  - ✓ Clean the house or wash the car (great help for your parents, too!).
  - ✓ Walk, run, skate, or bicycle more.
  - ✓ Play basketball, softball/baseball, or soccer on a team or with friends.
  - ✓ Do stretches, exercises, or pedal a stationary bike while watching TV.

Most important—HAVE FUN while being active!

But Really, Who Has the Time?

As one teen says, "Schoolwork gets in the way, and then I want to relax when I have a moment that isn't filled with schoolwork." You can make time for anything, if you choose to do so. But if you aren't athletic by nature, or school or work keeps you going nonstop, exercise is the first thing to go out the window.

However, you don't have to become a gym rat or run miles to get enough exercise. Longer workouts are great if you do them consistently, but you're better off getting little bits of regular exercise than just doing a huge workout every so often or never doing anything. And by "little bits," we mean 15- to 20-minute chunks. Add that to a fast walk to the bus, a frenzied private dance session in your room, or running up the stairs instead of taking the elevator, and you're exercising!

Regardless of how you choose to pump that muscle in the middle of your chest, the important thing is that you're doing something. You'll not only feel better about yourself, but you'll have increased energy to do other things, like study, go to work, or go out with friends.

What Does "Eating Right" Mean Anyway?

Eating right means eating a balance of good foods in moderate amounts. Your diet needn't be complicated or expensive. Dr. Michele Wilson, a specialist in adolescent medicine at the Children's Hospital of Philadelphia, notes that a teen's diet should be heavy in grains—especially whole grains—and light in sugars and fats. It should include a lot of fruits and vegetables and provide plenty of protein, calcium, vitamin A, B vitamins, iron, and zinc. Sound complicated?

Well, what's complicated about a bean burrito with cheese? How about pasta with vegetables, meat, or both in the sauce? A banana or some cantaloupe? Stir-fried vegetables with tofu? Carrot sticks with peanut butter? Yogurt? Cereal with milk and fruit? All of these are cheap, quick to make, and great for you.

One teen swears by microwaveable veggie burgers and adds, "Staying away from deep-fried anything is a good plan." Try to avoid things like chips and sweets, says Dr. Wilson, adding that if you're a vegetarian—and especially if you don't eat dairy products or fish—you should make sure you're getting enough protein and iron. And no matter what your diet, drink water—eight glasses a day.

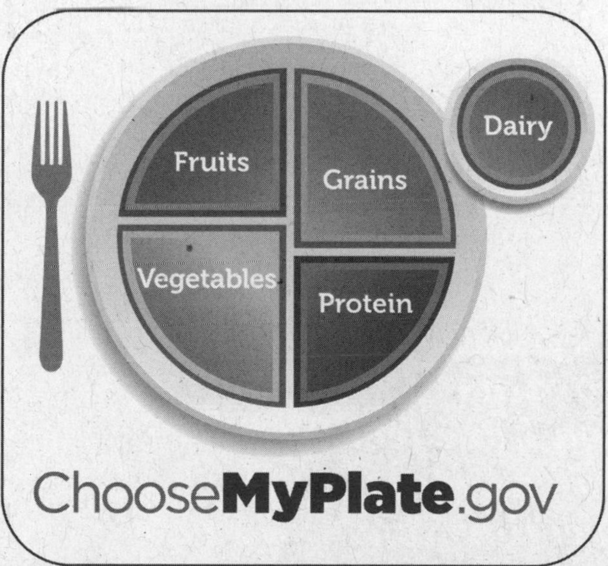

In June 2011, a colorful plate called "MyPlate," (http://www.choosemyplate.gov/) replaced the often confusing food pyramid as the official icon representing U.S. Dietary Guidelines. The simple, plate-shaped graphic is divided into four sections: green for vegetables, red for fruits, orange for grains, and purple for protein. Dairy foods are represented by a separate blue section, which is shaped like a drinking glass. It's clear that the green section is largest—providing a visual reminder that vegetables are the foundation of a healthy diet and should fill most of your plate at every meal.

As Long as I'm in Control of What I Eat, I'm Okay, Right?

That depends. Of course, having no control over what you eat is a problem. But "in control" can be good or bad. How severely do you control what and how you eat? Are you obsessed with getting thinner? Do people who love you tell you that you're too thin, and do you take that as a compliment? Do you ever binge secretly or make yourself throw up after a meal? If any of these is true, you may be suffering from anorexia or bulimia.

According to the National Association of Anorexia Nervosa and Associated Disorders (ANAD), eating disorders affect 7 to 10 million women and 1 million men in this country and can lead to serious health problems—even death. "The thing that convinced me to get help was fear—I had to be hospitalized, as I was literally dying from my anorexia," says one woman. Most Americans who are anorexic or bulimic developed their eating disorders in their teens.

We asked some women being treated for eating disorders what they used to see when they looked in the mirror. "Total ugliness," said one. "The smallest dimple in my flesh looked immense," said another. And a third said, "I got rid of the mirrors because they would set me off to where I wouldn't eat for days." What advice do they offer teens who are struggling with an eating disorder? "Treat yourself as you wish your parents had treated you," "Ask people you feel close to not to discuss your weight with you," and "Find ways outside of yourself to feel in control." Above all—get help! That means going to someone you trust, whether it be a parent, relative, sibling, friend, doctor, or teacher. Or call ANAD's Helpline at 630-577-1330, Monday through Friday from 9 a.m. to 5 p.m. CST, for a listing of support groups and referrals in your area or e-mail anadhelp@anad.org.

So, If I Eat Right and Exercise, Then I'm Healthy. Right?

Well, probably. But Dr. Michele Wilson suggests that you keep a few other things in mind, too. If you smoke, drink, or do drugs, you're asking for trouble. Aside from their many scarier side effects, all these habits can steal nutrients that you need. If all this sounds like the recipe for a dull and totally uncool life, remember that feeling and looking great are never boring, but that vomiting (or dying) after downing the most tequilas in the fastest time looks really uncool. If you're making short-term decisions that will hurt you in the long run, take some time to figure out why. Good health is priceless!

The next steps in life are yours. Whether you are starting high school, in the middle of your high school years, or close to graduation day, exciting times certainly lie ahead. The editors of Peterson's hope that the chapters of the *Teens' Guide* have provided valuable information as you head toward the future—whether it's to a four-year college, a vo-tech school or community college, a branch of the military, or a career. We wish you much success on your educational and life journey.

THE FUTURE IS YOURS

As Yogi Berra said, "The future isn't what it used to be." The next steps in life are yours, and you hold the key. Whether you are just starting high school, are in the middle of your high school years, or are close to graduation day, your future holds great, wondrous possibilities.

The editors at Peterson's hope that the chapters of the *Teens' Guide* have provided you with valuable information as you head toward a traditional four-year college, a vocational-technical school, a community college, a branch of the military, a gap year, a career, or some other exciting adventure. We wish you much success on your educational and life journey.

You have brains in your head. You have feet in your shoes. You can steer yourself in any direction you choose. You're on your own. And you know what you know. You are the [one] who'll decide where to go.

~Dr. Seuss

SPECIAL ADVERTISING SECTION

The ads placed by the following schools help make it possible for Peterson's Publishing to continue to provide you with the highest quality educational exploration, test-prep, financial aid, and career-preparation resources you need to succeed on your educational journey.

Saint Louis University John Cook School of Business
St. Mary's University Bill Greehey School of Business
Thomas Jefferson University School of Population Health
University of Medicine & Dentistry of New Jersey
The Winston Preparatory Schools